Walking Victoriously in the Power of the Spirit
by C. Matthew McMahon

Copyright Information

Walking Victoriously in the Power of the Spirit by C. Matthew McMahon
Edited by Therese B. McMahon

Copyright ©2020 by Puritan Publications and A Puritan's Mind®

Some language and grammar has been updated from any original manuscripts. Any change in wording or punctuation has not changed the intent or meaning of the original author(s) and has been made to aid the modern reader.

Published by Puritan Publications
A Ministry of A Puritan's Mind® in Crossville, TN.
www.apuritansmind.com
www.puritanpublications.com
www.gracechapeltn.com

All rights reserved. No part of this publication may be reproduced, stored in a retrieval system or transmitted in any form by any means, electronic, mechanical, photocopy, recording or otherwise, without the prior permission of the publisher, except as provided by USA copyright law.

This Print Edition, 2020
Electronic Edition, 2020

Manufactured in the United States of America

ISBN: 978-1-62663-687-3
eISBN: 978-1-62663-345-2

Table of Contents

Introduction 4
Chapter 1: Abundant Life 7
Chapter 2: The Holy Spirit's Person and Work 28
Chapter 3: Baptized with the Holy Spirit 58
Chapter 4: Indwelt by the Holy Spirit 77
Chapter 5: Unction and Anointing by the Holy Spirit 96
Chapter 6: Illuminated by the Spirit 114
Chapter 7: Filled with the Spirit 141
Chapter 8: Empowered by the Spirit 163
Chapter 9: Led by the Spirit 186
Chapter 10: Praying in the Spirit 206
Chapter 11: The Fruit of the Spirit 224
Chapter 12: Exercising the Gifts of the Spirit 243
Chapter 13: Walking in the Spirit 265
Chapter 14: Rejoicing in Abundance in Christ 283
Other Helpful Books by Puritan Publications 305

Introduction

One of the more neglected theological topics over the past 500 years of church history is a practical theology of the Holy Spirit; how the Holy Spirit works in your life as a believer every single second of every single minute of every single day in the grace of Christ Jesus. Keep in mind, there are some *very* good systematic theology books that deal in their respective chapters with the Holy Spirit as they cover the doctrine of God, and there are even some very well written single volumes on the Spirit compiled in a systematic fashion by divines looking to give us a "theological overview of the Spirit."[1] But there are relatively no books on the Holy Spirit that take a biblical and historic-confessional approach and marry that with *a theology of victoriously walking in the Spirit*, as it relates to the abundant life that Jesus Christ has promised to his church. Jesus did not come merely to give life, but to give believers *abundant life in the Spirit!* Is this what you experience in your daily walk?

This work is not merely about facts put together that apply to the idea of the "work of the Spirit of God" in Scripture to your life. Rather, it is taking the fundamental ideas of the Spirit's work in the life of the believer, and covering, chapter by chapter, a growing discernment on how to *walk victoriously* in the Spirit's work and how to please the Living Christ as you live before the face of God. It is here that you will come to understand the main role of the Spirit in your life day to day. We hear, *often*, that we should have "victory in Jesus" and a "Spirit-filled life." Do *you* have victory in Jesus?

---

[1] Consider John Owen's work on the "The Holy Spirit," "The Soul's Implantation," by Thomas Hooker, Jonathan Edwards' sermon, "A Supernatural and Divine Light," and the works of John Calvin (who was known as the theologian of the Holy Spirit).

Do you have victory in Jesus over sin? Do you have a Spirit-filled life conquering the world, the flesh and devil on a *daily basis?* Even though we *say* those things and ask such questions, what exactly does all that *practically mean*, and *how* does that work out in your own life as a believer? Could you explain this victory, *truly explain it*, to someone who asked you about how your life is different than theirs? I would imagine every Christian desires spiritual victory in Christ, and that they desire to walk victoriously in the Spirit as outlined by Scripture, but how would you explain that daily reliance, and how would you as a believer experience the fullness of the Spirit in your own course of life? Well, that is what this little volume is about. It is to arm you with the necessary biblical ideas surrounding a victorious and abundant life of walking in the Spirit day by day in order to please King Jesus, and experience true happiness as Christ promises.

    This study covers what abundant life is, who the Spirit is in Scripture as it relates to his work in a believer, what it means to be baptized in the Spirit, indwelt by the Spirit, anointed by the Spirit, illuminated by the Spirit, filled by the Spirit, empowered by the Spirit, and led by the Spirit. It also covers what it means to pray in the Spirit, how to exemplify the fruit of the Spirit, how to exercise your gifts in the Spirit, and *how to walk in the Spirit victoriously*. It concludes with a chapter on rejoicing in Christ in the Spirit, which ought to be a culmination of this abundant life for you as a born-again believer. Christians should be walking in abundance in Christ *right now through the work of the Spirit.* Are you? You should know what it means to walk victoriously in the Spirit, and understand the role of the Spirit in your life. You should also understand your role in following Christ's directives *to have* a victorious life in walking in the Spirit at this very moment; and that, abundantly. So why waste another moment wondering how all this works in your life?

Introduction to Reforming

Let's get started!

Chapter 1: Abundant Life

"Then said Jesus unto them again, Verily, verily, I say unto you, I am the door of the sheep," (John 10:7).

We begin our journey on a text which explains the parable of the door, porter, and shepherd. In these New Testament times in which Christ lived, several small flocks were sometimes kept in one field. The door was fastened from the inside with sticks or bars by the porter, who remained with the sheep during the night, and opened the door for the shepherds in the morning. The fold is the church, Christ is the door, the sheep are the disciples, and, consequently, the *shepherd* is also Christ. It is repetitive: the church and Christ, the church and Christ.

The porter represents God the Father. Who decides who shall enter through the door, to whom will he open the door? The Father opens the door, he decrees and sends Christ as the good Shepherd, Christ who is the door, the way, truth and life, so that the sheep he hands over to the Shepherd, or allows the Shepherd to bring in and out, in turn are blessed and find pasture and rest *in* the Shepherd.

Jesus contrasts his own care for his people with that manifested by the wickedness of the Pharisees, who had just cast out the beggar; they did not *care for him.* They abused people, and this is not what the Shepherd will ever do with the sheep that the porter has given him leave to bring in and out. They are safe in his hands. They are safe in his Father's hands.

Old Testament prophecies were full of declarations that false shepherds would arise to the injury of God's flock. "Woe be to the shepherds of Israel that do feed themselves!

Chapter 1: Abundant Life

should not the shepherds feed the flocks?" (Ezek. 34:2).[1] But other prophecies spoke of the true shepherding of God and his Messiah (Psa. 23; 77:20; Psa. 80:1; 95:7; Jer. 31:10; Ezek. 34:31; Mic. 7:14; Isa. 43:11). "And ye my flock, the flock of my pasture, are men, and I am your God, saith the Lord GOD," (Ezek. 34:31). The Pharisees were fulfilling the first line of prophecies in falsely leading the people, and Jesus was fulfilling the second in being the good shepherd.

The sheepfolds of the East are roofless enclosures, made of loose stone, or surrounded by thorn bushes, which make up a hedge of protection. They have but one door. Jesus, the true Shepherd, came in the proper and appointed way (and was the proper and appointed way as the Covenant Savior sent by the Father), in this way indicating his office as the Good Shepherd. A thief steals by cunning wiles when the Shepherd is away; a robber takes and steals by violence from another, things which are personal. The Pharisees were both thieves and robbers. They stole the sheep in the Messiah's absence, and they even *killed* the Messiah when he came. Actually, they were murdering the sheep through false doctrine, as much as they murdered the Shepherd when he came to save them.

These false teachers, of which much could be said, did not come in the ways ordained of God. What does a porter (a gatekeeper or caretaker) do in respect of thieves, the shepherd and the sheep? "To him the porter openeth; and the sheep hear his voice: and he calleth his own sheep by name, and leadeth them out." The right of free admittance is given, by order of him to whom the sheep belong. To him, God the Father, who is the porter of this spiritual door, gives willing entrance and admission to the sheep through the Shepherd; and the people of God, who are the Shepherd's sheep, willingly hear the

---

[1] *cf.* Ezek. 34:1–6; Jer. 23:1–6; Zech. 11:4–11.

Shepherd's voice. He is familiar with them and entirely at ease with them, and leads them forth to the green pastures of heavenly doctrine and to the waters of comfort and sustenance. He leads those who are with young, with his strong arm, he leads them, *gently*.

What does a door do in respect of thieves? The door protects the sheep; keeps them in and others out. It defines the place of protection; it shows the place where they will be safe. It defines the way to live life; there is but one door to enter in and out, to rest and to go for food.

"This parable spake Jesus unto them: but they understood not what things they were which he spake unto them," (John 10:6). Christ had to explain it, because the disciples did not understand it. The porter, is the one that recognizes and unlocks the way of the salvation. Verse 17 after this parable, then, is a commentary, "Therefore doth my Father love me, because I lay down my life, that I might take it again," (John 10:17). After this statement there is no further mention of the porter.

The simplifying of the parable revolves around a door, a porter, a shepherd and sheep which point to the Father, Christ and the elect. The Father decrees eternal salvation. He decrees it for the sheep which are his, all those he gives to Christ. "All that the Father giveth me shall come to me; and him that cometh to me I will in no wise cast out," (John 6:37). It is the Father's prerogative to give, or not give. (Shall the clay say to the potter why did you make me this way?)[2] It is up to the porter to decide to whom he will open the door.

The Son executes salvation and the Father is pleased for the true Shepherd to lead the sheep with all his benefits. "The Father loveth the Son, and hath given all things into his hand. He that believeth on the Son hath everlasting life: and

---

[2] See Romans 8-9.

he that believeth not the Son shall not see life; but the wrath of God abideth on him," (John 3:35-36). What does a Shepherd do? It is his job, to protect and mature the flock. Shepherds who fulfill this are *good* shepherds. Jesus, claimed and taught that *he* was the Good Shepherd. Such shepherds will protect their livelihood. They will protect that which means something to them. Christ, in his radical protection of the flock, gives his very *life* for them. "As the Father knoweth me, even so know I the Father: and I lay down my life for the sheep," (John 10:15). His giving of his life, then translates into his ability to lead them in and out of the fold, into green pastures and still waters to restore their soul and cause their lives to flourish as cups that not only get filled, but "runneth over," (Psalm 23). Not just cups that have a *little* in them, they have more than they could possibly ever have, and their cups spill over, run over, like a waterfall.

    The sheep hear the voice of the Shepherd. There is a great distinction in these sheep. They are called by name. They are known by name. The Shepherd leads them into the pastures by his calling. This voice is communicated by the Shepherd, Jesus, to the sheep, his church, by way of the Spirit and through the word; these are the pastures in which they feed.

    What does Christ do as the Shepherd for the sheep? He also *finds*. "And other sheep I have, which are not of this fold: them also I must bring, and they shall hear my voice; and there shall be one fold, and one shepherd," (John 10:16). "But he answered and said, I am not sent but unto the lost sheep of the house of Israel," (Matt. 15:24). "What man of you, having an hundred sheep, if he lose one of them, doth not leave the ninety and nine in the wilderness, and go after that which is lost, until he find it?" (Luke 15:4). He finds these sheep, he goes after them, appointed by the Father to do so as the Redeemer and Deliverer.

Jesus saves. The only way to eternal life is to be saved by the Good Shepherd to be a sheep in his fold. One door opens the pen of sheep; one door, one way, one truth, one divine mandate for eternal life. What does this one way and one truth *give* by way of the Shepherd? It gives life. It is the only way of life. "Verily, verily, I say unto you, I am the door of the sheep," (John 10:7). The only way of eternal life is to follow this Shepherd, and to be lead and guided through the gate in coming and going under his protection and nurture. "I am the good shepherd, and know my sheep, and am known of mine," (John 10:14). What is he *known* for? What does he *give and save* for? Not only life, but *abundant life*. Not common life, but abundant life. Not customary life, but abundant life. Not ordinary life, but abundant life. Not just life ... truly, it is abundant life.

Christ also protects the sheep; divine preservation of the sheep. The one who gives life, gives abundant life, and leads the sheep by his voice, communicating to them safety and nurture, protects them from robbers and thieves; the world, the flesh, the devil, murderers, liars and false teachers. Christ is in fact a hedge of protection for them. He gives them liberty and life (*true* freedom), to come and go by way of the door to sustenance. He leads them to the word, through the power of the Holy Spirit to come and go to grow, to come and go in his leading, to come and go under his watchful eye. "And when he putteth forth his own sheep, he goeth before them, and the sheep follow him: for they know his voice," (John 10:4).

Christ gives them pasture, the nourishment of the sheep. It begins with *his voice,* with his communication to them, telling them where to go, where it is safe to eat, where it is safe to lie down, or walk about, or drink of the water. They receive this pasture and by it, as they listen to his voice, grow into maturity. "My sheep hear my voice, and I know them, and they follow me: And I give unto them eternal life; and they shall never perish, neither shall any man pluck them out of my hand," (John 10:27-28).

Abundant life is given to the sheep by Christ. Jesus does not give life, but *abundant life.* περισσὸν (John 10:10) *abundantly.* It means exceedingly, over and above, more than is necessary, superadded, surpassing, uncommon, most remarkable, more excellent! They have this at the direction of the word, the communication from his mouth to their ears; the communication of his benefits as the Living Logos, the *Living Word of God.* With false teachers, "the sheep did not hear them," (John 10:8). With the Shepherd, "My sheep hear my voice...and I give unto them eternal life," (John 10:27-28). The work of Christ must be a great power indeed, not only to change the heart of a wicked sinner to himself, to regenerate the sheep, but also to bestow on them spiritual life when they were dead, and not only that, but give them abundant life. He does not give them just one thing, but *all things* concerning salvation. They are able of the Shepherd to come and go in this abundant life. They are given all his benefits as Shepherd, as he is the Covenant Mediator. "What shall I render unto the LORD for all his benefits toward me? I will take the cup of salvation, and call upon the name of the LORD," (Psa. 116:12-13).

In the covenant of grace an abundant provision is made to not only save the sheep, but through Christ, in the power of his Spirit, to give them this abundant life, a life continually pressing them on towards heavenly perfection. The Father opens the gate, the Shepherd leads them in and out, but what is that *life-giving principle which enlivens them?* Christ communicates spiritual life to all his sheep, all that the Father has given him. They are quickened, and lively, but how? This life he gives to his sheep is by quickening them by his Spirit, and continues that quickening by the continual supplies of living grace which he communicates to them every day. "...he that soweth to the Spirit shall of the Spirit reap life everlasting," (Gal. 6:8). "And if Christ be in you, the body is dead because of sin; but the Spirit is life because of righteousness," (Rom. 8:10). "The Spirit of God hath made me, and the breath of the Almighty hath given me life," (Job 33:4). A famous preacher, John Owen, said, "Neither does this living head communicate only a bare life to believers, that they should merely live and no more, a poor, weak, dying life, as it were; but he gives out sufficiently to afford them a strong, vigorous, thriving, flourishing life, (John 10:10). He comes not only that his sheep "may have life" but that "they may have it more abundantly;" that is, in a plentiful manner, so as that they may flourish, be fat and fruitful. It is this way with the whole body of Christ, and every one of its members."[3]

The eternal salvation which Christians have by Christ through the Spirit is a bountiful and abundant life. What is abundant life? Or it may be so deemed, *eternal life?* Jesus said in John 17:3, "And this is eternal life..." *What* is eternal life? This. What is "This?" He continues and says, "...that they know you the only true God, and Jesus Christ whom you have sent." Peter confessed in John 6:68–69, "You have the words of eternal life, and we have believed, and have come to know, that you are the Holy One of God." The very nature of faith in Christ, built on conversion, repentance for sin, belief in the Good News of the Gospel, stretching back all the way to Genesis 3:15, dictates knowing something about God's Savior. There are a great number of darkened philosophical atheists who think, because of their depravity, that Christianity is an irrational leap of faith. Not even remotely. It is a system of belief, set down by the voice of the Shepherd, found clearly in the infallible, inerrant, and inspired Scriptures, the

---

[3] Owen, John, *Works*, Vol. 6, 251.

inscripturated word, the Logos himself communicating abundant life through such knowledge – but quickened by the Spirit.[4] If people are to believe something, faith then rests on something to be believed. Christianity does not teach blind faith. It teaches a faith which has as its foundation knowledge. The sheep know Christ, they follow him. They hear his voice, and discern his presence and work among them. He is trusted. In this they follow. People have to assent to something they know or understand. If they assent to something, then, that presupposes knowledge.

Where does knowledge come from? In this case, concerning eternal salvation, it comes from the word of God, the living Christ, the Shepherd of the sheep, the one whom the Father has given into his hands all things. It is then enlivened by the regenerating power of the Spirit, where faith is like that reflex, that cannot but believe when the change is made. Faith is produced both internally and externally from the preaching of the word and by the teaching of Christ through the Holy Spirit. Internally, it stems from the new birth in the mind of the sheep, and externally it stems for the teaching of the word through preaching. There are specific things that one must believe in order to be saved. It is utterly absurd to think that one can be a Christian without *believing* something. They believe in the one sent of God, who comes to his sheep, who is the very Door himself, who is let in by the Father, and grants to his people the abundance of eternal life. This God does not do this for everyone, but only for his sheep, for there are no goats in that pen. Belief in Christ, in his work and salvation, is the constant exercise of the Spirit working faith in the believer, coming in and going out to pasture. It is a belief not only for some temporary fix, but for eternal and everlasting life. But this life must be thought of as life in abundance.

---

[4] See the *1647 Westminster Confession of Faith*, Chapter 1, of the holy Scripture.

Scripture is filled with this idea of not simply life, but abundant life; abundant life that begins now, in this life, but is forever, and is eternal life. Psalm 36:8 says, "They shall be abundantly satisfied with the fatness of thy house; and thou shalt make them drink of the river of thy pleasures." Song of Solomon 5:1 says, "I am come into my garden, my sister, my spouse: I have gathered my myrrh with my spice; I have eaten my honeycomb with my honey; I have drunk my wine with my milk: eat, O friends; drink, yea, drink abundantly, O beloved." Isaiah 55:7, "Let the wicked forsake his way, and the unrighteous man his thoughts: and let him return unto the LORD, and he will have mercy upon him; and to our God, for he will abundantly pardon." Ephesians 3:20 states, "Now unto him that is able to do exceeding abundantly above all that we ask or think, according to the power that worketh in us."

Abundant life is tied to the riches of Christ through his work. The work of Christ is a *treasure-house* of richness. "That in the ages to come he might shew the exceeding riches of his grace in his kindness toward us through Christ Jesus," (Eph. 2:7). Not just grace, not just life, abundant grace which gives abundant life from Christ in Scripture is often designated as the *riches* of Christ. "Riches and honour are with me; yea, durable riches and righteousness," (Prov. 8:18). "But ye shall be named the Priests of the LORD: men shall call you the Ministers of our God: ye shall eat the riches of the Gentiles, and in their glory shall ye boast yourselves," (Isa. 61:6). "If therefore ye have not been faithful in the unrighteous mammon, who will commit to your trust the true riches?" (Luke 16:11). "Or despisest thou the riches of his goodness and forbearance and longsuffering; not knowing that the goodness of God leadeth thee to repentance?" (Rom. 2:4). "And that he might make known the riches of his glory on the vessels of mercy, which he had afore prepared unto glory," (Rom. 9:23). "In whom we have redemption through his blood, the forgiveness of sins, according to the riches of his grace," (Eph. 1:7). "But my God shall supply all your need according to his riches in glory by Christ Jesus," (Phil. 4:19). "God would make known what is the riches of the glory of this mystery," (Col. 1:27). "...the unsearchable riches of Christ;" (Eph. 3:8). "...all riches of the full assurance of understanding," (Col. 2:2). Is that a belaboring of the point? I think Christians often miss this.

All that Christ did far exceeds anything Adam could have ever done in paradise. The reward of the work of the Shepherd for the sheep in his active and passive obedience of the Son of God is infinitely greater than anything Adam would have obtained, even if he would have obeyed God perfectly. Christ, by his active obedience (living out the law of God perfectly for his sheep) and by his passive obedience (as a perfect sacrifice on the cross for sin and justice for his sheep) has obtained a greater good, happiness and glory for his redeemed sheep, as the Good Shepherd, than anything the obedience of Adam would have ever gained. He gives them *the Spirit* abundantly. He gives them eternal life abundantly. The sheep of Christ's fold are raised up to sit with him on his throne. *What kind of a Shepherd is this?*

These redeemed sheep reign with him as kings and priests. They share in all the benefits of his work. They receive all his reward. They gain all the fruit of that reward and enjoy its blessings as if they had performed all those acts themselves. Abundant life is tied to the resurrected and ascended Son of Man who now sends the Spirit in abundance. "Not by works of righteousness which we have done, but according to his mercy he saved us, by the washing of regeneration, and renewing of the Holy Ghost; which he shed on us abundantly through Jesus Christ our Saviour;" (Titus 3:5-6). Christ's life endows to his people, as the Shepherd does to his sheep, the abundance of the Spirit, the richness of the Spirit, in a measure beyond even their understanding. Ask *airy fairy* Christians if they have an abundance of the Spirit, and they will say *yes.* But their understanding of that is emotional. "I feel spiritual. I feel the Spirit. I feel enraptured. I've lifted my countenance in something that makes me feel like I am more spiritual when the praise music is loud that when it is soft. I feel more spiritual when I pray longer than when I pray short. I feel spiritual when I wave my hand at the words of the jingle I'm singing than if not." Richard Sibbes said, "If Christ gives the water of life, he gives rivers, not small streams. If he gives peace and joy, he gives it in abundance; his scope is to fill up our joy to the full. As he is able, so is he willing to do for us far more abundantly than we are able to think or speak," (Eph. 3:20). Where Christ is present, he brings plenty with him. If there is no wine at first, he will rather turn water into wine, than there should be a fail."[5] The Spirit flows to his people from the work, life, death, resurrection, ascension and present intercession of Jesus, at his direction in the word. And has he not said that they shall have *life-abundant?* What will he give then? A *little* life? Some of the Spirit, part of the Spirit, or will he give abundant life in the Spirit? It will not merely be that they are alive, but that they are lively, enthusiastic, high-spirited in their life because of what they know to be true about God. They are not merely resuscitated like a person coming out of a coma in the hospital, but they are dancing and springing up in a lively manner. Christ sends the Spirit to his people which is the vital principle of abundant life *in* them.

But it is not about the Spirit, rather, the Spirit directs the sheep to look to, hear the voice of, and follow the Shepherd through the eternal word that brings eternal life. This is why the Spirit is compared to the flowing of life-giving water in the Scriptures. "...ye shall be baptized with the Holy Ghost," (Acts

---

[5] Sibbes, R. (n.d.). The Complete Works of Richard Sibbes Volume.

Chapter 1: Abundant Life

1:5). The Spirit shall fall on the Christian, on the believer, to shower them with all the benefits of Jesus Christ, submerged, in the word. They are sprinkled with the power and life of the Spirit, in the word. The Spirit does not baptize, so to speak; the Lord Jesus baptizes *with* the Spirit. He sprinkles them with the Spirit that they might have and cultivate that life-principle, and that more abundantly. Even, "out of his belly shall flow rivers of living water," (John 7:38). Out of his belly, rivers of water? What does Jesus mean? In the synagogues of old on the eighth day of the feast of tabernacles, called by the Jews Hosanna Rabbah, the great Hosanna, and by the Apostle John, "The last day, the great day of the feast," in his Gospel, four portions of scripture were accustomed to be read, *viz.* Deuteronomy, the last words of the prophet Malachi, the beginning of Joshua, and the passage concerning Solomon's rising up from his knees after his prayer and blessing the people with a loud voice in 1 Kings 8. Then Jesus, who was the fulfillment of the law and the prophets, He who is the true Joshua and Solomon, stood up, saying, "If any man thirst, let him come to me and drink. He that believeth on me, as the scripture has said, out of his belly shall flow rivers of living water," (John 7:38). Why *water?* Tremelius[6] says on this, "The Jews on that day used with much solemnity and joy to fetch water from the river Siloah to the temple where, being delivered to the priests, it was by them poured on the altar, the people in the meantime singing out of Isaiah, "with joy shall it draw water out of the wells of salvation," (Isa. 12:3). Jesus tells them of other and better waters, which they were to have of him, according to what he had elsewhere said by the ministry of the same prophet, "Lo, every one that thirsteth, come ye to the waters," (Isa. 55:1-2)."[7] Why labor for things of

---

[6] Immanuel Tremellius was an Italian Jewish convert to Christianity. He was known as a leading Hebraist and Bible translator.
[7] See John Arrowsmith's *A Chain of Theological Principles*.

no profit? Carrying water to the altar from a river in expectation, that comes and goes once a year? What about coming from the Messiah, with never ending water, that flows from within, instead of water that is looked at from without?

The indwelling Spirit, the living waters of abundant life, empowering believers for service before Christ are what Christ offers in the Gospel. *Come to the waters of life,* he says. Come through the door, come to the pasture, come to the still water, where they will flow out of the Christian. Christ is described as, "the fountain of living waters," (Jer. 2:13), who sends the living water of the Spirit into his people; an inexhaustible source of life. "And thus shalt thou do unto them, to cleanse them: Sprinkle water of purifying upon them," (Num. 8:7). "Then will I sprinkle clean water upon you, and ye shall be clean," (Ezek. 36:25). Water does not make one clean in the eyes of God, but rather, water, as a symbol of the Spirit, demonstrates the word-picture of being clean and constantly washed by the flow. Sprinkling by men is but for an instant. Sprinkling by Christ is done in abundance and does not ever stop. "Let us draw near with a true heart in full assurance of faith, having our hearts sprinkled from an evil conscience, and our bodies washed with pure water," (Heb. 10:22).

Abundant life is tied to the Work of the Spirit, this flow of living water, in applying Christ's merits to his sheep as they pasture and walk before him. How are people made partakers of the redemption purchased by Christ? By the effectual application of all the work of Christ to them by his Holy Spirit. How does the Spirit apply to them the redemption purchased by Christ? The Spirit applies to them the redemption purchased by Christ, by working faith in them, and by this uniting them to Christ in their effectual calling, the calling in the heart. By making them hear the voice of the Shepherd. By guiding them in his word. By causing them

Chapter 1: Abundant Life

to hear his sweet voice. By providing for them all the substance they need out of the word.

What benefits do those who are effectually called partake of in this life have as described by the word? They "partake of justification, adoption and all manner of sanctification, and the several benefits which in this life do either accompany or flow from them." This is how the *1647 Westminster Shorter Catechism* puts it.[8] It flows from them, in them, abundantly. This is the abundant life Christ's promises through his Spirit, to his sheep, for their plentiful and bountiful life as they pasture from the door to the place of abundant life. This not only happens here, but also continues into the life to come in heaven.

Abundant life is tied to Christ's work and blessing in both grace and comfort. What Christian is not looking for more grace, or if they think they have an abundance of grace, they look for some form of further comfort, or as might be said, assurance? Grace and comfort for the Christian only flow from the Shepherd to the sheep by way of the Spirit. It only flows to them by the Spirit. Christians look for the Spirit, more of the Spirit, a further working of the Spirit in his application of more grace and comfort. They look for a continual revival in their graces, and they look to be more lively and active in the service of God, as well as gain peace and consolation in their walk. They look for Christ to send more of the latter rain. They look to Christ to pour his Spirit out in abundance. What is the Christian life without the living Spirit? What is the body of Christ without the Spirit's work?

I've often asked people, "what would be left if Christ took the Spirit out of you? What good work would be done apart from the Spirit? What good part would be left without that vital union? What motion would be left without the

---

[8] See questions 33-35 in the *Westminster Shorter Catechism*.

Spirit's fruit?" "It is the spirit that quickeneth; the flesh profiteth nothing: the words that I speak unto you, they are spirit, and they are life," (John 6:63). Who said that? Is this not what Jesus, the Shepherd, said? There is nothing that can work any lively work in the soul other than Christ through the Spirit. How does he do this? Where will these rivers of living water flow from? Where is the fountain welling up in them for eternal life? It is by the Spirit through the word. Would Abraham have looked for a city whose builder and maker was God if not by the Spirit? Would Solomon have been wise if not by the Spirit? Would David have had a heart after God if not by the Spirit? Would Moses esteemed suffering better than the glories of Egypt if not by the Spirit? Would any of the prophets endured such hard lives without the Spirit? Would the apostles have been martyred without the fruit of the Spirit of Faith? The Spirit of God works on the soul by the means of grace, by motioning the soul to take the kingdom of God by force, and violence with the gracious habits of the Spirit's power working and producing righteous fruit in them. When the Spirit of God changes a man from darkness to light, he then indwells him, baptizes him, empowers his for service, resides in him and provides to him all the abundance of life in Christ. He works in that soul to change it and transform it into the image of Christ. He does this day by day, here a little, there a little, that they might have an abundant life *right now.*

    Reformation of life is useless without the Spirit of God. All the best things are nothing without the Spirit. One can have the most biblical worship service, the most intense bible study times, the longest seasons of prayer and without the Spirit of God working in those things they are nothing beneficial to the believer. Without the Spirit they tend towards cursing and not blessing. This is what the Pharisees did. All the most biblical duties a Christian can muster are nothing without living water flowing in and through them; the Spirit – this is where the Shepherd of the sheep leads them to and in. Without the Spirit, it is not even life, it is by no means abundant life; no life at all. All those things are dead without the Spirit of Christ. Apart from the Spirit, there is only death and hell. Bringing Christ to the work, bringing Christ in every action, bringing his work and life through the Spirit in all that the Christian does is to tap into the abundant life God seeks to embellish on his sheep. He does not simply give them puddles to drink from, but he fills their cups so abundantly as to cause them to overflow; as David said in Psalm 23. "The LORD is my shepherd; I shall not want. He maketh me to lie down in green pastures: he leadeth me beside the still waters. He restoreth my soul: he leadeth me in the paths of righteousness for his name's sake. Yea, though I walk through the valley of the shadow of death, I will fear no evil: for thou art with me; thy rod and thy staff they comfort me. Thou preparest a table before me in the presence of mine enemies: thou anointest my head with oil; my cup runneth over. Surely goodness and mercy shall follow me all the days of my life: and I will dwell in the house of the LORD for ever." (Psa. 23:1-6). This is the *Old* Testament. It is an abundant life idea. It is the parable Christ gave, as a precursor to set the spiritual stage of this psalm, truly. What is all this but by the Spirit of Christ?

    The Spirit enlivens and quickens all the means of grace for the Christian and points them to all the work of Christ in free grace and abundant mercy. Goodness and mercy through Christ, by the appointment of the Father, in the application of all the blessings of the Spirit sent from the intercessory throne of Jesus enables Christians to have abundant life. It is life to its fullest. Surely goodness and mercy shall follow the saints all the days of their life. If anything is accomplished in the Christian walk, in hearing the word, in reading the word, in praying, in drawing closer to God, in exercising the fruit of the Spirit, in any Christian duty, one must look to Christ, Christ at the right hand of the Father, interceding to send the life-giving Spirit in abundance to those things – he is the one who sends the Spirit who quickens and makes all things alive for the believer.

Do Christians take hold of the Spirit like Jacob did the angel, to not let him go without the blessing? And in those spiritual benefits it will not be that they will merely have life, but that they will have abundant life in the Spirit. This is coming and going from the pen, through the door, opened by the porter led by the Shepherd to abundant life.

You should be encouraged to live an abundant life in the Spirit. Christ came not to give you life, but abundant life. The Spirit is not sent by Christ, from his throne, to give little droplets of water. David's cup overflowed; does yours? Abraham's faith made him our father of faith; is your faith exercised in the same way. This is an abundant and growing supernatural and divine light that grows and grows day after day in the Spirit. Jonathan Edwards, "The Spirit of God ... unites himself with the mind of a saint, takes him for his temple, actuates and influences him as a new supernatural principle of life and action. ... The Holy Spirit operates in the minds of the godly, by uniting himself to them, and living in them, and exerting his own nature in the exercise of their faculties."[9] What does he exactly do to you in this? He communicates Christ to you, and edifies you in the love of the Father, and gives you abundant life *in* the Spirit.

The Spirit's treasures of grace are unsearchable; his storehouse is inexhaustible because it is a communication of Christ himself. He looks to improve in you all his supplies of grace to increase them in your life to such an extent that you

---

[9] Edwards, Jonathan, *Works*, Vol. 4, 440.

will say as David did, my cup overflows. Such grace from Christ, through the Spirit, communicated to you, is of abundant strength and power. The old puritan divines called it a, "virtuous medicine," that destroys disease, and comforts, refreshes, and strengthens our spiritual nature. You can have this *now*.

You can have abundant life now in the Spirit. Psalm 81 is most excellent to this, where God says, "open thy mouth wide, and I will fill it," (Psa. 81:10). This preserves us by his Spirit in attending us and encouraging us to be fed to the fill. Not simply open your mouth, *but open wide*. You cannot open wide enough for all that Christ will give you. You cannot take in enough of all that Christ accomplished. He leads you to rich pastures. "Who hath saved us, and called us with an holy calling, not according to our works, but according to his own purpose and grace, which was given us in Christ Jesus before the world began, But is now made manifest by the appearing of our Saviour Jesus Christ, who hath abolished death, and hath brought life and immortality to light through the Gospel," (2 Tim. 1:9-10). Not only life, but immortal life, eternal life, abundant life. He did this through the Good news of the Gospel. Where men were perishing in their sin, he sent his Spirit to save his sheep, and gather to himself one-fold. He did this to protect them, lead them, guide them, provide for them, secure them, watch over them, in fact to have abundant life while they live wherever they are. Our deliverance is spiritual, and it rides on the work of the Spirit in the pastures that Christ leads us to. "Being so delivered is not simply for you to be fat and full in him, but also to be useful in the Kingdom; "that being delivered from the justice of God, the condemning power of the Law, the reigning power of sin, the sting of an accusing conscience, the rage and malice of the Devil, and the intolerable torments of Hell, we might, with all love and thankfulness, cheerfully serve that God, whose mercy hath been extended towards us in those things, which are of highest and most precious concernment."[10] "Now our Lord Jesus Christ himself, and God, even our Father, which hath loved us, and hath given us everlasting consolation and good hope through grace," (2 Thess. 2:16).

You have comfort and consolation in the Spirit, for this comes with abundant life. Wayward charismatics who warp this doctrine of the Spirit look for an ecstatic experience of *feeling and emotion.* Feelings are fickle and often deceptive. Can one derive comfort and eternal consolation simply from a feeling? Or is it that the Spirit must flow through them as he works his fruit in them, filled up by the sweetness of Christ's voice in his word, where rivers of living water flow from them? "Grace be with you all," (Titus 3:15). How? By feeling? "...ye abound in this grace also," (2 Cor. 8:7). How? By mere subjective experience? "And now for a little space grace hath been shewed from the LORD our God, ... that our God may lighten our eyes, and give us a little reviving," (Ezra 9:8). How does the Spirit do this? Does one *feel* their way through abundant life? Is this what it means to have abundant life in Christ? To merely *feel* good?

Certainly, Christians feel good about what Christ has done, and feel excited, and we are certainly emotional beings, but all those emotions are informed by the word of God. Abundant life now in the Spirit is not based on the Shepherd cuddling up with the sheep to give them goosebumps. Where does Christ *ever* say that? He leads them, directs them, and he purposefully does this by his voice, which they in turn are ready to hear and to follow as his sheep. This is all accomplished through Christ's Spirit in the inscripturated word of God. We walk either by faith or by sight. A life in the

---

[10] Hopkins, Ezekiel, *The Works of Ezekiel Hopkins*, Volume 1 (Edinburgh: A. C. Black, 1841); reprinted., (Morgan, PA.: Soli Deo Gloria Publications, 1997), 271.

Spirit is a life of faith; a life of emotional goosebumps is not.

No Christian wants a life merely of sense. The life of faith is in Christ, and is built up in the Spirit, by the Spirit, through the Spirit and by no other way. Such a life is one of abundance, at least, that is what *Jesus says*. How could it not be? The Father gives the Shepherd the sheep he's protected, the Shepherd leads them through the door to an abundance of benefits in the Spirit in green pastures and besides still waters. How can eternal life, abundant life not be extravagant when the entire Trinity is behind the work?

You will also have abundant life in heaven in the Spirit. The promised bliss of heaven will be a furthering of abundant life in the Spirit. 2 Peter. 1:11, "For so an entrance shall be ministered unto you abundantly into the everlasting kingdom of our Lord and Savior Jesus Christ." Even your first steps into the entrance and gate of heaven are *abundant*. If you think you have an abundant life in the Spirit now, wait until heaven. "The Lord had shed forth the Spirit abundantly" in the renewing of his saints, so what will be that abundance when they are *fully transformed?* That which starts here continues there. But that does not detract from what Christ says of *this* life. He does not say only in heaven is your life more abundant. He says that abundant life is yours, *now* in the Spirit if you take hold of it, if you follow his voice.

Let us in all this see clearly the great need of Christ crucified and risen, who sends his Spirit to quicken our dead hearts, and subdue our strong temptations. Let us seek out his voice, and apply ourselves to his throne to shower down more of the Spirit, not that we will gain more, but that what he has bestowed we will in fact take advantage to hold fast to. At the throne of grace, where we find the floods of the living water flowing down on us, Christ is ready to answer all your requests, and supply all your needs by his Spirit. Remember, it was Christ's special work in the world, to bring abundant life to his people, as the good Shepherd, and to destroy the works of the devil, so that you may have life, and that more abundantly.

I have failed to give you particulars, about *how* to take hold of this Spirit, or *how* to take hold of Christ's benefits. In the next 13 chapters, or so, we will deal with each aspect of the Spirit, and how, piece by piece, to have a better practical theology of the Spirit to live the victorious Christian life in Christ, by his power. One cannot rightly have abundant life in Christ through the Spirit without knowing who the Spirit is, so our next chapter will deal with the person and work of the Holy Spirit.

Chapter 2:
The Person and Work of the Holy Spirit

"But the Comforter, which is the Holy Ghost, whom the Father will send in my name, he shall teach you all things, and bring all things to your remembrance, whatsoever I have said unto you," (John 14:26).

Throughout the greater part of church history, to a certain extent, one of the most neglected among biblical doctrines is the teaching concerning the Holy Spirit. Scripture is filled with truths identifying and explaining the person and work of the Holy Spirit in creation, through and in the Messiah, and in believers. Truths about the Holy Spirit are usually taught within the larger framework of the Trinity; or they concern specific other doctrines like mortification of sin or sanctification of the Christian. We need to consider the person and work of the Spirit in more general terms, as a precursor to coming chapters of walking victoriously in the Spirit.

The Spirit of God is the spark which gives that abundant life. And this Spirit is intimately related to the work of the Father and Son in the covenantal work of redemption. Truths surrounding the Trinity and the person of the Holy Spirit are directly related. There is one God; one divine essence. The same divine essence is common to the three divine Persons known as the Father, Son and Holy Spirit in one God. Between these three persons of the Godhead, there exists a natural order of subsistence and operation. This operation teaches that the first Person has life in himself (John 5:26) and that the second and third Persons subsist and act from the first; not in substance (their essence is not different) but only in operation, of the way they work in relation to our perception and what God has revealed in the word. This order of Persons is from eternity because they are all God. Their order of existence in relationship to one another as God is the ground and reason there are three names or designations of persons in the Godhead – Father, Son and Holy Spirit. But *who is this Spirit?*

As much as I don't like Bible drills, to some extent, I need to give you a survey of the person and work of the Spirit; it is purposeful in this regard. We cannot understand what it means to live victoriously in the Spirit unless we survey the work of the Spirit. He cannot merely be assumed. He must be pointed out and biblically proven. We do, however, have a starting point, John 14. We start there for the expressed purpose of setting the theological stage of the sending of the Spirit by the ascended Son of Man. First, we will concern ourselves with John 14, then we will run a purposeful bible drill to survey his work.

The context of John 14 is Jesus' discourse of departure and promise. Jesus is leaving, but not leaving the disciples alone. He promises to be with them until the end of the age (Matthew 28), and then bring them to himself in his kingdom. How will the descended, incarnate Son of Man be with them if he goes back to heaven? He will be united with them by the organic power of the Holy Spirit. This Spirit will teach them and remind them of all Christ said and did. He says in verse 15 – keep my commandments; in verse 21 – hath my commandments and keepeth them; in verse 23 – keep my words; in verse 24 – those who do not love him do not keep his commandments. These all point to the communication of God to his church. The Spirit's work here is set in the context and operation of the word of God given to the church, and its understanding of the Messiah, the Christ, the Redeemer, where the Shepherd leads the sheep to green pastures and still waters that flow to life eternal. In verse 26 the Holy Spirit is

Chapter 2: The Person and Work of the Holy Spirit

designated as "another" Comforter. Christ is a Comforter. He was born, lived with his disciples during this time of his coming, taught them, (was teaching them), about the Father's character and will; but he would leave. *Another* Comforter was needful. Why? Because Christ was going to ascend to the Father, and the Father and Son would in turn send the Spirit from the throne of the ascended Christ.

At no time in the history of the church of God, has the Son of Man come down from heaven, then depart and go back to heaven, other than in this one place and time. Once he fulfilled his covenantal obligations, he would, in interceding for his church, send another Comforter, which he, as the Son of Man, had never done before. That does not mean God had never sent his Spirit to his people to work and motion them and use them and gift them. That only means the *resurrected and ascended Christ* had not done that *as the exalted God-man*. How many Christians fail to understand that point has created immeasurable doctrinal error in the church. This Christ, the one who declares the Father in comforting with the word, would in turn send the Spirit and comfort them again through biblical illumination sent from his exalted covenantal position.

This Spirit is sent by the Father and the Son. "But when the Comforter is come, whom I will send unto you from the Father, even the Spirit of truth, which proceedeth from the Father, he shall testify of me," (John 15:26). In terms of the procession of the Spirit, He proceeds from the Father *and* the Son. John 15:26 says, "whom I shall send to you from the Father, the Spirit of truth who proceeds from the Father, He will testify of Me." The term "proceeds" signifies an ever-enduring procession. The Spirit proceeds forever from the Father.

He also proceeds from the Son. John 16:14 states, "He will glorify Me, for He will take of what is Mine and declare it to you." The Son is eternally generated from the Father, and hears what the Father commands and speaks. The Spirit proceeds from them both in order to speak what he hears the Son teach, and to confirm his teaching by supernatural power and divine illumination. As John 16:13 says, "for He will not speak on His own authority, but whatever He hears He will speak; and He will tell you things to come." What does the Comforter teach?

The Spirit teaches the Christ, the Living word. In terms of the deity of the Spirit, it is proved by the procession of the Spirit from God, and the incommunicable acts of creation and providence as ascribed to the Spirit (Gen. 1:6; Psalm 33:6; Job 26:13). Divine attributes are ascribed to him (1 Cor. 2:10-11; Psalm 139:7; Romans 8:26; 1 Cor. 1:13). He is placed in rank with the Father and the Son (such as at Christ's baptism – Matthew 3:16), and the name of God is directly given to him (Acts 5:3-4; *cf.* Psalm 95:7 and Heb. 3:7). "And Jesus, when he was baptized, went up straightway out of the water: and, lo, the heavens were opened unto him, and he saw the Spirit of God descending like a dove, and lighting upon him," (Matt. 3:16). He Teaches all things. He will teach all that which the word communicates. He will testify, or shine the light of God's truth on the Anointed Savior and Son of Man. He will make plain what he has said in Scripture, and what Christ has said to the disciples. In this way he makes plain the Old Testament, and the Messiah's witness to the Old Testament. He will also carry along the Apostles to teach the Old Testament clearly (since he was its inspirer as well), in their letters, Gospels and canonical writings. The Holy Spirit brings to remembrance, whatsoever Christ has exegeted of the Father, all things he said to them, (John 14:26).

Christ promised to send the Spirit in this way of teaching. This is something Christ has never done before, in that, the ascended Christ sends the Spirit when he enters into his glory. Again, this does not mean that the Spirit was not at work before. It *does* mean that the glorified and risen Christ had not ever, yet, sent the Spirit from a position of ascension, because he had not yet come in history. And now that he has come, and now that he ascends, he now sends the Spirit. The Spirit is spoken of as one of the fruits of Christ's death to his people. "Nevertheless I tell you the truth; It is expedient for you that I go away: for if I go not away, the Comforter will not come unto you; but if I depart, I will send him unto you," (John 16:7). All the gifts of the Spirit to his church are the fruits of Christ's purchase and work. They are not given by the Christ, until the Christ ascends into heaven.

There is a difference between the Spirit's procession from the Father and the Son all through Scripture, and the sending of *Another Comforter* by the Christ as the risen and ascended Son of Man. All the graces given by Christ, through the Spirit to believers proceed from this same Spirit who worked many works in the Old Testament in the Covenant of Grace. But when Jesus goes into heaven, he will send the Spirit, and attached to the Spirit will be all the benefits of his everlasting covenant given to all believers.

Jesus says there is a coming comfort of the Holy Spirit, παράκλητον, the Paraclete, or Advocate. This refers to one who is called in for aid; an advocate, one who pleads the cause of another and also gives him wise counsel. It is used of the Holy Spirit destined to take the place of Christ with the apostles (after Christ's ascension to the Father), to lead them to a deeper knowledge of Gospel truth, and give them divine strength needed to enable them to undergo trials and persecutions on behalf of the divine kingdom. He is designated by Christ as the πνεῦμα τῆς ἀληθείας (John 14:17), the Spirit of Truth. He is tasked with disseminating the truth of the Father and the Son as the τὸ πνεῦμα τὸ ἅγιον (John 14:26), the Holy Spirit. Separated to that holy work of saving, obtaining, mortifying and sanctifying the bride of Christ.

The Spirit is sent to teach the church *about Christ.* There must be belief in Christ as he is the Son of God, the Son of Man, that Advocate and Redeemer. The Son of Man has come to exegete the Father to his people; to teach them. The Spirit then, teaches through the word, reminding the disciples of everything said to them by the Christ; everything, that is, how Jesus Christ fulfills Scripture. And, what new institution or applications are made from a correct understanding of the Old Testament now written down in the New Testament. The Scriptures demonstrate the truth that Christ is God, and the Redeemer of men. That men are to believe on the name of the Son of God and to have life through his name, (1 John 5:11ff and John 20:31). Men are to know, to believe in Christ as the Mediator, that their faith and hope may be settled in God alone. If the Lord Jesus advocates on behalf of the Father for sinners, those sinners by no means will be plucked out of his hand. His relationship to God the Father assures believers that the intercession of Christ as High-Priest is irresistible, it is indisputable by the Father. All that Christ asks is fulfilled for them. The Son of Man was consecrated and perfected by covenant, fulfilled all things in covenant, and is able by his powerful intercession to save those to the uttermost who come to God by him, (Heb. 7:25, 28). God sent his Son to exegete the Father, to instruct. But upon the end of his work, he would be glorified and ascend and physically leave. He must, then, send another Comforter, another advocate, who will "teach you all things and remind you of everything I have said to you," who will be presently with you.

The one coming is termed *the Helper* in John 15:26, "But when the Helper comes, whom I shall send to you from the Father, the Spirit of truth who proceeds from the Father, he will testify of Me." His designation is to confirm the work and person of Christ, and teach believers the truth as in John

16:14, "He will glorify Me, for he will take of what is Mine and declare it to you." Being taught all things by the Spirit does not mean the disciples will know all things, or know things comprehensibly. Men learn imperfectly. They would have an advocate that teaches them and reminds them as forgetful men. They would in turn teach the church, and the Spirit would be with them to teach in a way as to take what is Christ's glory, and be a witness and testimony through preaching and teaching the word to the church. Having the Holy Spirit, you will be taught all things, and he will make you prepared to do all things that are necessary for your salvation and the salvation of the church. They shall have power and direction from the Holy Spirit. "For it concerned them not only to know what they should do, but whence they should have strength to do what was required of them," said Thomas Manton rightly.[1]

    The Holy Spirit is God who is sent by the Father and the Son to apply Christ's saving benefits to the elect. This Holy Spirit, the Comforter, sent by Jesus Christ, as a result of Christ's intercession (John 14:16). He is sent in the name of Christ, (John 14:26), to teach the saints, (John 14:26), dwelling in the saint, (John 14:17), abides forever with the saints, (John 14:16), is known by the saints, (John 14:17), whom the world cannot receive, (John 14:17) and is known as Yahweh, the Lord God, (Exod. 17:7 with Heb. 3:7–9).[2] He is known as Yahweh of hosts, (Isa. 6:3, 8–10; Acts 28:25), as Yahweh, Most High, (Psa. 78:17, 21; Acts 7:51), invoked as Yahweh, (Luke 2:26–29; Acts 4:23–25; 1:16, 20; 2 Thess. 3:5) and in this way called God. "But Peter said, Ananias, why hath Satan filled thine heart to lie to

---

[1] Manton, Thomas, *The Complete Works of Thomas Manton*, Volume 21, (Worthington, IL: Maranatha Publications, 1979), 290.
[2] Num. 12:6; "I will speak to them in a vision or dream." "For the prophecy came not in old time by the will of man: but holy men of God spake as they were moved by the Holy Ghost," (2 Peter 1:21).

the Holy Ghost, and to keep back part of the price of the land? Whiles it remained, was it not thine own? and after it was sold, was it not in thine own power? why hast thou conceived this thing in thine heart? thou hast not lied unto men, but unto God," (Acts 5:3-4).

The Spirit is joined with the Father and the Son in the sacrament of baptism, Matt 28:19, "in the name of...the Spirit." He is eternal, (Heb. 9:14), omnipresent, (Psa. 139:7-13), omniscient, (1 Cor. 2:10), omnipotent, (Luke 1:35; Rom. 15:19), called the Spirit of glory and of God, (1 Peter 4:14), Creator, (Gen. 1:26, 27; Job 33:4), is equal to, and one with the Father, (Matt. 28:19; 2 Cor. 13:14), is the Sovereign Disposer of all things, (Dan. 4:35; 1 Cor. 12:6, 11), is the Author of the new birth, all those born of the Spirit, (John 3:5, 6; 1 John 5:4), has power to raise Christ from the dead, (Acts 2:24; 1 Peter 3:18; Heb. 13:20; Rom. 1:4), inspires Scripture, (2 Tim. 3:16; 2 Peter 1:21), is the source of wisdom, (1 Cor. 12:8; Isa. 11:2; John 16:13; 14:26), the source of miraculous power, (Matt. 12:28; Luke 11:20; Acts 19:11; Rom. 15:19), appoints and sends ministers, (Acts 13:2, 4; 9:38; 20:28), directs where the Gospel should be preached, (Acts 16:6, 7, 10), dwells in saints, (John 14:17; 1 Cor. 14:25; 3:16; 6:19), comforts the church, (Acts 9:31; 2 Cor 1:3), sanctifies the church, (Ezek. 37:28; Rom. 15:16), is a witness to the truth, (Heb. 10:15; 1 John 5:9), and convinces the world of sin, of righteousness, and of judgment, (John 16:8-11).

This Holy Spirit has a personality and is not a mere force, shown that he creates and gives life, (Job 33:4), appoints and commissions ministers, (Isa. 48:16; Acts 13:2; 20:28), directs ministers where to preach, (Acts 8:29; 10:19-20), directs ministers where not to preach, (Acts 16:6-7), instructs ministers what to preach, "Which things also we speak, not in the words which man's wisdom teacheth, but which the Holy Ghost teacheth; comparing spiritual things with spiritual," (1 Cor. 2:13), spoke in, and by, the prophets. (Acts

Chapter 2: The Person and Work of the Holy Spirit

1:16; 1 Peter 1:11, 12; 2 Peter 1:21), strives with sinners, (Gen. 6:3), reproves, (John 16:8), comforts, (Acts 9:31), helps our infirmities, (Rom. 8:26), teaches, (John 14:26; 1 Cor. 12:3), guides, (John 16:13), sanctifies, (Rom. 15:16; 1 Cor. 6:11), testifies of Christ, (John 15:26), glorifies Christ, (John 16:14), has a power of his own, (Rom. 15:13), searches all things, (Rom. 11:33-34; 1 Cor. 2:10-11), works according to his own will, which is God's will, (1 Cor. 12:11), dwells with saints, (John 14:17), can be grieved, (Eph. 4:30), vexed, (Isa. 63:10), and resisted, (Acts 7:51).

He is known as the Teacher who is promised, (Prov. 1:23), as the Spirit of wisdom, (Isa. 11:2; 40:13-14), given in answer to prayer, (Eph. 1:16-17), given to the saints, (Neh. 9:20; 1 Cor. 2:12-13), and necessary for their spiritual well-being. 1 Cor. 2:9-10. As such he reveals the things of God, (1 Cor. 2:10, 13), reveals the things of Christ, (John 16:14), reveals the future, (Luke 2:26; Acts 21:11), brings the words of Christ to remembrance, (John 14:26), directs in the way of godliness, (Isa. 30:21; Ezek. 36:27), teaches saints to answer persecutors, (Mark 13:11; Luke 12:12), enables ministers to teach, (1 Cor. 12:8), and directs the decisions of the church, (Acts 15:28).

In the Old Testament the Spirit of God is first introduced as the Creator of all things. "And the earth was without form, and void; and darkness was upon the face of the deep. And the Spirit of God moved upon the face of the waters," (Gen. 1:2; cf. Job 26:13; 33:4). Man, one being among "all things," is also created and filled with the breath of life, or a special operation of the Spirit imparting his image on man, "made like unto one of us." Adam attained knowledge, righteousness and holiness originally. This Christ would later reconstitute in some fallen men through the gift of the Spirit. As a result of the fall of man, the Spirit spiritually withdrew from him by way of benefit and he was then designated as "flesh" (Gen. 4:3).

The image of God that Adam was first created in was wholly corrupted and defiled by his sin in the garden under the temptation of the devil (Gen. 3:1-15; John 3:6). "That which is born of the flesh is flesh; and that which is born of the Spirit is spirit," (John 3:6). The Spirit's work is the *reversal* of that. Since the fall, the plan of salvation has encompassed the replenishment of the defiled image of God by the operation of the Spirit upon wicked men who receive mercy through Christ's mediation and covenant.

Throughout the Old Testament the Spirit worked upon and in men for the glory of God. Never believe the false teachers who tell you the Spirit did not indwell men in the Old Testament. The Spirit of Christ animated the prophets and indwelt them as those speaking on behalf of God. "Searching what, or what manner of time the Spirit of Christ which was in them did signify, when it testified beforehand the sufferings of Christ, and the glory that should follow," (1 Peter 1:11). Abraham himself, called a prophet, had the Spirit indwelling him (Gen. 20:6). Even Joseph is said to have the Spirit of God in him when Pharaoh commented, "Can we find such a man as this – a man in whom the Spirit of God is?" (Gen. 41:38). The blessing of Abraham and the promise of the Spirit were always bestowed on all those that believed God and his promises, "unless a man is born again..." Though the Spirit may have been more sparingly imparted to fewer people, this never voided the same work of the Spirit to save men by the Messiah in the Old Testament as he works to save men by Christ in the New Testament (Num. 11:17; 27:18; Deut. 34:9; Neh. 9:20; Isa. 63:11-14). "Then he remembered the days of old, Moses, and his people, saying, Where is he that brought them up out of the sea with the shepherd of his flock? where is he that put his holy Spirit within him?" (Isa. 63:11). Even in the book of Judges we find God raising up supernaturally gifted men who were endowed with a special portion of the

Spirit for service. Samson was raised up, "And the Spirit of the LORD came mightily upon him," (Judges 14:6). The prophets themselves required the operation of the Spirit in order to fulfill their special duties as well as being carried along by the Holy Spirit to write the inspired Scriptures. "For the prophecy came not in old time by the will of man: but holy men of God spake as they were moved by the Holy Ghost," (2 Peter 1:21). Even the kings, such as David, were endowed with special office-gifts in order to fulfill their function as king by the Holy Spirit. Psalm 51:11 states, "Do not cast me away from Your presence, and do not take Your Holy Spirit from me."

There are certainly a host of passages that deal with the work of the Holy Spirit through the Old Testament. Psalm 139:7 says, "Where can I go from Your Spirit? Or where can I flee from Your presence?" Psalm 143:10 says, "Teach me to do Your will, For You are my God; Your Spirit is good. Lead me in the land of uprightness." Paul the apostle quotes Psalm 116:10, "And since we have the same spirit of faith, according to what is written, "I believed and therefore I spoke," we also believe and therefore speak, (2 Cor. 4:13)." The same Spirit of faith in the Old Testament is the same Spirit of Faith of the New Testament; and immutably so. Even Proverbs 1:23 says, "Turn at my rebuke (*wisdom says*); Surely I will pour out my spirit on you; I will make my words known to you." Such a pouring out of the Spirit is not uncommon for those seeking truth. And it is not merely found in Joel or in Acts.

The prophets also have a great amount to say about the Holy Spirit. Joel 2:28 prophesies about the gathering of Israel and the outpouring of the Spirit in connection with the Messianic sending of the Spirit. "Poured out on all flesh…" all kinds. Isaiah sets forth a vivid picture of the Spirit in numerous passages (Isa. 9:2; 42:1; 44:3; 59:19-21; 61:1). Ezekiel was extraordinarily involved in the Spirit's prophetic work "And the spirit entered into me when he spake unto me, and set me upon my feet, that I heard him that spake unto me." (Ezek. 2:2).[3]

The Holy Spirit was active in the Old Testament in the work of imparting the supernatural gift of prophecy to a few, and the comforting power of the Spirit to many. The divine personality of the Spirit was not less known and not less recognized in the Old Testament in comparison to the New Testament. Even through the Old Testament the Holy Spirit was recognized as a divine Person. He was simply not seen as clearly.

In the New Testament the Spirit's work is more clearly seen, but at no time was his work ever called into question unless it meant committing the unpardonable sin. "But the blasphemy against the Holy Ghost shall not be forgiven unto men," (Matt. 12:31). Jesus and the apostles in speaking of the Spirit's work were not speaking some new language or with new ideas that threw off their hearers. The fundamental idea that the Messiah should be anointed with the Spirit and come in the power of the Spirit was consistent with what the Jews understood in that day. They expected a Spirit enabled Messiah who would bring forth waters that caused their cups to overflow.

All the Gospel evangelists refer to the Spirit's work in connection with Christ's birth, baptism and temptation. But the title Christ or Messiah was given to the Redeemer from the peculiar unction of the Spirit which was given to him by nature and unlimited degree.

In terms of the coming of the Messiah, the forerunner, John the Baptist, was filled with the Spirit even from his mother's womb (Luke 1:15-17). With Elizabeth, Zacharias and Simeon they were filled with the Holy Spirit and gave forth divine announcements of the divine will (Luke 1:42, 67, 2:25).

---

[3] See Ezek. 8:3; 11:24; 36:25-27.

Chapter 2: The Person and Work of the Holy Spirit

With Christ, though, it is very much different. The fullness of the Spirit was given to him constantly and uninterruptedly unlike believers who had the Spirit indwelling them, but not uninterruptedly because of sin. His Father's will was to send the Holy Spirit in his name (John 14:26) and that the Spirit would be dispensed by his own hand to them. He, being filled with the Spirit beyond measure could dispense the Spirit by way of divine sending at the completion of his work without measure.

With the teachings of Christ, there are two main divisions about the Spirit. [1] Those which describe the Spirit's work in conversion. [2] Those which describe the Spirit's work on the mind of the apostles and of the church in general for sanctification. Oftentimes, the teaching of the Spirit surrounded discourses on living water (John 7:37-39). "...out of his belly shall flow rivers of living water. (But this spake he of the Spirit, which they that believe on him should receive: for the Holy Ghost was not yet given; because that Jesus was not yet glorified.)," (John 7:38-39). Such blessings are announced as gifts to those that come and repent of their sins. The Holy Spirit sent from the throne this way is a gift of the Christ. Such repentance and reception is done by faith which involves the teaching of the Father (John 6:45), the drawing of the Son (John 12:32) and the life-giving power of the Spirit (John 6:63).

When the apostle John speaks of the Spirit not yet being given, he is not talking about *location*. The Spirit is everywhere where he will be forever since he is infinite. When the Apostle says "the Spirit was not yet given," (John 7:39) he is speaking comparatively, not absolutely, as is always the case between the Old Testament and the New Testament. Nor is it strange when Christ says, "Receive ye the Holy Spirit (John 20:22)." This refers to the gifting of the Holy Spirit for service, in which the apostles would take up in Jerusalem.

They would receive even more of the Spirit in Jerusalem as they awaited a greater outpouring for their Gospel service. The waters were flowing, but to what extent they had no idea to the great blessing that would well up in them as rivers. The greatest event in all of history next to the incarnation, death and resurrection of Jesus Christ is the giving of the Comforter by the Ascended Messiah. This event following the Messiah's departure was inaugurated at Pentecost. There the Holy Spirit took the place of Christ's physical bodily presence, and instead, was sent to fill that void spiritually in every believer. Now the enthroned Messiah seated at the right hand of God would send the Holy Spirit. The Spirit was poured out upon the one hundred and twenty of the Upper room – those who waited upon the Lord's command. The tongues of fire baptized them for service, and touched them on their heads. *Baptized* on their heads. This effusion of the Spirit made a great change on all the powers of the apostles, whether we look at the further sanctification of their heart (since they had previously been converted before their empowerment for service). They received extraordinary gifts by the Holy Spirit at an appointed time, but these would cease after the Church was founded upon the inspired Scripture.[4]

In the New Testament letters apostolic epistles demonstrate an acute awareness of the person and work of the Holy Spirit. Paul draws attention to the reality that Christ and the Spirit work together for the good of the church and the glory of God (2 Cor. 3:17). He is called the Spirit of God (Rom. 8:9), the Spirit of His Son (Gal. 4:6) and the Spirit of Him that raised up Christ from the dead (Rom 8:11).

---

[4] Referring to gifts such as tongues (1 Cor. 14:22), the interpretation of tongues (1 Cor. 14:5), the word of wisdom (1 Cor. 12:8), the gift of faith (Mark 16:18; Acts 28:5) – which is not the same as faith in believing, but the faith of miracles, gifts of healing, and other gifts which were supernatural by the Holy Spirit sovereignly disposed to them in his own right for founding the church.

Chapter 2: The Person and Work of the Holy Spirit

In believers, the writer of Hebrews notes that the Spirit is the Spirit of grace (Heb. 10:29), Paul calls him the Spirit of adoption (Rom. 8:15) and the Spirit that dwells in believers (Rom. 8:11). The Spirit is involved throughout Paul's writings as the action of the whole application of Christ's redemption. He washes, sanctifies and justifies his church (1 Cor. 6:11). He reveals his word to his people (1 Cor. 2:14). He is the author of saving faith (2 Cor. 4:13) who produces such faith by a saving call and change of the depraved heart, one of stone, into a heart of flesh that beats for God.

The work, seen here thus far, is the same work that the Spirit accomplishes all through redemptive history, whether in the Old Testament or New Testament. The contrast between one and the other mainly rests on the extent the Spirit was given by the Messiah, and his actions to send the Spirit from the throne of God. The Spirit is always working, but was not always sent by the exalted Christ. In comparison with the numbers of people who had the Spirit on the Old Testament, and were made partakers of the Spirit, Paul makes a differentiation between the economy of the "letter" and the economy of the "Spirit," (2 Cor. 3:6). It is by the scope and extent of the outpouring of the Spirit that marks that difference.

In the practical application of the work of the Spirit upon the Christian, one may divide his work into the three sections that Paul outlines in Romans: regeneration, spiritual-mindedness, and walking after the Spirit (Romans 8:4, 6, 9). Such a gracious salvation and indwelling of the Spirit (walking in Him) is for the Christian in any age. For Paul says in Romans 8:9, "But you are not in the flesh but in the Spirit, if indeed the Spirit of God dwells in you. Now if anyone does not have the Spirit of Christ, he is not His." If one does not "have" the Spirit, meaning to have, *i.e.* to hold in the sense of *wearing*, then he is not God's and not Christ's. He declares that sanctification is so joined and knit to a believer's grafting into Christ, that it can by no means be separated.

All the saints, in any age, were saved, filled, and walking in the Spirit in this sense or they were not of Christ in *any* saving sense. They are evidenced to be children of the Spirit, adopted by God, and having a filial relationship with God as his children, *or they are not.* For the Christian, the Spirit is also the Spirit of prayer (Eph. 1:17; James 1:26) in which the Christian prays in the Holy Spirit, and by the illumination of the Spirit, the Christian is able to understand the things of God and of Christ and help the believer to pray effectively according to the will of God. The Spirit is also the Christian's seal and earnest (Eph. 1:13; 4:30). This means that believers are God's inviolable property and known to be so by the Spirit dwelling in them.

One of the most comprehensive treatments of the New Testament witness to the Spirit is through the Apostle John and his letters. The Spirit is known as the Spirit of God (1 John 4:2), sent forth from God (1 John 4:3), providing powerful unction from the Holy One (1 John 2:20-27), the Spirit of truth (1 John 5:6), and the one who abides in all believers (1 John 3:24). The Holy Spirit is not a mere divine influence or a created force. The Holy Spirit is God, sent by the Son of Man, the Anointed Christ himself in conjunction with the decree of the Father. When the Bible speaks about the personality of the Spirit, it speaks in terms of mind, will and spontaneous action. The Spirit is not the Father and is not the Son, but distinct from both. He is intelligent, has a will, power and wisdom that he acts upon. Jesus said he would send another Comforter, which, if Christ is the first Comforter than that statement alone demonstrates the personality of mind, will and affections of a-n-o-t-h-e-r Comforter. If the Spirit is denied as a person from that text (John 14:16-17), "And I will pray the Father, and He will give you another Helper, that He may abide with you forever "the Spirit of truth," then one must also deny the personality of the Christ, which is impossible. The Spirit teaches (John 14:26), guides (John 16:13), and glorifies Christ (John 16:14). The personality of the Spirit is seen in the personal actions ascribed to him (John 14:26; 1 Cor. 12:11).

His distinction from the Father and the Son, and his mission from both, prove his personality (John 15:26). The co-ordinate rank and power that belong to him equally with the Father and the Son prove his personality (Matt. 28:19; 2 Cor. 13:14). His appearance under a visible form at the baptism of Christ and on the day of Pentecost proves his personality. The sin against the Holy Ghost implying a Person to sin against, proves his personality. The way in which he is distinguished from his gifts proves his personality (1 Cor. 12:11).

The work of the Spirit in the anointing of Christ, according to his work in the Covenant of Grace, is of great importance in all this. The Lord Jesus taught about the nature of the Covenant when he spoke of himself as receiving the Father's command (John 10:18), and of the Spirit as not speaking of himself, but glorifying Christ, and of taking of his teachings and showing them to the disciples (John 16:14). The great fact of the incarnation of the Son in human flesh takes for granted that Christ's manhood was immediately filled to its capacity in being led by the Spirit. Passages that refer to Christ being filled with the Spirit, or the Spirit given to him without measure are stated historically; they are part of the historical narrative of the Gospels. In the office of Mediator, in human flesh, the Lord Jesus received the unction of the Spirit. He was anointed by the Spirit so far as the call to the office of Messiah was concerned. He supplied Christ with actual gifts and power, so that he has all necessary gifts for the function of his office. The first degree of this anointing of the Spirit took place at his incarnation (Luke 1:35; Luke 2:40). The second degree was given at his baptism (John 1:33). This descent was intended to confirm and encourage the Lord Jesus before entering on his formal work of salvation. The symbolic dove demonstrated the resting of the Spirit upon him for the task (Isaiah 11:2).

The Spirit anointed him supremely for his official work (Matthew 3:11). This was also part of his temptation in the wilderness where the Spirit drove him there to be tested. And when such a time of testing was completed, Luke tells us that he returned with the power of the Spirit (Luke 4:14). When he offered himself upon the cross as a sacrifice, he did this through the power of the Spirit. Hebrews 9:14 states, "how much more shall the blood of Christ, who through the eternal Spirit offered Himself without spot to God, cleanse your conscience from dead works to serve the living God?" The Son of God, moved by the Holy Spirit, offered himself without spot or blemish as an atoning sacrifice. He was endowed with power by the Spirit for his exaltation and sending of the Spirit. Acts 2:33 says, "Therefore being exalted to the right hand of God, and having received from the Father the promise of the Holy Spirit, He poured out this which you now see and hear." This is where the actual mission of the Comforter is stated and is sent by the Messiah from his throne room to the Church organically binding together the whole church to the Head, which is Christ.[5]

The inspiration of the Scriptures is from the Holy Spirit. The Spirit gave inspirational power called *carrying*, to fabricate the final result of the inspired Scriptures.[6] He carried along the prophets to speak and write down the word of God

---

[5] Make this note, in the Old Testament the Holy Spirit is never actually said to be "sent" since this would be done officially by the office of the Mediator.

[6] "For the prophecy came not in old time by the will of man: but holy men of God spake as they were moved by the Holy Ghost," (2 Peter 1:21).

without violating their personalities. Peter states, "for prophecy never came by the will of man, but holy men of God spoke as they were moved by the Holy Spirit," (2 Peter 1:21). The prophetic Spirit imparted a supernatural divine illumination in virtue of what the apostles and prophets understood fully and what they were commissioned to announce on behalf of God and Christ. The Holy Spirit accommodated the message through prophets which resembles a mother's accommodation to the capacity of her infant. He spoke in a manner that human beings would understand the divine message. And he gives them now Spiritual illumination which is different than being carried along by the Spirit to confer a divine message. Conferring divine revelation was officially binding upon the church, where divine illumination helps the believer understand the word of God.

The Spirit applies the redemption of the Christ to sinners. This is initially called *regeneration or being born again*. The efficacious operation of the Spirit presupposes God's sovereign election on certain individuals to receive the benefits of Christ's death for them. This application of Christ's work is done by the Spirit's divine application on the human soul. Men do not have the Holy Spirit as fallen humans (Jude 19), and as a necessary consequence of that void, they are sensual and carnal (1 Cor. 2:14). This withdrawal of the Spirit as a result of the fall is called, "spiritual death," (2 Cor. 3:5; 1 Cor. 2:14; Romans 8:7). Now, men must be regenerated and endowed with the Spirit of God since they are imputed with Adam's sin from conception and are devoid of all spiritual good. Jesus demonstrates, emphatically, that men must be born again, or born from above, which is the work of regeneration on the heart of the wicked (John 3:3). As John 6:63 states, "It is the Spirit who gives life; the flesh profits nothing." Such a sovereign regeneration (a change of the heart from stone to beating flesh) is by the blowing will of the Spirit (John 3:1-8). The Spirit then convicts and sanctifies the individual by purging unbelief (John 16:8). Those regenerated are then made new creatures (2 Cor. 5:17). The Spirit inhabits the whole man and renews him (Romans 8:9). These are adopted as sons, and are assured by the Spirit of their sovereign election (Rom. 8:16; 1 John 3:2).

    The Spirit sanctifies the believer. In the work of sanctification, it is important to note the work of Christ for the Christian in comparison to the work of the Spirit in the Christian. One leads to a first conversion, the other to a continual holiness. The Spirit enables regenerated Christians to discern good from evil, or sin from holiness. He disposes the mind to accept truth and to know what the Scriptures contain. Here the Spirit aids the Christian in expounding Scripture in order to apply that Scripture to the Christian's life and further grow in the mystical union he now has with Christ (1 Cor. 6:17). The Spirit illuminates through his indwelling presence within the individual (John 16:16; 2 Tim. 1:14; Rom. 8:9; Gal. 4:6; 1 Cor. 3:16; 1 John 4:13; Eph. 1:13). Those who are illuminated and are indwelt by the Spirit are called by the Spirit (Gal 5:18; Rom. 8:14; Ezek. 36:27). In the New Testament his function is poured out over the whole covenant community, and in the Old Testament he chose specific people to be anointed for service. Love is the principle here, and only through the power of the Spirit can there be true Christian love reflecting Christ (1 Cor.13). The degree of the Christian's sanctification and ethics will differ according to the Spirit's will. Romans 7 gives Christians a glimpse into the real struggle in which every believer fights against sin. They sometimes lose and sometimes win. Ultimately, they *will be* glorified. But the Spirit of grace enables them to fight their way out of every temptation (1 Cor. 10:13) although believers do not always arrest that opportunity to please God and rather, they grieve the Spirit. As Ephesians 4:30 says, "And do not grieve the Holy Spirit of God, by whom you were sealed for the day of redemption."

The Spirit unites the church in Christ. Christ's cause on the earth is advanced through the Spirit, through individuals who are indwelt by the Spirit. The Holy Spirit joins together every regenerated member of the Church to the Head to create a complete body. There is and has only been one church and one Spirit in the Old Testament and the New Testament. The same Spirit of faith in the New Testament filled believers in the Old Testament for spiritual service (2 Cor. 4:13). "We having the same spirit of faith," (2 Cor. 4:13).

The Holy Spirit has worked throughout history. There are three main epochs in which the miraculous giftedness of the Spirit worked through the church for the good of the church: 1) in the days of Moses, 2) in the days of Elijah, and 2) in the days of the Messiah and his apostles. At other times, such as the Great Awakenings under the preaching of men like Jonathan Edwards and George Whitefield, we find curious outpourings of the Spirit on his people for the purpose of revival and sanctification. In all cases, the mission of the church (to worship, be sanctified, to convert souls and proclaim the kingdom) in their primary relationship to Christ has *never* changed. The church has never been afraid to say in its corpus of writings and literature about theological issues, "I believe in the Holy Spirit," for he is their Comforter.

The doctrine of the Spirit has always been violently attacked by various writers through the centuries, and defended by others who uphold orthodoxy. Though Justin the martyr speaks of the Holy Spirit, Tertullian is the first to use the term "Trinity" dogmatically. The Greek Church was overrun, so to speak, with allusions to the Holy Spirit all through their worship liturgy. This does not mean the Greek Fathers were perfect in their conceptions of the Spirit theologically – far from it. But it does demonstrate that from early second century writings that the Holy Spirit occupied a place of prominence in theological literature.

Though solid teaching on the Holy Spirit abounded in the early church and its literature, so did the heresies. From AD 157-171 the Montanists arose in Mysia, who believed in the continued supernatural gifting of the Holy Spirit upon believers, which is where the charismatics of today literally get their doctrine of the Spirit.

Sabellius arose around AD 200 and taught that God wore three masks (Father, Son and Holy Spirit) which completely detracted from the reality of a triune God and made out of him a single entity that deceives through personality schizophrenia. Sabellianism was the first anti-Trinitarian heresy found in the church.

In the fourth century it was Arianism that denied the Son and the Spirit as God, and instead, made the Son a created being and the Spirit a force. Arius laid stress on the subordination of the Son and Spirit to the Father, and denied they were coequal, (these are the Jehovah's Witnesses of today).

However, the principal assailants of the deity of the Spirit were the Macedonians. They believed the Holy Spirit was a creature that derived its life from Christ. They were brought before the second General Council of which Athanasius was a part, and they were condemned as heretics. The much-needed Council of Constantinople convened in AD 381 and added an addendum to the Nicene Creed. The addendum reads, "And I believe in the Holy Ghost, the Lord, and Giver of Life, who proceedeth from the Father and the Son; who with the Father and the Son together is worshipped and glorified; who spake by the Prophets."

The arguments surrounding the procession of the Spirit are historically viewed and classified in three epochs:

the first epoch was during the rise of Greek theology until the time of Epiphanius. During this time, the Spirit was seen as proceeding from the Father and the Son. The second epoch of Greek theology and encompassing the Council of Ephesus (AD 431) there are statements that the Spirit proceeds from the Father only. Here we find the filioque clause that was debated between the Eastern and Western Church. The Western Church (of which Augustine was part) believed the Holy Spirit proceeded from the Father and the Son, where the Eastern Greek Church believed he proceeded only from the Father. In the third epoch of controversy there is Photius in the Latin Church (AD 867) who tried to set forth his own ideas that mimicked the Greek church and condemned the Western Church as heretical. In all this, though, the Greeks and Latins were overwhelmed by the teachings of the Western Church by exegesis rather than just attempted human logic. Though they did not change their minds on the subject, the formulated creeds of Christendom teach that the Spirit proceeded from both the Father and the Son. This view, of the Western Church, was that of the magisterial reformers of the 16th century Reformation, and the Puritans and the *1647 Westminster Confession of Faith.*

In terms of the historical nature of the Spirit's work, the early fathers often did not set forth the best theology. Chrysostom, for instance, denied the correct order of regeneration then faith, and his views of Christ's work and the application of it to the believer were defective. It is not until Augustine that we have a more biblical and exegetical understanding of salvation and election, and the application of this by the Holy Spirit. Augustine, in contrast to the British monk Pelagius who opposed sovereign grace, wrote vehemently against Pelagius for the truth. Augustine's work on free will and the Spirit's role in man's will was written against the Manicheans who held to a defective view as well.

Augustine's work on predestination and his anti-Pelagian writings also demonstrate more than adequately the truth of the biblical position of the Sovereign Spirit's work in the application of redemption to men's souls. His maxim still stands, "Lord, command what Thou will, but grant to us what Thou commandest."

Later, after Augustine's battles with Pelagius, semi-Pelagian's taught that man's sinful nature was inherited from Adam, but was not completely corrupted. This precursor to the Arminian position was refuted and condemned at the Synod of Orange in AD 529.

During the period of the Reformation and later, the term "grace" was used interchangeably with the phrase "the work of the Holy Spirit." Luther debated Erasmus on this issue surrounding the work of the Spirit when Erasmus wrote his Diatribe and Luther responded with his greatest work *The Bondage of the Will*. Luther says, "We have need of the Spirit of Christ, without whom all our works are worthy of condemnation." The Reformed Confessions echo these sentiments. In Article 18 of the *Augsburg Confession* it states, "they teach that man's will has some liberty to choose civil righteousness, and to work things subject to reason. But it has no power, without the Holy Ghost, to work the righteousness of God, that is, spiritual righteousness; since the natural man receiveth not the things of the Spirit of God, 1 Cor. 2,14; but this righteousness is wrought in the heart when the Holy Ghost is received through the word."

In chapter 12 of the *Scottish Confession* it states, "Our faith and its assurance do not proceed from flesh and blood, that is to say, from natural powers within us, but are the inspiration of the Holy Ghost; whom we confess to be God, equal with the Father and with his Son."

In point 33 of the *Irish Articles* it states, "All God's elect are in their time inseparably united unto Christ by the effectual and vital influence of the Holy Ghost, derived from him as from the head unto every true member of his mystical body. And being thus made one with Christ, they are truly regenerated and made partakers of him and all his benefits."

The Thirty-nine Articles of Religion state, "Wherefore they which be endued with so excellent a benefit of God be called according to God's purpose by His Spirit working in due season; they through grace obey the calling; they be justified freely; they be made sons of God by adoption; they be made like the image of His only-begotten Son Jesus Christ; they walk religiously in good works; and at length by God's mercy they attain to everlasting felicity."

The Synod of Dort fought for the Sovereign work of the Spirit: In Head 3/4:8, "Nevertheless, all who are called through the Gospel are called seriously. For seriously and most genuinely God makes known in his word what is pleasing to him: that those who are called should come to him. Seriously he also promises rest for their souls and eternal life to all who come to him and believe."

Head 3/4:9 states, "The fact that many who are called through the ministry of the Gospel do not come and are not brought to conversion must not be blamed on the Gospel, nor on Christ, who is offered through the Gospel, nor on God, who calls them through the Gospel and even bestows various gifts on them, but on the people themselves who are called. Some in self-assurance do not even entertain the word of life; others do entertain it but do not take it to heart, and for that reason, after the fleeting joy of a temporary faith, they relapse; others choke the seed of the word with the thorns of life's cares and with the pleasures of the world and bring forth no fruits. This our Savior teaches in the parable of the sower (Matt. 13)."

With other articles (3/4:10-13) they reinforce the same and condemned the doctrines of the Arminians as pestilential heresies and errors, overthrowing the Spirit's sovereign work.

The Puritan movement during the 17th century was a pristine time of theological development for the application and work of the Spirit. Rutherford, Blair, Henderson, Owen, Charnock, Goodwin, Howe and others wrote extensively on the work of the Holy Spirit. Owen's masterpiece, *The Work of the Holy Spirit,* is one of the best treatises in print on a systematic and practical view of the subject, though very theologically dense in its writing. These men continued the line of Reformation Theology that placed preeminence on the sovereign power of the regenerating work of the Spirit on the believer. Other figures are worthy of noting who wrote extensively on the Spirit, such as Jonathan Edwards in his *Religious Affections*, and Charles Hodge in his *Systematic Theology*.

Errors still abound on the work of the Spirit as such writings as Junckheim in Germany (of which they never recovered from his combination of Pelagianism, Arminianism, Amyraldianism and Naturalism all rolled into one), and the Schleiermacher School (which is a refined sort of Sabellianism). Arianism is still active today through the Jehovah's witnesses, and various other cults such as New Age have turned the Spirit into a force, such as the Manicheans of old. It can be said, though, that no group today has a new angle on heresy. It is simply old heresy drudged up again from ignorant people who have no sense of the theological history of the church.

Do *you* have a practical theology of the Holy Spirit? Such a practical overview of the Spirit should lead You to be excited about the work of the Spirit in your life as a Christian. "Be filled with the Spirit," (Eph. 5:18). Are you filled? Do you *feel* filled? Do you *know* you are filled? The apostle writes to regenerate men who have the Spirit; and when he bids them not to be drunk with wine in which is excess, he takes for granted that he is setting before those to whom the Epistle was sent a source of joy, exhilaration, and comfort to which nothing else could be compared. Nothing can compare to being indwelt, anointed, illuminated, empowered, baptized, motioned, and walking in the Spirit, whom our Lord says is *our Comforter.*

As a believer, you are among all those true Christians that have the Spirit of Christ dwelling in them. There is a distinction between people of the world and you as a true believer, for you have the Spirit in you with his operations and motions. It is not only having him, but discerning that he is there. Do you have love to Christ? Do you live as a member of his mystical body? 1 John 2:13, "Hereby we know that we dwell in God, and he in us, because he hath given us of his Spirit." What is it to have the Spirit in you? Indwelt, anointed, illuminated by, empowered by, baptized in, motioned by, walking in, praying in the Spirit. Is this how you think of your spiritual walk in Christ? It is to have new life flowing out of you like rivers of living water. He leads you, guides you, makes you more holy...because he is in you. You have a right to him because of what the Messiah has done for you and that you believe him by faith. He is given to you as a gift, as a sealing benefit of Christ's work and the covenant of grace.

Who can say that the Spirit is ours, that the Father is our Father, that Christ is our Savior? God satiates you by his Spirit and does this in your very heart. The Spirit motions you in your heart and in your mind. You are his very temple, (1 Cor. 3:16, 6:19). He moves you, motions you, warns you, excites you, and directs you to the throne of Christ. He does not wish to be stifled. He does not wish to be grieved. He does not wish to be quenched. He desires to sanctify all those whom he possesses.

The Spirit of God is close to you. He lives in you. John 14:23 in our text, "We will come to him, and make our abode with him." It is never merely a momentary visit by the Spirit, but he lives in us. Thomas Manton said, "Some have fits and qualms of religion, motions of conviction and joy, but not a settled bent of heart towards God and heaven."[7] That only happens when one is indwelt. He indwells you to govern, direct and motion you to do everything that is pleasing to God.

There are so many things the Spirit does; and we will cover them in turn, but he looks to take your sin-laden broken and battered spirit and body and transform it into something which is Christ glorifying. He points you to Christ. He beckons you to walk in Christ's light, but his light is that which points to Jesus. He is the light that shines to demonstrate the glory of the Redeemer who has done everything acceptable to save you. It is a great evidence that the Spirit is in you based on your interest both in his light, and what that light shines on. The old preachers always said, "Get an interest in God, and in Christ." The reason was that an evidence or proof of being a Christian, was having this interest in Christ. This interest is cultivated by the Spirit who dwells in you.

The Spirit does everything in connection with the Redeemer and the word of the Redeemer so that you have an interest in him. He applies the benefits of salvation to you for the glory of Christ. He mortifies sin in you for the glory of Christ. He motions you to good works for the glory of Christ. He sanctifies you for the glory of Christ. He comforts you for the glory of Christ. Anything religious, any good biblical duty, any work of grace, it is the Spirit moving and prodding you to do that so Christ would be glorified in it. Do you see how practical all that is? I hate bible drills, but in an echelon of such truths housed one upon another, does such a survey not bring great excitement to your soul?

---

[7] Manton, *Works*, Volume 17, 502.

Chapter 2: The Person and Work of the Holy Spirit

The Spirit is Christ's gift to you. There is an intimate connection between the gift of Christ in salvation and the gift of the Holy Spirit. Do you like gifts? People love to get gifts. Christ died for all those the Spirit indwells and sanctifies. What kind of a gift is that? Christ's death and atonement, and the giving of the Spirit to you who believe, are always joined in Scripture as cause and effect. What a gift! "Nevertheless I tell you the truth; It is expedient for you that I go away: for if I go not away, the Comforter will not come unto you; but if I depart, I will send him unto you," (John 16:7). "And he that keepeth his commandments dwelleth in him, and he in him. And hereby we know that he abideth in us, by the Spirit which he hath given us," (1 John 3:24).[8] The gift of the Spirit, and the atonement of Christ go together, they cannot be separated. Christ does not purchase redemption for anyone other than believers to whom the Spirit is given to apply the salvation he has obtained for them. Francis Turretin said, "It is plain that the Holy Spirit is given to none but the elect."[9] Christ was given to die for the elect, and the Holy Spirit is given to the elect, in fact, through the Spirit; and in this Spirit he gives you, his elect, all things. "He that spared not his own Son, but freely delivered him up for us all, how shall he not with him also freely give us all things?" (Romans 8:32). He who gave us his Son, will he not give us the Holy Spirit? Christ, by dying on a cross for the sins of his people, has merited for us, together with salvation, all those Holy Spirit gifts. He will comfort you, teach you, and shine the light of Christ on your heart and mind for the glory of God if you are a believer.

And yet, I have still failed to give you the "how" of all

---

[8] cf. Galatians 4:4, 6; Romans 8:9.
[9] Turretin, Francis, *Institutes of Elenctic Theology*, Volume 2, (Phillipsburg, NJ: Presbyterian and Reformed Publishing Company, 1992-94), 461.

this: *how to take hold of this Spirit. How* to be moved by this Spirit. *How* to cultivate the power of the Spirit in your life. The next chapter will begin to cover that...the baptism of the Spirit of God is on all believers; what it is, and how it is obtained.

Chapter 3:
Baptized with the Holy Spirit

"And as I began to speak, the Holy Ghost fell on them, as on us at the beginning. Then remembered I the word of the Lord, how that he said, John indeed baptized with water; but ye shall be baptized with the Holy Ghost," (Acts 11:15-16).

Peter's report to the church at Jerusalem concerns the continued reports of the Gentile conversion and admission into the mystical body, the church of Jesus Christ. Luke writes Acts to demonstrate the continued work of Jesus Christ, in the world, by the power of the Spirit. All that Jesus began to do and teach, Luke records, now, "through the Holy Spirit", the apostles take all Christ did and taught, to the world. This included Gentiles. The book of Luke records the work of Christ as the anointed Savior coming to fulfill the Father's will in the power of the Spirit. It records the work of the ascended Christ, glorified, exalted, at the right hand of the Father who reaches down to his people through the Holy Spirit. Truly, it is the acts of Jesus through the Spirit in the work of the apostles.

Christ intercedes and sends the Spirit to all those for whom he died, for all his life, work, death, intercession is all one thing, it is all covenant fulfillment, and so he gives the Spirit, sends the Spirit to his people to be with them until the end of the age. "O praise the LORD, all ye nations: praise him, all ye people," (Psa. 117:1). Is this not to convert the nations?

In Acts 1:3-5 Jesus is quoted as reminding them that they are to go into the city of Jerusalem, and wait for *the gift* of the Holy Spirit; the power from on high to be sent to them. It was promised of the Father. It was confirmed in Christ's words. The Spirit is a gift given by the ascended Christ who in turn gifts people for service to God, for worship to God. It was contrasted with John the Baptist's water baptism, and it was now called the baptism of the Holy Spirit. Peter had in mind an Old Testament text, "And it shall come to pass afterward, that I will pour out my spirit upon all flesh," (Joel 2:28). Pour out from heaven, from the side of the exalted Christ, from the throne of the Ancient of Days, onto the church in the world. It means to *pour*, interestingly, *not to submerge*. It concerns, for the disciples at this point, power, service, and ability. "And, behold, I send the promise of my Father upon you: but tarry ye in the city of Jerusalem, until ye be endued with power from on high," (Luke 24:49). "John answered, saying unto them all, I indeed baptize you with water; but one mightier than I cometh, the latchet of whose shoes I am not worthy to unloose: he shall baptize you with the Holy Ghost and with fire," (Luke 3:16).

In contrast to John's baptism, new converts would receive the presence and power of the Holy Spirit (2:38b). In Acts, new converts generally experienced three things, the gift of the Spirit, repentance in conversion, and then water baptism for them and their household. They received the baptism of the Spirit in regeneration. It is the baptism of the Spirit continually outpoured on them for service. Water baptism as a sign of what had taken place inwardly.

Peter, in preaching in the beginning of Acts, links the prophecy of Joel's pouring of the Spirit as that which was fulfilled at that day. The Spirit is poured out continually on the church. He was the preaching minister under the pouring out of the Jewish Pentecost, Jews who had been scattered all over in the dispersion, who heard the preaching of the word in the miracle of tongues, languages of their varied countries from which they came out of the dispersion. And yet, now, he sees this amazing event on the Gentiles.

Peter further witnessed to this pouring in Acts 11. He

had been convinced that the Gentiles were included in the church. It was at this point that he gave the Jerusalem church a testimony of events as to how this occurred, that they would too be persuaded that God was drawing in his people from all over the world.

Some of the circumcision, brothers who had been converted but still held onto their Jewishness, thought that the Gentiles needed to do a great many things to "get into" their fellowship. Peter is corrected on this directly by the Holy Spirit, and he is now relaying to the elders of Jerusalem that what the Jews received, so, the Gentiles received also. The main point was that there were no unclean people in this light.

In recounting events in Acts 10 at Cornelius' house, he tells the Jerusalem church what occurred as it is laid out in chapter 11. Verses 13-16 summarize the vision of Cornelius. The angel instructed Cornelius to send for Peter in Joppa. Peter was to bring a message to Cornelius "through which [he] and all [his] household [would] be saved." What an *amazing* statement to be made to a sinful man. Peter comes to Cornelius' house and begins to preach. While he preaches the "Holy Ghost fell upon them." They were, again, not submerged, but the Spirit was *poured out* on them; pouring, falling, effusion, *upon the head*. At this point, Peter is reminded of what Christ had said, and what had happened to the Jews at Pentecost in fulfillment of the Christ sending the Spirit and the Spirit being poured out. This is where the contrast between John the Baptist's baptism and the baptism of the Spirit is distinguished. He does not say that the Holy Spirit fell on Cornelius' house, "just as it does with everyone." He says it came upon them just as it was on "us" in the beginning. The Spirit fell on the Gentiles like the Spirit did on the Jews.

Peter does not explain his sermon to the elders, but

shows how the baptism of the Holy Spirit interrupted his sermon. The Spirit came upon them just "as he had come upon us at the beginning." The *us* being *the lost Jews* of the house of Israel, and so now, the Spirit took the opportunity during the preaching of the word to baptize these people. He is reminded of "but ye shall be baptized with the Holy Ghost." (Acts 11:16). This phrase "baptized with the Holy Ghost" is only used in two places in the New Testament. In Acts 1:5 at Pentecost with the Jews, and here in chapter 11 at the Gentile Pentecost. Are there two Pentecosts? Somewhat; one promise with two applications. But consider that the usual phrase used is "receive the Holy Spirit" which is synonymous with what happened at Pentecost (Acts 2:38; 8:17; 10:47; 19:2).

In verses 17-18 the same gift of the Spirit given to the Jews, is now given to the Gentiles. Who is Peter to tell God that such is unfair, or wrong? Gentiles are part of God's sovereign plan of salvation? Was not *Abraham* a Gentile? Was not Nineveh converted under the preaching of Jonah? Was not Nebuchadnezzar brought close to God? Did not Jesus long to see the elders of Jerusalem gather together the people of God scattered among the nations? "O Jerusalem, Jerusalem, thou that killest the prophets, and stonest them which are sent unto thee, how often would I have gathered thy children together, even as a hen gathereth her chickens under her wings, and ye would not!" (Matt. 23:37). These were people they were to teach from every tribe tongue and nation, "O give thanks unto the LORD; call upon his name: make known his deeds among the people. Sing unto him, sing psalms unto him: talk ye of all his wondrous works," (Psa. 105:1-2).

What was this gift given here in Acts 11 on Gentiles? The gift was the Holy Spirit falling upon them, baptizing them. The gift, as verse 18 says, that God had granted "repentance unto life" to the Gentiles as well as to the Jews. The baptism of the Holy Spirit is connected, synonymously,

Chapter 3: Baptized with the Holy Spirit

with repentance unto life. If one repents of their sin and is saved by Jesus Christ, one is baptized in the Spirit and continues to be so. To have repentance is to have the baptism. Peter's recounting rests on the witness of the divine word, on the witness of Jesus Christ. Consider that the object of faith is not "in the Holy Spirit," but through the Gospel, in Christ, and when they believed, when the Spirit worked regeneration in them, the gift of the Holy Spirit is given, they are baptized in him, and he is poured out on them. Peter explains this to the Jerusalem elders, and they in turn glorify God, seeing clearly that the Gentiles, believing on Christ, have been given the gift of repentance to life in Christ, they too are baptized in the Spirit.

Christ's gift of the Holy Spirit in repentance and remission of sins (to believing Jews and Gentiles) is the baptism of the Spirit, both initially and in a continued outpouring. Christ's continued work in the church through the Spirit is through the fire of Holy Spirit Baptism. "...he shall baptize you with the Holy Ghost and with fire," (Luke 3:16). In contrast to John the Baptist's pouring of water on the head as a preparation of the *coming* of the Christ and the Spirit's work, this way of pouring water on those who came to John in the wilderness signifies Christ's baptizing with the Holy Ghost and with fire also poured out on the head, so to speak. John said, "'I indeed have baptized you with water: but he shall baptize you with the Holy Ghost,'" (Mark 1:8). John spoke of Christ's baptizing with the Spirit as prefigured by his baptizing with water. The baptism in the Spirit is a phrase applied both at the times of conversion and also in conjunction with the initial pouring out of the Spirit on those called into service with the term surrounding "fire." It is being ignited for service, being empowered for service. It is taking that which exists and igniting it. This was fulfilled when the Holy Spirit was poured out on the 120 at Pentecost, which lighted on their heads in the appearance of cloven tongues like fire for service to God. It is expressly called baptizing with the Holy Ghost, in opposition to John's baptizing with water. God shed forth his Spirit on them. That is why Peter's direct reference to Pentecost, "as wilt us" he remembered the word of the Lord, "how he said, John indeed baptized with water; but ye shall be baptized with the Holy Ghost," (Acts 11:15-16).

The apostle Paul alludes to this baptism when he says that God saves us by the washing of regeneration, and renewing of the Holy Ghost, which He shed on us abundantly through Jesus Christ our Savior (Titus 3:5-6). This baptism of fire, this baptism of the Spirit, as the phrase is given, the concept is found throughout the New Testament. "There is one body, and one Spirit, even as ye are called in one hope of your calling; One Lord, one faith, one baptism," (Eph. 4:4-5). A person is first converted by the baptism of the Spirit, and then they are gifted for service through the subsequent continued pouring of the Spirit in fire on them. If one is lost, and in need of regeneration, they are baptized in the Spirit through repentance for the remission of sins, and then empowered. This baptism is given at conversion, but a further filling or igniting of this fire is also prayed for by the disciples for service. It is a further pouring, like tipping the bowl more to pour out more. It is the Spirit's power of filling the Christian up, and heating the fuel implanted there by the initial regenerating work of the Spirit. They are not to grow weary in well doing as a new Christian. Instead, they are to walk in the Spirit. "For by one Spirit are we all baptized into one body, whether we be Jews or Gentiles, whether we be bond or free; and have been all made to drink into one Spirit," (1 Cor. 12:13). And so, subsequently, they are regenerated into one body.

In Acts 11:15 Peter declares the gift of the Spirit, which fell on the Gentiles, by the ministry of the Gospel (through preaching), to be the baptism of Christ, or the baptism of the Holy Spirit and fire, which Christ promised at his ascension into heaven. The entire church of Jesus Christ is set under this baptism. Did you think all this was *water* baptism? This is not baptism by water, but of the Spirit; which after such occurs, one is then marked outwardly by the sacrament of baptism by water as entrance into the visible body of believers, by pouring on the head showing forth the baptism of the Spirit poured out from Christ's throne, effused onto and in them. That which had happened by fire inwardly, is given water outwardly as a mark of cleansing to the visible body. The fire has burned up the old man, and the water washes the new man, and the fuel ignites for service, which is initially the worship of the Triune Godhead. The Father seeks worshippers (John 4). He changes them and baptizes them with a fiery zeal for worship. The pouring out of the Spirit, the baptism of the Spirit, the power of the Spirit in this work, is to drink from Christ by the one Spirit he sends from his ascended throne. It is to partake of a never-ending fountain of living water that will flow out the inner man for all time, to be with him, and to be one with him. It begins as a pouring on them, figuratively speaking, and then flows out continually from the inner man. Every service or duty the Christian does ought to remind them by way of their water baptism, of the living water that now constantly flows through them and out of them in the baptism of the Spirit.

    The outward agent of the baptism of the Spirit is the word of God. "And as I began to speak, the Holy Ghost fell on them, as on us at the beginning," (Acts 11:15). Preaching was the outward agent, and the baptism of the Spirit was the inward affect. The Spirit used the word, and in the midst of preaching, the Gentiles were converted, as on us, that is the Jews on Pentecost. The Gospel is called *the ministration of the Spirit*, because it proceeds from the Spirit, and communicates the work of the Spirit, who in turn points all things to Jesus Christ who is the giver of the Spirit, and has all his saving benefits given to them. "How shall not the ministration of the spirit be rather glorious?" (2 Cor. 3:8). Christ baptizes with the Spirit through the work of the Spirit, which is the preaching of the Gospel. "That he might sanctify and cleanse it with the washing of water by the word," (Eph. 5:26). Washing renders those images of baptism, rivers of water. Christ sanctifies the church through baptism, through the washing of the water of the word.

The water with which the word washes is the Spirit, for by the word the Spirit is given, and the word cleanses by the Spirit, and the Spirit by the word, and in this way, believers are washed and prepared for service. The baptism of the Spirit, the reception of the Holy Spirit in the life of a repentant believer, is through the ministration of the Spirit. This is his work on their soul, baptizing them into a new man.

There are six qualities of the gift of the Holy Spirit in Spirit baptism. [1] The Baptism of the Spirit regenerates, or gives men a new nature. "Except a man be born of water and the Spirit," (John 3:5-6). The baptism of the Spirit, according to Christ, *gives* the new birth. This is a new nature. Dead sinners, they are made, new by regeneration of the Spirit upon their baptism in the Spirit. "That which is born of the Spirit is Spirit." And, 3:10, in Christ's rebuke of Nicodemus, it's found that Christ says, "You are Israel's teacher and you do not understand these things?"

This baptism of the Spirit is an *Old Testament work,* yet, it holds a New Testament fulfillment. Pictures change, but the substance of what is going on does not. Circumcision changes to water baptism, but the reality of both is the underlying work of regeneration in the soul by the Spirit applying all the benefits of Christ. And then the fire of God is ignited in them for service. All of which is referred to by the baptism of the Holy Spirit. Abraham was baptized in the Spirit, as is every other Old Testament saint. What is different, is that the risen Christ, now, sends the Spirit from the throne of God to his church. This could not happen until he ascended into heaven after finishing his work. This does not squelch the work of the Spirit in any Old Testament saint. But the fulfilled promise of the Father poured out on all flesh occurs at the time in its fullness when Christ is enthroned. Its extent is larger than in the beginning but no less powerful. "Not by works of righteousness which we have done, but according to his mercy he saved us, by the washing of regeneration, and renewing of the Holy Ghost," (Titus 3:5). The baptism of the Spirit is called the laver of regeneration, or washing. All those from any time in history who are regenerate, are baptized by the Spirit. To be *born from above* is a blessing all believers have.

[2] The baptism of the Spirit translates believers from the dominion of darkness into the Kingdom of Christ's mediatorial reign over his church. The work of Christ endows the extensive gift of the Spirit. "For by grace are ye saved through faith; and that not of yourselves: it is the gift of God," (Eph. 2:8). Where do gifts from Christ flow from? Where are these rivers flowing from? But this work, this Christ, this Messiah, is the highlight. One repents at Christ's throne, but they repent by the baptism of the Spirit in regeneration. If men are not regenerated, they are not going to repent. They cannot repent, for they have not been baptized by the Spirit, they have not been given the gift of the Spirit.

If they are given the gift of the Spirit, they are taken out of the kingdom of darkness and now placed in the kingdom of light. The baptism of the Spirit makes a new creature, and this new creature enters in to a new world. "Giving thanks unto the Father, which hath made us meet to be partakers of the inheritance of the saints in light: Who hath delivered us from the power of darkness, and hath translated us into the kingdom of his dear Son: In whom we have redemption through his blood, even the forgiveness of sins," (Col. 1:12-14). Repentance leads to the forgiveness of sins in Christ. In this way, all believers are baptized into one body by one and the same Spirit. Then the Spirit gifts them by igniting that baptism and gifting them for whatever service they are to take up.

[3] The baptism in the Spirit makes believers one with Christ who is the Head of the body. "For as many of you as have been baptized into Christ have put on Christ," (Gal. 3:27). This is not water baptism, but Spirit baptism. So many Christians think that every time the bible says "baptism" that it is referring to water baptism. The truth of the matter, it is far less to speak of water baptism than it is to speak of spiritual baptism in regeneration. By the baptism of the Spirit believers actually put on Christ, and are made one with Christ. This is not by water, but by the Spirit. Water does not unite to Christ in a spiritual saving manner. That does not mean that baptism is not a good time for the Spirit to baptized with fire.[1]

What is the most opportune time for the Spirit to save but in the sacrament? I only mention that to make the stark contrast between water and fire baptism in the Spirit. Water and regeneration are not intrinsically linked. The Spirit is not bound to regenerate someone at baptism. But it seems to be the most opportune time for him to do. (But I digress.)

The Spirit carries believers into Christ, is poured out in baptism on them, and unites them together spiritually to

---

[1] Cornelius Burgess, a Westminster Divine, wrote a great book on covenant infants being saved at the time of baptism as the most opportune time for baptism by the Spirit. The work is called "Presumptive Regeneration, or, the Baptismal Regeneration of Elect Infants," by Cornelius Burgess (1589-1665).

the Head and gifts them by igniting the fire within them. This fire baptism, this baptism in the Spirit, unites believers to Christ in his death and resurrection, or, baptized into the death of Christ. "Know ye not, that so many of us as were baptized into Jesus Christ were baptized into his death? Therefore we are buried with him by baptism into death: that like as Christ was raised up from the dead by the glory of the Father, even so we also should walk in newness of life," (Rom. 6:3-4). The Spirit always points to Christ, applies the benefits of Christ, makes alive in Christ, joins to Christ, *etc.* Believers have the death of Christ, by the Spirit, uniting them in Spirit baptism. They are baptized into Christ's death, meaning, as a result of this baptism there is now a walking in newness of life. They are translated from the dominion of darkness to the light of life and they are born again, now with rivers of living water flowing in them and out of them. In this conversion the death of the old man is killed, the body of sin is destroyed, and they walk in newness of life. This does not remove remaining sin completely. It places them in the kingdom of light to fight the remaining remnants of it until glory.

All this occurs in the baptism of the Spirit that unites the believer with the death of Christ. They are unable to walk in newness of life outside of the baptism of the Spirit. Walking in life is only through the gift of the Spirit. How is sin mortified, or sanctification furthered but by the Spirit applying the death of Christ to the soul and igniting that fire? They are baptized into the benefits of the Resurrection of Christ. Do believers die with Christ in his death? Do believers live in him? "For if we have been planted together in the likeness of his death, we shall be also in the likeness of his resurrection," (Rom. 6:5). The same baptism of the Spirit which buries the believer in Christ, also quickens them in the power of the resurrection. It is like the title of Henry Scudder's book, "The Life of God in the Soul of Man." It is the life of God in them. Fire, life, light, kingdom living in walking in the Spirit in a most victorious manner due to the work of Christ and the Spirit in the soul.

[4] The baptism of the Spirit makes believers one with Christ, the Head, in this way, one with the body of Christ, his church. "For by one Spirit are we all baptized into one body, whether we be Jews or Gentiles, whether we be bond or free; and have been all made to drink into one Spirit," (1 Cor. 12:13). There is no other way to be joined to the Head, no other way to be joined to the mystical body of Christ, than through being baptized in the Spirit. If one calls themselves a Christian, if they are changed, they are baptized in the Spirit. It is important to point out, that charismatic churches abuse this idea, because they believe that a Christian can be saved, and then get the baptism of the Spirit later on. Some Christians have it and some do not. Some are running on unleaded spiritual gas and other have high octane spiritual gas. And they believe that the evidence of this is speaking in babbling tongues. But by one Spirit are believers all baptized into one body. No one is united to Christ in his death and resurrection, as the head of the church, into one body, who is then gifted for service who is not baptized by the Spirit. There is one Lord, one faith, *one baptism.*

[5] The baptism in the Spirit has a continual affect for the believer. Water baptism shows the entrance of the covenanted believer and family into the visible church. It is a *picture* of Spirit baptism. This baptism in the Spirit washes and cleanses from sin. The Spirit is poured out like water on the believer, and kills sin. There is no other way to kill sin than through the baptism of the Spirit. "That he might sanctify and cleanse it with the washing of water by the word," (Eph. 5:26). Nothing will make the church holy, until it is thoroughly cleansed from all spots and all blemishes, except the initial baptism of the Holy Spirit and the ongoing fire of the Spirit

enlivened in the grace of Christ.

The baptism of the Spirit, sent from the throne of God, sent from the Son of Man, sent from the Christ, is a continued baptism. Water baptism happens once. Fire baptism in the Spirit is continual. There are rivers of water now flowing from the "internals" of a believer. The life of a believer is forever under the continual baptism of the Spirit poured out on him until he reaches glory and is made perfect. For, whoever is not baptized in the Spirit does not belong to Christ. Whoever is not baptized with the Spirit, is not regenerated, or made new, or translated from the kingdom of darkness. If a person is not baptized in the Spirit, if they have not received the gift of the Spirit, they are not washed from all filthiness of flesh and Spirit, nor do they have any renewing in the Holy Spirit. They are not renewed. They are not translated. They then have not been given power from on high. They are not new creatures. They are not regenerated. They are not spiritually gifted. They are not connected to Christ. They are not united in his death nor resurrection. They are not conformed to his image. They do not have fellowship with him. They are lost; they are a "dry country." "And the LORD shall guide thee continually, and satisfy thy soul in drought, and make fat thy bones: and thou shalt be like a watered garden, and like a spring of water, whose waters fail not." (Isa. 58:11). They do not have rivers of living water.

[6] The baptism of the Spirit and the gift of the Spirit are conjoined together and represents a whole package. Repentance is a gift of God linked to this. "Forasmuch then as God gave them the like gift as he did unto us, who believed on the Lord Jesus Christ," (Acts 11:17). Spirit Baptism is an abundant supply of the graces of God. The word brings people to Christ; which is the fountain where all believers are baptized with the Holy Spirit.

How will, then, a person know whether they have

received the baptism of the Holy Spirit or not? One must look at their fruits, and affects. This baptism of the Spirit endows with illumination. The baptism of the Spirit illuminates to the light of the Gospel. It is a new light shining into the renewed soul of man. It is as Jonathan Edwards called it, "a supernatural and divine light."[2] The apostle says, "God who commanded the light to shine out of darkness, hath shined into our hearts, to give the light of the knowledge of the glory of God, in the face of Jesus Christ," (2 Corinthians 4:6). This baptism of the Spirit endows faith. "For by grace are ye saved through faith; and that not of yourselves: it is the gift of God:" (Eph. 2:8). This baptism of the Spirit endows continual sanctification. He is baptized with the Holy Spirit and fire. The Holy Spirit is poured out on the believer in such a way as to set him completely on a fire. Set him against sin, having an indignation of it as that which God hates. He feels the spiritual use and profitability of reading the word, the preaching of the word, God's ordinances, as a work of the Holy Spirit in his soul, which in turn begins to work in him assurance that he is a child of God. What does he do with these motions of assurance but walk a closer walk with Christ? He seeks to glorify Christ in life, in troubles, in times of joy, in all things. He is baptized by the Spirit and prepared for service to God – whether by cloven tongues of fire on their head, or fire in the heart.

    Are you baptized in the Spirit? If you are a Christian, if you are born again, you are baptized in the Spirit. It is intrinsically linked to the first infusion of divine illumination by the Spirit. The early church anciently called Holy Spirit baptism (or regeneration) by the name of *illumination.* Hebrews 10:32, says, "after ye were illuminated." Those who are baptized with the Holy Spirit have their minds

---

[2] http://www.apuritansmind.com/puritan-favorites/jonathan-edwards/sermons/a-divine-and-supernatural-light/

illuminated with the beams of this divine and heavenly light, light, fire, motioning. Without the first act of illumination in the heart by regeneration, there is no salvation. Remember, "Unless a man is born again he cannot see..." He has no perceptive ability. It is from divine light that this twofold state of man, the state of nature and the state of grace, are called darkness and the other light. "Ye were sometimes darkness, but now ye are light in the Lord," (Ephesians 5:8), and a, "calling out of darkness into a marvelous light," (1 Peter 2:9). Light, fire, as our God is a consuming fire, as our God is light, so we are brought into the Kingdom of Christ by the baptism of fire in the Spirit.

Now, have we received the baptism of the Spirit, this divine and supernatural change and light? Has this light shined to and in us? Has it shined into our minds and shined into our hearts? Is it set in our minds, enlightening our understanding with some measure of knowledge and spiritual and heavenly mysteries? Have we been supernaturally enlightened and illuminated to the mystery of godliness in Christ and the Gospel of God? Without this baptism of the Holy Spirit, without that light, without that fire, there cannot be any true work of conversion, any spiritual resurrection. Christ does not bring men out of their graves blindfolded. He must first open their hearts, their minds, their eyes to know they are in a casket, and they are now ready to break free by the Spirit. "Paul was sent to the Gentiles to open their eyes," (Acts 26:18). They were to be turned from darkness to light; from the darkness of ignorance to the light and knowledge, which shines into the mind. And this supernatural light shines into the heart; the apostle says, "he hath shined in our hearts." To, "receive a love of the truth," (2 Thessalonians 2:10).

Has the supernatural and divine baptism of the Holy Spirit shined in your heart? In your mind? If he has, then we may say that we have received the gift of the Spirit of Christ, the quickening Spirit, the beginning of this work of a spiritual resurrection in our souls, having been baptized by the Spirit into Christ. Otherwise, if we still sit in darkness, we are still under the shadow of death. There is no living water there.

Christ gives us gifts bound up in the gift of the Holy Spirit. At Pentecost you have a very clear presentation of this gift. The Jews had bleeding hearts, bleeding under sin, and they were now looking at salvation. In Peter's preaching they saw no hopes of it, and they did not know how to attain it. Cuthbert Sydenham says, "The Apostle bids them to repent and be baptized. They might have said, "What shall we do the better?" The Apostle says, "You shall receive the gift of the Holy Spirit, for the promise is unto you." What promise? Of gifts, of tongues and miracles? What is this to our souls? How will this save us? They might well object. It would be but a poor comfort to a wounded soul to tell him of a promise of gifts, not of spiritual grace."[3] The Baptism of the Spirit was about spiritual grace from Christ, the gift of the Spirit, renewing grace given to them, baptizing them, *saving them.* They were not myopic to think that baptism is merely having some spiritual gift to exercise. What good would that have done them to have the Spirit like *Balaam*, who prophesied and yet, was as lost as the day is long? (Num. 22:29-41; Jude 1:11). The Gospel carries with it the gift of the Holy Spirit, the baptism of the Holy Spirit; *salvation.*

Faith in Christ gains the gift of the Spirit. It does not gain the gift of tongues or knowledge or whatever Christians think is fantastical and within their reach as something to strive after. Those who seek the Spirit by gifts, "Woe unto them! for they ... ran greedily after the error of Balaam for reward, and perished," (Jude 1:11). It is a gift from Jesus to you

---

[3] Cuthbert Sydenham, *A Discourse on Covenant Theology and Infant Baptism*, (Coconut Creek, FL: Puritan Publications, 2014) 56.

Chapter 3: Baptized with the Holy Spirit

as a faithful believer. I asked in the last chapter, who does not like a gift? Natural gifts are often very nice. A gift at a birthday party, or a gift out of the goodness of someone's heart to you. They take the time to choose the gift, or make the gift, wrap the gift, address it to you, and come and give it to you. The gift takes some work, and so it is appreciated because it often shows the heart of the giver.

What shall we say of a supernatural gift, even more so, of the supernatural divine light of the Holy Spirit himself given to you by the Redeemer, the ascended Son of Man, who died for it, decreed by the Father? What gift is better than the first and best of beings given to you as a gift, the Spirit himself, his personal baptism to you? The Gospel itself and the joy one receives as a result of having all the benefits of Jesus Christ in the Gospel given to them, rests in the baptism of the Holy Spirit. Paul explains in Romans 14:17, "for the kingdom of God is not eating and drinking, but righteousness and peace and joy in the Holy Spirit." Christians, then have the benefits of Christ applied to them and sealed to them in the baptism of the Holy Spirit. Paul again writes in Ephesians 1:13, "...you were sealed with the Holy Spirit of promise..." And it is this Spirit in Ephesians 4:30 that seals into the coming of the ages, "by whom you were sealed for the day of redemption." All of this is a result of the work of the Spirit in the lives of the saints because Jesus gives them a gift. As Paul instructs Timothy in 2 Timothy 1:14, "That good thing which was committed to you, keep by the Holy Spirit who dwells in us." So, we see the Bible overflowing with theological direction about the work of the Mediator, applied by the Holy Spirit, on behalf of the elect of God.

The gift of the holy Spirit is *given*. It cannot be bought with money as Simon the sorcerer thought. It is given freely by Christ to you. "But unto every one of us is given grace according to the measure of the gift of Christ," (Eph. 4:7).

"According to the gift of the grace of God given unto me by the effectual working of his power," (Eph. 3:7). How does one get it? Do they climb a mountain? Do they traverse a dangerous journey with wild beasts on every side? What work do they do to get it? What work did Cornelius do in the text? *Nothing.* They merely listened to the word and the Spirit fell on them. The Spirit descended on them, was poured out on them, baptized them, and by faith they believed the message. They grasped the gift, because the light shone in a dark place, the darkness of their mind and heart.

The gift of the Holy Spirit is given to you in Spirit Baptism to renew and sanctify your soul. Bound up in it are the exceedingly great and precious promises, privileges, and engagements of the new covenant in Christ Jesus; and the present comfort and future inheritance of the Lord's adopted children. The very faith you have is a gift. "Every good gift and every perfect gift is from above, and cometh down from the Father of lights," (James 1:17), the shining light of the fire of the Spirit, the baptism of the Spirit. "...but the gift of God is eternal life through Jesus Christ our Lord," (Rom. 6:23). "Know ye not, that so many of us as were baptized into Jesus Christ were baptized into his death?" (Rom. 6:3). Synonymous with "gift" is being baptized into his death, which is the gift of the Spirit. It is a free gift of God. It is a gift from the Father. It is a gift from the Son. It is a gift that renews. It is a gift that saves. It is a gift that enlightens the mind. It is a gift that comforts the heart. It is a gift of righteousness. It is a gift of justification. It is a supernatural gift. It is a gift of living water flowing out from you because the Spirit indwells you. "Jesus answered and said unto her, If thou knewest the gift of God, and who it is that saith to thee, Give me to drink; thou wouldest have asked of him, and he would have given thee living water," (John 4:10). This is Holy Spirit baptism. It is a gift of the mercy of God. It is a gift of remission of sins. It is a gift of everlasting life. It is a gift meticulously purchased by Christ. It is a gift which frees us from sin and death. It is gift which excludes any works of our own. It is a gift which causes us to honor God, give the sacrifice of praise, give much thanksgiving, and enables us to live in a holy manner before him. It is a gift which points and rests in Christ's merits, through faith, in the blood of Christ, who is our Savior and Advocate. It is the gift of the Holy Spirit. *It is the baptism of the Holy Spirit.* "Thanks be unto God for his unspeakable gift"! (2 Cor. 9:15).

There is no victorious life in the Spirit without his baptism. Take hold of the Gospel, take hold the preaching of the word, take hold the word itself, take hold of the promises, take hold of the Christ found in it all. He is the one sending the Spirit, sending the baptism of the Spirit in the regenerating power of God. The next chapter we will study being able to live that victorious life by considering the word "indwelt," being *indwelt by the Spirit.*

Chapter 4:
Indwelt by the Holy Spirit

"Know ye not that ye are the temple of God, and that the Spirit of God dwelleth in you?" (1 Cor. 3:16).

Paul's exhortation against divisions in the Corinthian church answers the rhetorical question, "How can Christ's body be divided?" The Corinthians placed preaching ministers in different camps, because they worked among them having brought them to faith, or improved their faith. Some then were by affinity close to Apollos, some Paul, some Peter (take a moment to read 1 Cor. 3 in its entirety). There is a certain truth to the reality that ministers who work among a given people have an affinity with them if they have brought them into the truth. If under some preaching they are converted or have some measurable pivotal spiritual growth, there is an attraction to continue it. Christians who are baptized in the Spirit and then cultivate that fire of the Spirit through the preached word have an affinity to hear certain ministers, or read certain *kinds* of books. Even in this, the Apostles constantly call believers in various New Testament letters, their "children" in various ways. "But we were gentle among you, even as a nurse cherisheth her children," (1 Thess. 2:7). "As ye know how we exhorted and comforted and charged every one of you, as a father doth his children," (1 Thess. 2:11). "My little children, these things write I unto you, that ye sin not," (1 John 2:1).

These divisions, *playing favorites*, are unnecessary since the union which the mystical body of Christ has as one body, and with one another, is by the sent Spirit which indwells them both individually, but for the collective purpose of joining them to Christ as a body to the head. It does not matter who has planted, it does not matter who has watered, God gives the increase. Such divisions ought not to exist.

To explain the importance of removing divisions, Paul uses three images. Keep in mind, he is looking to explain why the church ought not be divided in such a way as to prefer a particular preacher over another. And keep in mind, this does not include unqualified or poor preachers, or bad preachers. Here Paul uses the examples of Peter, Apollos and himself. The three images he uses is a field, a building and a temple. The field is where seeds are sown and grow. Some plant, others water and tend. The building is shown how it is built up together on the foundation of Jesus Christ. The temple is the finished work where holy service is found. The temple is where God dwells by way of covenant. "Behold the man whose name is the BRANCH; and he shall grow up out of his place, and he shall build the temple of the LORD," (Zech. 6:12). This is speaking of *the Christ.* Christ came to build his spiritual temple, and to empower that temple for spiritual service. In this Paul exhorts the Corinthians. "Know ye not that ye are the temple of God, and that the Spirit of God dwelleth in you?" (1 Cor. 3:16). *Division,* how can this be? The Spirit dwells in you knitting together the body. "What? know ye not that your body is the temple of the Holy Ghost which is in you, which ye have of God, and ye are not your own?" (1 Cor. 6:19).

The Spirit mystically indwells the believer as a consequence to Spirit baptism. "Ye are of God, little children, and have overcome them: because greater is he that is in you, than he that is in the world," (1 John 4:4). "The Spirit itself beareth witness with our spirit, that we are the children of God," (Rom. 8:16). They are vitally joined. He dwells in the believer not only by his work of saving and applying the benefits of salvation, but also because he is there as God is in his temple. Andrew Gray said, "As a carnalist's heart is the devil's heaven, so a saint's soul is God's dwelling house."[1] It is a special kind of temple. It is not made with bricks and stones like the Old Testament physical temple that typified all this. It is a spiritual house for a spiritual purpose. In 1 Peter 2:5 this spiritual house is made up of living stones. It will never decay, and instead, each time a soul is added to the church, the building grows. It is a living temple because living stones are set on Christ, the living one, the foundation, the chief cornerstone, that makes other stones alive by his Spirit. It is a living temple because the Spirit indwells it, causing it to grow continually to greater heights of glory in Christ.

In the Old Testament the temple was used for sacrifices, fleshly ordinances, and only had some impression of spiritual glory; and they had to do these things in the temple as God so required. But in the temple now, the entire temple is indwelt by the Holy Spirit sent from the Son of Man from heaven. "Ye are builded together an habitation of God through the Spirit," (Eph. 2:22). No longer is the temple, necessarily, a place to visit with carnal sacrifices, spiritually considered, rather, the stones are the indwelt temple of God. What divisions should be found in such a spiritual temple as this?

It is a great privilege to be part of this current temple, indwelt by the Holy Spirit, and should press the Corinthians never to divide themselves between ministers, who, for their good, build them up into a holy priesthood, together. How can this spiritual temple, this place where the Spirit dwells himself, be found to be at odds with one another? Instead of being at odds, rather, they should be offering up spiritual sacrifices common to such an indwelt spiritual temple. Are they not individuals knit together by the Spirit? Then they ought to exemplify a synchronized universal holiness since

---

[1] Gray, Andrew, *A Door Opening into Everlasting Life*, (Coconut Creek, FL: Puritan Publications, 2013) 330.

they all have been baptized in the Spirit. They ought to be, as the Apostle exhorts, pure in their soul and body. Which is part of the point of the text. They ought to be striving to serve Christ in his house, in their station, for an increase in grace, and edification. The Spirit of God is given to believers to dwell in them as his special dwelling. He will be there forever. He will be to them a principle cultivating a new nature, with new perspectives and new spiritual understandings. They are to be his proper house, an everlasting dwelling-place. Is this not the teaching and prayer of Christ in John 14 and 17? And the Father is answerable to all Christ prays for to fulfill all the desires of his beloved Son. He says this, "And I will pray the Father, and he shall give you another Comforter, that he may abide with you for ever," (John 14:16). This is not a short visit. It is a baptism that continually flows from the Spirit in believers and out as rivers of living waters to abundant life; to eternal life.

  The Spirit is so joined to the believer in his indwelling, that he becomes their principle motivation for all service and all holiness in union with Jesus. There is nothing found emanating from the believer that is good in God's sight, because anything good is from the fruit of the Spirit. It is not Paul's fruit, Apollos' fruit or Peter's fruit, *but the Spirit's fruit.* Paul is prompting the Corinthian believers to grasp the idea that division is opposite to the union of the indwelling Spirit in Christ's temple, in his body. The Spirit communicates grace to the soul which is in the hearts of the saints and gives them the tastes of God's divine nature. That spiritual nature, they now exercise in walking in the Spirit, has no excuse for any division. They are to walk in the light of God. Walking in the light allows, as John says in 1 John, one to walk in fellowship with God, and this works itself out in fellowship with the rest of the body of Christ.

  These believers, then, live by Christ who lives in them

by his indwelling Spirit. He does not merely operate by the Spirit in them, but he lives in the Spirit with them. Both the Father and Son make their abode in the believer through the Spirit. They are one. They partake of Christ, who sends them his Spirit, and dwells in them with the Father in the Spirit, in the temple of their soul and body. Jonathan Edwards said, "The Spirit of God being in this way communicated and united to the saints, they are from there properly denominated from it, and are called spiritual."[2] Believers are *spiritual*, with this new spiritual perspective because of the Spirit in them. They are baptized in the Spirit and they are united by the dwelling of the Spirit *in them.*

Consider the temple in progression. First, it was merely an altar in various places in the early days of the patriarchs. Then the tabernacle was shown to Moses. It was *movable* called, "tabernacle of assembly" and "the tabernacle of testimony." Spiritual service was rendered there to God. This was the place God designated at the time after altar worship, to serve him spiritually. Later, David wanted to build a temple, but God gave that privilege to Solomon. What was its difference? The temple was now to be fixed, immovable. It was a type of Christ; fixed, immovable, where the fullness of God dwells in him bodily, and where the Father is fully exegeted to the world in Christ. It is also though, a picture of the church. In the church is found salvation. It is temple of God in the Spirit. It is the house of the living God (1 Tim. 3:15). Believers are now this very temple of God (1 Cor. 3:16; 6:19) in whom Christ dwells and they are so exercised in the fire of the Spirit by faith (Eph. 3:17).

Spiritual service is now fixed and immovable in Christ, in the very body and soul of believers to perform spiritual sacrifices to God. The progression, types, shadows,

---

[2] Edwards, Jonathan, *The Works of Jonathan Edwards* (Vol. 3), <u>Religious Affections</u>, (New York: Levitt and Allen, 1851) 68.

fulfillment are all orderly in God's administration of the covenant in Christ.

Believers are indwelt for service through *covenant*. What was the point of the temple, but to offer sacrifices to God in worship by his covenant people? God desires worship. He seeks that. Does he not say that very thing in John 4:23-24? Christ's fulfillment of all that which the temple was, now points to the church in a new manner (it is a *refreshing* kind of service that is accomplished), not on a hill, or a mountain, but in daily living in them. The acceptable service of worship in a daily walking of the Spirit. The holiness of service in a daily walking of the Spirit. Even so far as to apply this holy service to the holiness of the body. Both the church, and the body of the believer, and the spirit of the believer. All these things, in Christ, in the Spirit, are exercised by believers. They are priests all day long and temples of the Holy Spirit who indwells them. The indwelling of the Spirit is a promise to those in the covenant of grace.

When did that covenant start? Did you think that Spirit was somehow indwelling believers only *now?* Only after Christ came? Jesus instructed Nicodemus in John 3 that as Israel's teacher, he should have known that the Spirit indwells all his saints and people, that the baptism of the Spirit is something all believers have that all are born from above and filled and empowered and saved in the same way in this new covenant of Grace that was inaugurated in Genesis 3:15; (John 3:10). Ezek. 36:27 says, "I will put my Spirit within you, and cause you to walk in my statutes." God's Holy Spirit will be placed within his people, in their heart, in their mind, in their soul. Such who have this new heart, a new principle of grace in them, perceive the very existence of abundant life in a new way. It is not merely working a little grace here and there in a person. They are *baptized* in the Spirit. They are *indwelt* by the Spirit and the Father and Son make their abode in them. It is a whole renovation of man's nature. It is a union with God in a way which carnal men cannot fathom. Caleb and Joshua "were of a different spirit," (Number 14:24). Different, in light of being saved or lost, being baptized in the Spirit, regenerated in the Spirit, placed on fire in the Spirit, born from above *or not*. Isa. 59:21 says, "This is my covenant with them, saith the Lord; My Spirit that is upon thee shall not depart from thee." The Old Testament is filled with such ideas and types. Types don't mean spiritual things didn't exist. *Types* mean they are not so *clearly seen.* The substance of such things remains the same, but the full understanding of such things is explained in the New Testament. Yet, this indwelling of the Spirit is *not new* in the New Testament: *all* God's saints are indwelt. But with Christ's fulfillment, it is certainly renewed, and clearly seen and explained in a new way and new perspective. Did not the Lord teach, "If ye then, being evil, know how to give good gifts unto your children: how much more shall your heavenly Father give the Holy Spirit to them that ask him?" (Luke 11:13). Was this the New Testament, or did he say this before he went to the cross? Was Christ exalted yet? There is so much presumption by so many in dealing with passages like this, that somehow they slide it over to the New Testament idea, when Jesus, the great rabbi, was exegeting the Father and the work of the mediator and the work of the Spirit from the Old Testament. John Owen said, "Our Savior instructs his disciples to ask the Holy Spirit of God upon the account of his being so promised; as Acts 2:33. All our supplications are to be regulated by the promise, Rom. 8:27. That Spirit which the Lord Christ instructs us to ask of the Father is the Spirit which he has promised to bestow on us as that he shall dwell in us. That the Spirit which Christ instructs us to ask for, and which himself promises to send unto us, is the Holy Ghost himself, the Holy Spirit of promise, by whom we are sealed to the day of redemption."

This is so plain that Owen said, "this requires no labor to prove."³ If Jesus tells them that if they ask of the Spirit, and that such should be granted, is he lying to them? Or is this an idea that they would have been very familiar with? Did anyone question it? Were they walking about saying, "What is this Holy Spirit that Jesus keeps talking about?" Should it be new to them? Nicodemus needed instruction on the Spirit's work of being born again. But Christ makes this of no less importance to the hearer of his preaching, that the Holy Spirit *is given to those who ask.* I wonder if after he taught them this, *they asked for it.* And if they asked, did God grant that? What divisions could be had among those who are forever fixed together, indwelt by the promised Spirit, in the immovable covenant of Christ's grace? The indwelling of the Spirit is a unifying Spirit, and so you see that Paul could not see having a church with such divisions.

The Holy Spirit indwells all believers, and he does this for spiritual service in the worship of God's Christ. Consider this in the realm of personal holiness by way of instruction. We've considered that Jesus demonstrates, emphatically, that men must be born again, or born from above, which is the work of regeneration on the heart of the wicked (John 3:3), they must be baptized by the Spirit. As John 6:63 states, "It is the Spirit who gives life; the flesh profits nothing." Such a sovereign regeneration (a change of the heart from stone to beating flesh) is by the blowing will of the Spirit (John 3:1-8), it is the baptism of the Spirit to rivers of water towards abundant life, all the work of the Spirit both in the Old Testament and the New Testament. The Spirit then convicts and sanctifies the individual by purging unbelief (John 16:8). Those regenerated are then made new creatures (2 Cor. 5:17). They will now be as Joshua and Caleb, of a different kind of

---

³ Owen, John, *The Works of John Owen*, (Edinburgh: Banner of Truth Trust, 1998) 330.

Spirit than the world has. The Spirit then inhabits the whole man and renews him (Romans 8:9), indwells him, and the Father and Son make their abode with them. These are adopted as sons and daughters, and are assured by the Spirit of their sovereign election in Christ, (Rom. 8:16; 1 John 3:2). "Beloved, now are we the sons of God," (1 John 3:2). In the work of sanctification, in continual holiness, in the rivers of water that flow out of believers, the Spirit enables baptized Christians to exercise their lives in Spirit-fire, to discern good from evil, or sin from holiness. He disposes their mind to accept biblical truth and to know what the Scriptures contain through indwelling them. Here the Spirit aids the Christian in expounding Scripture in order to apply that Scripture to the Christian's life and further grow in the mystical union he now has with Christ (1 Cor. 6:17). This does not mean they understand everything perfectly, but they have the Spirit to teach them as they hear the word and read the word and study the word because the Comforter is in them always. He *indwells* them. Through His indwelling presence he enables them to consciously work towards holiness for the glory of Christ, (John 16:16; 2 Tim. 1:14; Rom. 8:9; Gal. 4:6; 1 Cor. 3:16; 1 John 4:13; Eph. 1:13). "That we should be to the praise of his glory, who first trusted in Christ. In whom ye also trusted, after that ye heard the word of truth, the Gospel of your salvation: in whom also after that ye believed, ye were sealed with that holy Spirit of promise, which is the earnest of our inheritance until the redemption of the purchased possession, unto the praise of his glory," (Eph. 1:12-14). *But there is more.*

There is collective holiness by way of instruction, which is not merely personal. This is why people can never say, "Religion is personal to me, it is a private thing." No, it's not. Paul's rejection of division in the body is predicated on the advantage of being one in the mystical body of Christ. Being of the same heart in love is Christ's New

Chapter 4: Indwelt by the Holy Spirit

Commandment, urged by way of Christ's work, to continue in spiritual service to the body. It is a badge or character of Christ's disciples. "By this shall all men know that ye are my Disciples, if ye have love one to another." There are no divisions in the Spirit. There are no divisions with those unified by the indwelling of the Spirit. If there are divisions, it is due to sin. If people don't want to be part of organized religion, it is because *they are lost.* Christians, indwelt by the Spirit, are part of the body of Christ, having unity and oneness of mind and heart. Is it not both, "Good and Pleasant for brethren to dwell together in unity?" Some things are good, but they might not necessarily be pleasant; like affliction, or even acts of repentance. Some sins are fun for a season, as Hebrews points out; which is deceptive. But unity in the mystical body of Christ is both good and pleasant to them both – such a unity, stemming from the indwelling Spirit, is at opposition to any division. This is because the Spirit of God dwells in them, unifying them wholly as Christ so desires. Aaron's Holy oil which ran down his head onto his face onto his beard and such, is like the Spirit, who is designated by oil in the Scriptures, in covering and baptizing from the head downward in an anointing for service. From Christ's throne, in the power of the Spirit, flowing down onto the church, and into them, permeating their very being. "It is like the precious ointment upon the head, that ran down upon the beard, even Aaron's beard: that went down to the skirts of his garments," (Psa. 133:2). Believers walk worthy in holy service (worship) to God which is the reason *they are called out of the world.* They are sons and daughters of their heavenly Father, saved by the Father's covenant Mediator, the Christ, who is God, and is to be worshipped, and is the one with whom all acceptable sacrifices are brought to God. "And will be a Father unto you, and ye shall be my sons and daughters, saith the Lord Almighty," (2 Cor. 6:18). This is directly set, to the

Corinthians, in the context of being the temple of God. "And what agreement hath the temple of God with idols? for ye are the temple of the living God; as God hath said, I will dwell in them, and walk in them; and I will be their God, and they shall be my people." (2 Cor. 6:16). They are to be *temples* of the Holy Spirit, (1 Cor. 3:16-17; Eph. 2:21-22), *members* of one mystical body, united to the body of Christ, the church, (Eph. 5:30, 32; 1 Cor. 12:12-28), of which the Christ permeates every believer by this indwelling Spirit and knits *the body together.* They profess one faith, (Eph. 4:5), are baptized by one Spirit, (Eph. 4:5), fed by one Supper, (1 Cor. 11:20, 23, 10:16), live by one Gospel, (Titus 2:1) are heirs of one hope, and partakers of one Kingdom in Christ.

How shall they live then with an indwelling of the Spirit? How shall they honor this one calling they were called with, that they would not have divisions, but be united in their heart and mind to serve God acceptably with reverence and godly fear? How shall they answer the upward call of God in Christ? They do this in unity of mind and service to the Christ. Anything less than this is division.

You think to yourself, there is much division in the body of Christ. You would be right. Francis Roberts said, "Oneness adorns this, and dividedness shames it."[4] There must be a striving in the body for holiness in spiritual service. 1 Cor. 3:16-17 says, "know ye not that ye are the temple of God, and that the Spirit of God dwelleth in you? If any man defile the temple of God, him shall God destroy; for the temple of God is holy, which temple ye are." Collective holiness is motioned by the Spirit in his indwelling to the whole body. The heart does not pump blood only to one member of the body; it's to the whole body for service of gold, silver and precious jewels over an against hay and stubble and all

---

[4] Roberts, Francis, *Mystery and Marrow of the Bible* (London: R.W., 1657) 1171.

manner of lesser things burned up in judgment. Would those who are the temple of God serve God with wood, hay and stubble? What lasting eternal value is there in works or actions which will be burned up? Being indwelt by the Spirit in this way, for spiritual service, is directly related to rewards for good works. They bring forth fruits worthy of repentance. They bring forth spiritual works worthy of such an indwelling. For the Spirit in indwelling them fans the flame of his baptism in them. Holiness and purity are to be cultivated because of the indwelling of the Holy Spirit. Divisions create wood, hay and stubble. All divisions will be burned up. Eph. 2:21-22 says, "In whom all the building fitly framed together groweth unto an holy temple in the Lord: in whom ye also are builded together for an habitation of God through the Spirit." Believers are instructed collectively by Paul to keep themselves pure as an appropriate temple for the Spirit who dwells there; who dwells in them. Will the Spirit reside in an *unclean house?* What will sin of all kinds do to the temple of the Holy Spirit, or the Spirit in that temple? Sin must never dwell where God dwells. This is why, again, as Scripture states, that the indwelling Spirit can be vexed, grieved, resisted, and such.[5]

The indwelling Spirit is to guide them into holy worship, and by the Spirit this temple has guidance and direction. Godly wisdom is given to the body to live and move and have their being in God daily through the word and weekly through the preaching of the word. And remember, "The LORD loveth the gates of Zion more than all the dwellings of Jacob," (Psa. 87:2). He loves the church gathered together, all those indwelt by the Spirit, collectively together to praise and worship the Father, through the mediation of Christ, by the power of Spirit-fire. There must be a great

---

[5] Eph. 4:30, 1 Thess. 5:19; Isa. 63:10; compare with Psa. 51:11; Gen 6:3, *etc.*

discernment between acceptable works and sinful works. Christ gives this character of his sheep, that they "hear him, know his voice, and follow him," but "a stranger they will not follow," (John 10:3-5). Christ speaks to his people by his Spirit, where he guides and directs his body through the word. The indwelling Spirit feeds the Christian by movements in the soul through the word. What a frustrating thing it must be for the Lord to direct his Spirit filled body that goes in so many different ways and divisions in the world because of so many and so much sin. "He that hath an ear to hear, let him hear what the Spirit saith unto the churches," (Rev. 2:29). *Hear.* Do you have an ear? *Hear.* Paul says, 1 Cor. 2:15, "He that is spiritual judgeth all things." Why? They discern between the voice of the Spirit which dwells in them and the voice of the spirit of sin, and the spirit of the world, and the spirit of Antichrist. The Spirit will direct the believer and the church to do nothing but what is according to the mind of Christ. This is delivered to God's people in his revealed will, the word. This is the rule by which all believers walk.

Imagine being the Spirit in a believer who looks little to the word? What guidance will he gain? Does the Spirit merely work by way of *feeling?* Does he work by merely *zapping* the Christian? How will waters flow if there is no cultivation of the word in a believer by which the Spirit-fire of baptism is kindled in them? Believers are guided by the Spirit according to the standards of God's righteous character. He does not move in believers to give them new feelings, but rather, new light and power which reside wholly in the word and this will in turn excite them because the indwelling of the Spirit gives them an enlightened mind which then translates down to a zealous heart. Such commands and directives for the church are received happily, *if they hear it.* "Where the Spirit of the Lord is, there is liberty," (2 Cor. 3:17). Such directives cause the believer to live in a happy estate. If they are not led by the Spirit by the word, then they are influenced by the, "spirit of bondage," (Rom. 8:15) which is wholly set in opposition to the Spirit's fruit. Do they have a fire in their heart? Or is there just some smoking flax? Does such walking in the indwelling Spirit stir them up to offer spiritual sacrifices to God, pleasing and acceptable? Do they walk closer with God? Do they know Christ more? God looks, by his Spirit to rouse them up to have his graces exercised in them, and their souls strengthened by being obedient to Jesus to worship acceptably, with reverence and godly fear. This indwelling Spirit works and motions all these things in the listening believer.

Consider personal and collective holiness by way of warning. The Spirit indwells the believer, and the church, because of the union to Christ. 2 Peter 1:4 says we are, "by the promises made partakers of the divine nature." The mutual indwelling of Christ and his saints is in their union exemplified by the indwelling Spirit. 1 Cor. 12:12 says, "As the body is one, and hath many members, and all the members of that one body, being many, are one body, so also is Christ." The body is one, and the saints are one body in Christ. I have used the phrase *the mystical body of Christ* in many of my teachings, and this is the meaning behind it. The church is mystically, spiritually, joined in union with Christ. It is a spiritual connection by way of being baptized in the Spirit. Such temples of the Holy Spirit must be holy temples. Christ, "is the head of the church, and the savior of the body," (Eph. 5:23). He is "the head of the body, the church," (Col. 1:18). By his Spirit, he indwells this one body, and gives life to the body, and animates the body by the fruit of his holy Spirit. He looks for acceptable service to be rendered by every part. The hands, the legs, the fingers all must be holy. Consider a man with gangrene in his leg. It must be cut off, for it is no good, it has no life. It is dead rotting flesh.

Jesus likens the body of the church to a vine with branches (John 15:4-5). The sap in the midst which gives life flowing through the channels of the veins is the Spirit by which flows living water, living sap. If such branches are not fruit-producing branches, filled with spiritual life, they have to be cut off and thrown into the fire. They are not really connected by the vitality of the Spirit. The church is unified in Christ by the indwelling Spirit. The motivation for holiness, then, is a direct result of the Spirit's indwelling power, shining a light on the work that Christ has fulfilled, and all that he procured. The Spirit bids the church, bids each believer, to put on Christ.

What do they put on when they are baptized and indwelt by the Spirit sent from Christ? What is this putting on of Christ? It is synonymous with the indwelling of the Spirit. It is the unction and anointing of the Spirit. It is continued illumination by the Spirit. It is continual filling by the Spirit. It is empowerment by the Spirit. It is exercising the Gifts of the Spirit, praying in the Spirit, walking in the Spirit, and exemplifying the Fruit of the Spirit. All these are a direct result with the new principle of grace, the quickening, by the Spirit, applying the work of Christ and his cross on the soul.[6]

You should have motives to holiness by the Spirit's indwelling. The Holy Spirit indwells you who believe. You are his dwelling, his temple, (1 Cor. 6:19, 3:16-17; Eph. 2:21-22). You are to be holy in all your walk, for all your service to Christ, (1 Peter 1:14-18). "For as many as are led by the Spirit of God, they are the sons of God," (Rom. 8:14). Spiritual service is at the heart of the Spirit's indwelling. It is not only salvation. Salvation is only the beginning. The Holy Spirit does not baptize you, save you, indwell you for you to sit as a couch potato. It is not merely attending a church service. He

---

[6] Every one of these chapters will cover each part of those ideas, now that we understand being baptized and indwelt by the Spirit.

is looking for servants, worshippers, who are ignited by the indwelling Spirit-fire of his continued work in your soul. You are the temple of the Spirit. "Your body is the temple of the Holy Spirit, which is in you, which ye have of God," (1 Cor. 3:16). Do you not know this? "Know ye not," (verse 17), "the temple of God is holy?" God has no physical temple today. Spirit and truth are to emanate from his temple which is you. He has chosen to live in the Spirit indwelling you, in your heart and soul. Paul's emphasis is that knowing this should guard you against all manner of sin.

Your temple is far more lovely than the old physical temple. You are washed clean. It was covered in blood. You are washed by the blood of Christ, with a sweet smelling savor. They smelled the rankness of animal sacrifices. You are adorned with the graces of all his saving spiritual gift, the entirety of his spiritual blessing in the Spirit. They looked forward to benefits to come more fully. You are readied by the Spirit as a bride made ready for her husband; the, "King's daughter," is said to be, "all glorious within," (Psalm 45). The inside of their temple was really, a mere building. You are part of the holy assembly of God's anointed people. Their assembly had to stand far off and watch from a distance. You are in the assembly of the saints described as God's temple. This is where they come together for the Father's purpose of worship *to him*, through Christ, in the power of the indwelling Spirit. God dwells in the midst of his people in this way. You are the holy of holies. The Spirit dwells *in you.* You are far more glorious today, even without being perfectly sanctified and in heaven, than anything the Old Testament had that was even spoken of as glorious. Count yourself blessed to be in a New Testament, in opposition to the Old Testament, made at Mount Sinai.

The Covenant given at Mount Sinai, called *the Old Covenant*, is a precursor to the *New Testament*, of the covenant made *after the fall.* This old *Testator Moses,* contrasts with the new *Testator Jesus.* These two, being in substance the same, are in outward administration different. They had one and the same Testator as it concerns eternity, that is *Jesus Christ,* but differently considered. Jesus *promised* was Mediator and Testator of the Old Testament, typically and obscurely; under the types of Moses of the death of Levitical sacrifices, and of their blood sprinkled. But Jesus Christ came and actually exhibited and performed in his perfect flesh all that was required by the Mediator and Testator *of this New Covenant,* to see Christ and his substance clearly, *without types,* without sacrificial hints of the Old Testament. He did this by means of his own death and blood, that all you who are called into service by the Spirit may receive the promise of the eternal inheritance. This is why the new covenant is called New, in opposition to this Old way of looking at types and shadows under the testator of Moses. It is Christ's established work as the God-man. It revokes all types and shadows. It is fulfilled by *Christ himself in his person.* It is established on better promises dedicated with the death and blood of *the promised Christ.* It is taught in a manner which is extensively applied and confirmed to the mind and heart by being baptized in the Spirit, and ratified visibly by New Testament seals showing the glorious change in administration by his manifested indwelling through acceptable worship. It is the everlasting covenant, seen fully, seen in Christ, given to you as a gift, where the Spirit is poured out on you, and indwells you to connect you and the church to the Spirit never to be revoked, but to remain new until Christ's final coming.

Christ is your Head, the Head of the body, the Head of the church. He came to die for sin to make a special habitation of you *in the Spirit.* You are together in church "a building fitly framed." You are partakers of the promised eternal spirit who can never be taken away from you. But never being taken away is not a license to sin. For those who are saved will show forth, outwardly, that the Spirit indwells them. Your temple is to be used for holy purposes. The old temple, with carnal sacrifices, was a type fulfilled in Christ, but still pointing and used of spiritual things. God set the temple apart for holy purposes, and the Jews saw anything occurring in that temple not in accordance with the word as *defiling it;* (that is, once they were not dissuaded by wickedness or sin to defile it, such as the terrible time under Manasseh's reign). But they saw the temple as a means of grace where the means of grace for them at the time was used. There were many provisions and directives to use that means the right way. Even the headband of the high priest said "Holiness to the Lord."[7] In the temple, everything was holy. The holy oil. The holy candles. The holy furniture. The holy bread. The holy fire. The holy incense. The holy place. The holy of holies. How does one describe you as a holy temple of the holy Spirit that indwells you? Holy affections? Holy fruits? Holy desires? Holy love? Holy contemplations? Holy zeal? Holy devotions? Holy worship? *You are to be holy,* separate, separated to God, who *indwells* you. You are his temple. He is present with you, not only as he is with the heathen, present in upholding their very being (Acts 17:28), but with you, for he lives in you and produces fruit *from that indwelling.* He is there in a more special manner; a *saving* manner.

Do you not know you are not your own if you are a professing Christian? If the Spirit resides there, whose house is it? It is not only his house, but it is a bought house. It is bought by Christ's life and blood. You are not your own. God has a very high view of the body. God has a very high view of you and your body. It is a body that he fashioned that can have

---

[7] "And thou shalt make a plate of pure gold, and grave upon it, like the engravings of a signet, HOLINESS TO THE LORD," (Exod. 28:36).

the Holy Spirit indwell it. How should you think about this? Consider it this way, think about it this way as a Christian:

> God has taken me, a vile wretch, a poor worm, and made a house of it for his own Spirit. The Lord tells me in his word that he has a delight to do this, and that he will dwell with me, by promise, forever. He does not live in a temple made with hands. He does not place his name on stones or wood. Instead, Jesus says that the Father and he will come and dwell in me by his Spirit, forever. Is it unfathomable that the infinite Spirit of Truth, the eternal Spirit of holiness, the Spirit of Christ dwells in me? He is utterly pure and holy, and yet, he desires, no, he promises to dwell in me also. Will I quench the Spirit? Will I grieve the Spirit? Will I act in an uncomely manner while the eternal Holy Spirit resides in me? What will I do with my thoughts? What will I do with earthlimindedness? For I know, he is not just the Spirit, but he is in me the indwelling Holy Spirit.

The next chapter will deal with the *anointing* of the Holy Spirit who indwells the Christian.

Chapter 5:
Unction and Anointing by the Holy Spirit

"For all the promises of God in him are yea, and in him Amen, unto the glory of God by us. Now he which stablisheth us with you in Christ, and hath anointed us, is God; Who hath also sealed us, and given the earnest of the Spirit in our hearts," (2 Cor. 1:20-22).

In these verses we find Paul's *thesis* on the believer's assurance. In verse 20 he makes this emphatic that "all the promises of God in him are yea, and in him Amen, unto the glory of God by us." The word by him, fulfilled in Christ, is *yes and amen* to everything Paul has been teaching from the word of God itself to the church; from the inception of the Old Testament to the Christians of the New Testament. God's promises found in the Old Testament are *yes and amen* in Christ. "Now he," that is God, "which stablisheth us with you," which refers to all believers at Corinth, are united with the same salvation Paul has by being united in Jesus Christ. He is pressing that the one who is confirming us is also confirming you, "in the Anointed One." This anointed one is the only means of salvation. It is only in the Christ, God's anointed Messiah. It is God himself in the flesh. He "hath anointed us," or literally has, "touched us with his hand." The Anointed one establishes us, and anoints us. *He touches the church with his hand.* This "is God." No other but God could establish or confirm salvation in his Anointed, and anoint believers in him. It is the One, "who hath also sealed us," which is a term taken from commerce, that means "a mark of ownership." It is placing a seal upon something indicating possession. God has put a sign of ownership on them to show that they belong to him. He touched them, and by such a touch owns them. In fact, he has, "given the earnest of the Spirit in our hearts," (2 Cor. 1:21-22). It is "the guarantee of the Spirit." The Spirit *himself* is the guarantee. The word *earnest* or *guarantee* is also a term taken from commerce, a down payment, a partial payment of the purchase price, which guaranteed that the full price would be paid later. The gift of the Holy Spirit to the believer is God's guarantee that eventually he will finish the work he has begun in confirming them in Christ. He will fully redeem his people. If he begins it, he will end it.[1]

All these verses are predicated on the preaching of the Gospel, and the truth of all Old Testament promises in Christ. "For the Son of God, Jesus Christ, who was preached among you by us, even by me and Silvanus and Timotheus, was not yea and nay, but in him was yea. For all the promises of God in him are yea, and in him Amen, unto the glory of God by us," (2 Cor. 1:19-20). These are all the Old Testament promises. He, that is the Anointed One, confirms and establishes all believers together, in sending an anointing by the hand of the Holy Spirit who is the guarantee that they belong to God. They are baptized in him. They are indwelt by him. They are *touched and anointed* by him with the Spirit. This anointing confirms the Corinthian believers, the "us," in the truths of the Gospel of the Anointed One.

The word *anointing* is used in various ways in Scripture, both in the Old Testament and the New Testament and is generally connected with oil. This oil is a type of the Holy Spirit. There was a holy ointment Exod. 30:25 which typifies the pouring of the Spirit by Christ on the people. Anointing oil in this way was used to install men into any office. Kings were anointed, priests were anointed, prophets

---

[1] 2 Cor. 5:5; Eph. 1:13.

were anointed; that holy oil poured on Aaron and his sons. Jesus was anointed. "God anointed Jesus of Nazareth with the Holy Ghost, and with power," (Acts 10:38). The apostles were anointed. The Spirit was *poured* on them, (Acts 2). *All* Christians are *anointed*, 2 Cor. 1:21, "Now he that stablisheth us with you in Christ, and hath anointed us, is God." They are made kings and priests to God *by this anointing*.

1 John 2:20-21 compliments the Corinthian text, "But ye have an unction from the Holy One, and ye know all things. I have not written unto you because ye know not the truth, but because ye know it, and that no lie is of the truth." The medicine prescribed against antichristian doctrine is that you have an, "unction from the Holy One, and know all things." The author of this unction is called *the Holy One*. Those who have this unction, *know all things*. What do they know? All things. What are "all things?" They know the promises of the *yes and amen* in Christ taken from the Old Testament.[2] *Unction* is a metaphor. It is an indirect expression, which works from the Old Testament idea of anointing with oil. Anointing is with the Spirit, which is like using the oil of the Old Testament for anointing. Isa. 61:1 says, "The Spirit of the Lord is upon me, because the Lord hath anointed me..." The Spirit is vitally tied to this anointing. Peter says in Acts 10:48, "God anointed Jesus of Nazareth with the Holy Ghost." This is the same anointing of our main text. The Spirit of God, with his gifts and graces, *is* the unction. Oil mixed with anything generally retains its properties and remains oil. The Spirit, in this light, *will not be mixed*. He gives an unction, a touching, that is pure oil of a lasting character. Water evaporates, but oil holds in itself its virtue. It is of *great worth*. Ezek. 16:19, "I gave her corn, and wine, and oil, and multiplied her silver and gold."

---

[2] How many Christians can actually say yes and amen to this?

This anointing is attached to the Spirit, such an anointing is of transcendent value. It is of heavenly value; eternal value. In the Old Testament oil is used for a great many things. Oil poured on wounds heals. Christ comes to heal, "The Spirit of the Lord GOD is upon me; because the LORD hath anointed me [*to do what?*] to bind up the brokenhearted, ... to give unto them beauty for ashes, the oil of joy for mourning, the garment of praise for the spirit of heaviness; that they might be called trees of righteousness, the planting of the LORD, that he might be glorified," (Isa. 61:1). How? Through preaching and heralding the word of God. When there is no oil, there is disease, as Isa. 1:6 says, "They have not been mollified with ointment." This is to soften them; to heal them. Anointing the face with oil makes it beautiful. Psa. 104:15 says, "oil to cause the face to shine." Naomi tells Ruth, before she went to Boaz, *to anoint herself*, (Ruth 3:3). Anointing the head with oil is special. Eccl. 9:8 says, "Let thy head want no ointment." Anointing the eyes with oil is also metaphorical in that oil *in lamps* so maintains light. "Oil for the light, spices for anointing oil, and for sweet incense," (Exod. 25:6). It revolves around consecration, separation, holiness; setting people apart for holy service. "Then shalt thou take the anointing oil, and pour it upon his head, and anoint him," (Exod. 29:7). The ascended Savior, the anointed Savior who had the Spirit without measure, sends the Spirit, who is the anointing which Christians have from the Holy One. Christ gives this gift of the Comforter, the Spirit, in his anointing. And Scripture does not say one gets an anointing *from* the Spirit, but *with* the Spirit. The Holy Spirit, sent by Christ, to touch the mind, to touch the heart, pours out his gladness into them for abundant life, to baptize them, to indwell them, *that is the touch,* the *anointing.* Christ, being the Anointed Holy One, sends the Spirit and anoints *with* the Spirit *his people.*

Christ, in both his natures, as God and as man, was eminently holy. It is an undeniable attribute of God. It is the crown of God's attributes. Christ communicates himself in holiness by the Holy Spirit in holy anointing with the Spirit on the minds and hearts of his people. Psa. 141:17, "He is holy in all his works." In this sending of the Holy Spirit, from the holy Christ, the Spirit first births or baptizes the believer in regeneration. Then he gives affect to both the anointing of Christ, and his sealing. He enlightens the mind and heart, and then seals or confirms what Christ did through an anointing, or knowledge of the truth which the Spirit works in believers by touching them. In this, both Paul and the Corinthians share in this anointing. *All believers* share in this anointing. All believers in Christ are anointed to serve Christ through the Holy Spirit, by which they are anointed. This anointing is not a speculation, but a certain establishing knowledge which grows into assurance. Those who are anointed are sanctified and consecrated to God, and they are under the confirmation of Christ in the truth, by the sealing of the Spirit, who motions their mind to serve God. They are under his spiritual care. To be anointed, here, is the idea of *consecration*; they poured oil onto something for setting it apart for holy service throughout the Old Testament. This is a setting apart for holiness. As we saw in the last chapter, such people are indwelt, and now *anointed for God's special use*.

Believers, as God's servants, are set apart, confirmed and qualified for holy use by the grace of the Spirit of the *Anointed One* who anoints them with his Spirit. They are special to God, set apart by God and protected by him through Christ, through the anointing of the Spirit. Psa. 105:15, "Touch not mine anointed." *I have touched them,* God is saying, *with my Spirit, they are my anointed ones.* This anointing by the Spirit is to bring them into the truth of the word. Interestingly, this is the fulfillment of all *Old Testament promises*, and all New Testament *application.* They are *yes and amen* in Christ. The Father and the Son send God the Holy Spirit to continually abide in believers (John 14:16–17). He is the spring of eternal life welling up in the elect. He is the Author of their seal of salvation confirming their election (Ephesians 1:13; 2 Corinthians 1:21-22; 2 Timothy 2:19). He gives to them a down payment of their eternal salvation in his work in their hearts by this anointing. Ephesians 1:14 says, "Which is the earnest of our inheritance until the redemption of the purchased possession, unto the praise of his glory." Paul uses in these verses three equivalences to express what he had said plainly in these verses. He establishes, confirms, and guarantees the believer, which is the anointing.

The Spirit is given to guide the believer into all truth. He teaches believers all things and they know Christ is yes and amen to all the Old Testament prophecies. See how important all Scripture is in this light? He assures believers of their interest in God and in Christ by his anointing and guidance in all the Bible, not just the New Testament. Guiding into truth, teaching the truth, sealing the truth, anointing the believer, assures them of their interest in the Anointed One.

The Holy Spirit does not make salvation sure. *Christ has already done that.* All the promises are *Yes and Amen* in the Anointed Savior. What the Spirit does is point this out in the heart of a believer. Salvation in Christ is *already sure*, it is held out in the preaching of the Gospel, it can be yours, and as a matter of fact, all the promises of God are yes and amen in Christ, so you believers in Corinth are confirmed in the Anointed One just as I am, Paul says. Gospel, faith, salvation, sealing, confirming, establishing, anointing, assurance all are poured out on them. Salvation can be had, and it can be known as something sure. One can gain great assurance from all this. The Spirit does not seal up the inheritance believers have, but Paul says the believer is sealed.

Chapter 5: Unction and Anointing

Then, the Spirit is not given in his anointing to making salvation sure, but to make believers sure of it by teaching them all things. The inward work of being baptized and indwelt by the Spirit, regenerated, is this use of being sealed by the Spirit, being anointed in all of this. The seal of the Spirit, the anointing, is a fruit of indwelling.

The believer is sealed by the Holy Spirit of promise for the expressed purpose of being confirmed in the same anointing of Christ, but to a lesser degree, for the assurance of salvation. God establishes all believers in Christ by the Spirit, by the anointing. And this anointing is a confirmation, and continued belief and cultivation in what the Gospel teaches them about the promises of God. The powerful working of the Holy Spirit is the only one who can take the drifting mind of the believer, who is very forgetful, and remind it of everything Christ has said to them. Without the inward, spirited anointing of the redeemer in the believer through the Spirit, no other help will be sufficient to assure them of their confirmation in Christ.

Christ confirms all believers savingly by the anointing of the Holy Spirit. There is a great deal of *charismatic chaos* in the world today in regard to this idea. In charismatic circles, the anointing of the Holy Spirit is partly attached and partly separated from the baptism of the Spirit, and the baptism of the Spirit is partly separated from salvation and partly attached to spiritual service; *it's all a mess.* They think, one is saved and they are baptized into Christ, but later, if they seek it, they can gain the full reception of Holy Spirit baptism, which, for them, is evidenced by the gifts of talking in babbling tongues, this was a doctrine begun by the Montanists, *heretics* in the early church. Interestingly they do not choose to evidence this baptism by the gift of healing, or the gift of future prophecy. Those are far too *hard* to easily replicate. Not even by the gift of tongues, *to speak in a known tongue perfectly by the Spirit*, do they "prove this" but by an imaginary "gift of babbling tongues" which anyone can do because *they make it up personally*. They use a non-biblical idea of speaking in some angelic language, as if angels were somehow unintelligible in Scripture by babbling in gibberish, which they term *glossolalia*, found nowhere in Scripture as an evidence of being baptized in the Spirit after salvation. In their mind, to be baptized is to be supernaturally, experientially, and in full consciousness, immersed in or submerged in the power of the Holy Spirit. This very concept of babbling in prayer, *is expressly forbidden by Christ*. "But when ye pray, use not vain repetitions, as the heathen do: for they think that they shall be heard for their much speaking," (Matt. 6:7). This is Christ's directive *against* many words over and over, meaning to *stammer* or *to babble*.

These charismatics call it *a second work of grace;* some people have it and some don't. Some Christians are regular gas, and some are high octane. They believe that every believer is baptized *into Christ,* but not every believer is baptized *into the Spirit*. Once baptized in the Spirit, one is then further anointed to continue that fresh power in utilizing the gifts of the Spirit, and one must be open to be the conduit of the Spirit to fully adore and make useful this mystical anointing; it is all very much *man centered*. It's making one's self available to be used by the Spirit with fresh power, because one is seeking *power,* not holiness.

Now, the theological term given to all that charismatic tongue-speaking is...hogwash. All of this is complete nonsense. It is all fabricated, it is all a delusion. All regenerate believers are anointed with the Holy Spirit's unction. In the Old Testament it was no less real, yet it was also typified by external signs of its fullness to come. In other words, Abraham had the anointing and unction of the Spirit. He is the father of the faith of believers. Whatever he had, believers have. He is *the father of the faithful.* Signs were also given to him and others, word pictures, of this anointing, "And thou shalt put them upon Aaron thy brother, and his sons with him; and shalt anoint them, *[why?]*...and consecrate them, and sanctify them, that they may minister unto me in the priest's office," (Exod. 28:41). They are consecrated and sanctified. So they may be assured of God's power working in them for service; is assurance something all believers are to obtain and cultivate? Then all believers are under the unction of the Spirit. Why? So they can serve God. Otherwise, there would be no confirmed believers, and instead, fearful slaves. Is this not a forerunner of understanding the priesthood of all believers to a certain extent? That they are a kingdom of priests and a holy nation? Are they not all anointed? Do they not all have unction? Have they not all been set apart if they are touched by God and born again by the Spirit from above and have comfort in their conformation as sons and daughters? "But ye have an unction from the Holy One, and ye know all things," (1 John 2:20). Unction, anointing, is set in the context of "knowing things" not feeling things, or ecstatic things. "But the anointing which ye have received of him abideth in you, and ye need not that any man teach you: but as the same anointing teacheth you of all things, and is truth, and is no lie, and even as it hath taught you, ye shall abide in him," (1 John 2:27). Nathaniel Hardy said, "All who are taught by the unction, need not that any man should teach them, and consequently not the holy men of God; But all Christians are taught by the unction which they receive from Christ."[3]

Spiritual illumination (which we have not covered yet) is conjoined with this unction. Men cannot empower others; God does that by his Spirit; he touches them and gives

---

[3] Hardy, Nathaniel, *The First General Epistle of St. John the Apostle Unfolded and Applied*, (Edinburgh: James Nisbet and Co., 1864) 372.

them guidance through the word of God. "Unless that divine Spirit is present in the heart of the hearer, the word of the teacher is to no purpose."[4] One can never assign credit to the teacher, but by the Spirit, because all these things concerning Christ are *spiritually discerned*. They cannot be carnally discerned. The testimony given by the Holy Spirit to the truth of the Gospel (the word given to believers) is this "unction."

In the New Testament we have a more clear and distinct knowledge of the mysteries of faith (Isaiah 11:9; 54:13; Jeremiah 31:34; 1 John 2:27), a more generous, sublime degree of holiness (Isaiah 33:24; 35:9; 60:21–22; Zechariah 10:5; 12:8) a more delightful consolation (Isaiah 40:1–2; 60:1–2; 55:11; 66:12–14; John 14:16; Acts 9:31; Ephesians 1:13; 2 Corinthians 1:22), and a boldness to come to God, which is now greater, for believers come *boldly* before the throne of grace. Adopted as sons and daughters; the affects of such a salvation are more clearly seen. Galatians 4:6 tells us, "And because ye are sons, God hath sent forth the Spirit of his Son into your hearts, crying, Abba, Father." Those that are established and anointed, and have the sealing and earnest of the Spirit, cannot fall away; they are anointed for service and *assured* of it. This is again mentioned in Eph. 1:13-14. The Spirit's unction, his anointing, his confirmation in a believer, is by way of spiritual instruction, through the Gospel, by divine illumination, that supernatural divine light, demonstrating the mystery of godliness in the Gospel of the Anointed Savior. Through this spiritual unction by the Spirit, these works cultivate assurance.

The anointing cultivates assurance. Where does one find the Gospel and what do they find in it? Start it at Genesis 1:1 and end it at the last verse of Revelation. In the word the Christ is found. Believers have an unction from the Holy One

---

[4] Ibid.

to understand this if they are born again. The Spirit in his divine Person is the believer's seal, his confirmation, his unction, *power* resulting in the nurturing of Gospel assurance. *You* like *us* are confirmed, Paul says. This is assurance and it is vitally conjoined to the anointing.

Christ is the Anointed One who sends the anointing Spirit to comfort believers. Christ anoints all believers with the Spirit. He does not anoint a select group. He anoints his whole body. He does not anoint part of his body, as if one part is greater or better than another. He does not anoint the hand and not the arm. He pours the Spirit out from the head which then anoints and travels down to the ground itself, as the illustration of Old Testament anointing is seen. It covers the whole man to further the metaphor.[5] The Spirit is sent by the Father and the Son from the throne of the ascended Son of Man to anoint his whole body. As Jesus was anointed by the Spirit without measure. "...for God giveth not the Spirit by measure unto him," (John 3:34). "The Father loveth the Son, and hath given all things into his hand," (John 3:35). He has the fullness of the Spirit in every respect. He imparts a measure of this Spirit as he sends the Spirit to baptized and indwell every believer. They are anointed by the Spirit in measure, from Christ's anointing. Such an anointing is the Spirit of Christ which indwells and empowers the believer. He gives gifts to men, the Holy Spirit's anointing them. He is the fountain by which rivers of living water flow out forever. He is an inexhaustible fountain, the fullness of God, from the Christ, who has the Spirit without measure, who sent him to comfort, the Comforter, the one who will teach you all things and remind you of everything he said to his disciples. Christ, who is the Holy One, sends the Holy Spirit, as a result of being

---

[5] "It is like the precious ointment upon the head, that ran down upon the beard, even Aaron's beard: that went down to the skirts of his garments," (Psa. 133:2).

the Holy Anointed Messiah and deliverer. He was the first anointed, and has all the fulness of the Spirit of Grace flowing from himself. He purchased the covenantal benefit of this for believers in fulfilling all his work, in his death and in his resurrection. He sends it to them by way of his ascension and intercession.

Christ shed his blood hanging on the cursed tree, and then he deposited his Spirit into the hearts of his people, touching them for service. Titus 3:6, "Which he shed on us abundantly, through Jesus Christ our Savior." He sends his anointing to us through his Spirit abundantly. John 1:16, "Of his fulness have we received, and grace for grace." By his anointing believers are anointed. Why? Why not save, and then simply throw believers a bible?

Christ sends the anointing of the Spirit in assurance to his people. There is a special encouragement imprinted in the heart by the Holy Spirit where believers look to understand their confirmation in Christ to themselves. Many great and precious promises have been made to them, and they look to apply them. All the promises of Christ are *yes and amen* for them, and the more they know the more they are assured of this work of the Spirit on them. Matt. 9:2 says, "They brought to him a man sick of the palsy, lying on a bed. And when Jesus saw their faith, he said to the sick of the palsy, Son, be of good comfort, your sins are forgiven thee." Gal. 2:20, "I live, yet not I now, but Christ lives in me. And in that I now live in the flesh, I live by the faith of the Son of God, who have loved me, and given himself for me." Such a confirmation is a beckoning to Christ to give more grace. Matt. 15:22, "A woman, a Cananite, came out of the same coasts, and cried, saying to him, Have mercy on me, O Lord, the son of David, my daughter is miserably vexed with a devil," *etc.* (see verses 23-27.) John 20:29, "Jesus said to him, Thomas, because you have seen me, you believest. Blessed are they which have not seen, and have believed." Heb. 11:1, "Faith is the ground of things hoped for, and the evidence of things which are not seen."

Faith consents to the word of God. It is *opposite* to doubt. Faith is to grow into assurance; into the full assurance of faith and this can only happen through the anointing of the Spirit. Jesus says that it is the work of the Comforter to do this in believers; to teach them, to remind them, *etc.* It cannot be done unless they are anointed by the Spirit. 2 Chron. 20:20, "Put your trust in the Lord your God, and you shall be assured. Believe his Prophets, and you shall prosper." It cannot be done, it cannot be believed, without the *continued* anointing of the Spirit. Those who doubt their salvation, who really doubt it, walk a difficult walk because they do not cultivate a comfort by the special motions of the Spirit who indwells them and anoints their mind and heart through the word; find a Christian without comfort, without assurance, really, and you find a Christian who does not know the promises of God, and has not applied them to their soul; for if they are saved, they have the anointing; but if they neglect the word, that anointing is not cultivated.

What assurance might believers take from being confirmed, sealed and anointed in Christ by the Spirit? Christ preserves his people from falling away. *God* is the Savior. Many Christians really don't believe the depth of that statement. But, for true believers, the world and the devil try to take *that* away from every believer. He gives his people the very promises resting on his immutable counsel. Paul says to the same Corinthians, "He will confirm us," in and to the end, "that we may be blameless in the day of our Lord Jesus Christ. For our God is faithful, who hath called us to the fellowship of his Son Jesus Christ our Lord," (1 Corinthians 1:8-9). Is his decree immutable? Does the foundation of God remain sure in Christ? Is God strong enough, faithful enough, immutable enough in his love and power to save sinners? Is there a sinner greater than Christ is a Savior? "We are kept by the power of God to salvation," (1 Peter 1:5). For, "he which hath begun a good work in us, will perform it till the day of Christ," (Philippians 1:6). Believers *have* the seal and the anointing of God until that day and beyond.

Everyone that believes, is, "sealed by the Holy Spirit of promise." Is there any other way than being established in Christ? He, "will put his Spirit into them, which shall lead them into all truth, and cause them to keep his statutes, and to do them, (John 14, Ezekiel 36). Nicholas Byfield said, "He will uphold them, and order their ways, and keep their feet, that they do not fall. "The steps of the good man are ordered by the Lord, and he delighteth in his way." "Though he fall, he shall not utterly be cast down. For the Lord upholdeth him with his hand," (Psalm 37:23-24). "He holdeth our soul in life and suffereth not our feet to be moved, (Psalm 66:9). "He will keep the feet of his saints," (1 Samuel 2:9). God will work their works for them, and continually assist them with his presence, and blessings, (Isaiah 36, Ezekiel 36, Philippians 2:13). From this, believers may gather many comforts from God."[6]

The saints have a special anointing from Jesus Christ, to confirm them in the truth of the word. The preaching of the Gospel speaks of the Anointed Savior forgiving sin, imputing his righteousness to sinners and taking their sin to satisfy the justice of God; in *either* testament. Acts 5:31-32, "Him hath God exalted with his right hand to be a prince and a saviour, for to give repentance to Israel, and forgiveness of sins. And we are his witnesses of these things, and so is also the Holy Ghost whom God hath given to them that obey him."
Such a work of the Spirit, on a believer, for assurance comes in three parts. They are enlightened by the Holy Spirit. They

---

[6] Byfield, Nicholas, *The Promises of God*, (Coconut Creek, FL: Puritan Publications, 2013) 103.

are converted by the Spirit. They are comforted by the Spirit. Will believers take that comfort? Will they cultivate the promise of the oil of gladness? Will they cultivate the anointing they have been touched with?

The anointing of the Spirit and your comfort is where God presses his promises into your mind and heart. Hannibal Gammon said, "...you must press God on his promises, that he would perform them to you; and you must entreat his favor with your whole heart, (as David does, Psalm 119:58), that he would persuade you by his Spirit to rest on his gracious promises for your justification, for sanctifying your afflictions, and for perseverance, (Romans 11:29; John 1:14 and 9:12; 1 Peter 1:5, 23; Matthew 16:18; Luke 8:15; Ephesians 4:10; 1 John 2:19, 27; 2 Corinthians 1:21, 22; Luke 22:32; John 17:15, 20, 10:28-29 and 6:37, 39 and 15:16; Matthew 24:24; Romans 8:38-39; 2 Samuel 7:14, 15)."[7]

How will you get this anointing? Believers have it! If every believer has it, why can't you simply turn it up, and never turn it down, much like the volume on a car stereo? Why not jack it up, and keep it at optimum level? What can't the fullness of the assurance of faith be at the highest bar *all the time* in that *Holy Spirit unction and anointing?* Though Jesus gives you everything generously and freely, it does not argue that you use it all diligently for your own good all the time, to the best that it could be used. How does the Spirit come to you? He comes to you in the use of the means of grace. He comes according to God's prescription. Don't want to follow God's prescription for life and godliness? What kind of assurance can you expect? And there are so many things to use. Bible reading, godly meditation, prayer, worship, praise, the Lord's Supper, preaching, fellowship, *etc.* Further degrees of assurance are cultivated upon its use. The anointing is

---

[7] Gammon, Hannibal, *God's Desertion of the Unjust and Other Works*, (Crossville, TN: Puritan Publications, 2016) 136.

enhanced by the common and ordinary use *of those means.* Acts 10:44, "The Holy Ghost fell on all them which [*desired it*] heard the word." Imagine your life if you optimally cultivated the anointing of the Spirit, which you have if you are born again, always? How victorious would your life be? How abundant would it be?

Cultivating assurance is done through the anointing through the word. The best way to cultivate the anointing, assurance, is to increase your faith in the things of God. It's ordinarily done through the ministry of hearing the word preached, reading the word, and studying it, as well as by partaking of the sacraments, prayer, and Christian fellowship. In all of these, it is increased and strengthened. You see, true believers may have the assurance of their salvation shaken in a number of ways. It can diminish and sometimes even be intermittent. Do you feel, [using the *feel* word on purpose there] like this is the most spiritually beneficial time in your life? What if you are not using the means well, and such? How will you *feel* then? This waxing and waning of this feeling sometimes happens as a result of being negligent in the means of grace. Sometimes Christians fall into some special sin which wounds their conscience and grieves the Spirit. Eph. 4:30 says emphatically, "Grieve not the holy Spirit of God, whereby ye are sealed unto the day of redemption." What sin will stifle the truth of your own assurance? One dead fly in the ointment, what does *that* do? It spoils the whole box, (Eccl. 10:1). Sometimes a Christian may be overtaken by some sudden or horrible temptation. It may be that God withdraws the light of his countenance on them for a time. But even things like this happen to a Christian, they are never left utterly destitute of the life of faith. They always have the love of Christ and the love of the brethren and they always have the anointing on them. They merely need to cultivate that mind and heart in the word. The sincerity of their heart and the conscience they have to do their duty before God will be rekindled. The Spirit's anointing cultivates this further.

The anointing is cultivated through the word. That means Christians need to rely constantly on Christ at the throne of grace asking for more of the Spirit's influence, his anointing, his unction, in their lives. But they must use the means as well as the petitions. Praying to be *zapped* into holiness or duty is not the answer, *ever*. God will never leave them in utter despair or without the operation of the Spirit; and assurance is always gained in due time.

The fruit of the unction of the Spirit is assurance. "The oil of gladness," does it fill your heart? It fills the heart with spiritual joy. Why? Because it ministers comfort. *Confirmed* as the Apostle was in comfort. There are no people more cheerful in all conditions than anointed ones. St. Jerome said, "Many see our affliction, but not our unction; our troubles, but not our comforts; our tribulation, but not our consolation, which far exceeds them."[8] You must make use of this unction for the end which Christ designed it. If oil is kept in the jar and hid in the closet, what use will it be? You must be wise to use it and improve it.

You must walk in the Spirit, in the word. God looks for more from you who have his word, and his Spirit. 1 Thess. 4:1, to "walk worthy of their high and heavenly calling," so walk worthy of this high and heavenly unction. It is one thing to have it, it is another thing to manifest it. On my property, there might be a vein of gold under the ground. I own the very ground itself, and I own all the mineral rights to what is under it. But I don't know if it's there or not. If I don't know it's there, though I own it, what good does it do for me? It is one thing to have the Spirit, and another thing to be filled with the Spirit. Where is our unction; where is its power? How do you

---

[8] Hardy, *1 John*, 318.

exercise it? Where and what is that sword of the Spirit you are to wield so fearlessly? If you exercise the unction of the Spirit, the anointing of the Spirit in the truth of the word to your mind and soul, what kind of life will you have before God? It will be ever growing. It will be continually cultivated. It will assure you of your eternal life in Christ. 1 Thess. 1:5-6 says, "Our Gospel came to you not in word only, but in power, and in the Holy Ghost, and in much assurance. And ye became followers of us, and of the Lord, having received the word in much affliction, with joy of the Holy Ghost." 1 Thess. 2:13 states, "We thank God without ceasing, because when ye received the word of God, ye received it not as the word of men, but as the word of God, which effectually worketh in you that believe." Want real change in your soul, and greater height of power in your daily walk? Do you want victorious living? Cultivate the exercise of that unction for your spiritual good. Get into the word and be in the word and stay in the word. Thomas Manton said, "If there be but a form of knowledge, there will be but a form of godliness. But where this anointing is, there we are made partakers of the divine nature, and live a holy life."[9]

The next chapter will deal with being *illuminated* by the Spirit.

---

[9] Manton, *Works*, Vol. 22, 103.

Chapter 6:
Illuminated by the Spirit

"Howbeit when he, the Spirit of truth, is come, he will guide you into all truth: for he shall not speak of himself; but whatsoever he shall hear, that shall he speak: and he will shew you things to come. He shall glorify me: for he shall receive of mine, and shall shew it unto you," (John 16:13-14).

In this text, Jesus is speaking to his disciples because he is going away. The disciples are saddened. But they will be comforted, which Christ promises. The Christ must leave and then he will send the Spirit. The Anointed Savior, exalted and glorified has never sent the Spirit before. The Anointed Savior had not yet come until now. The Anointed Savior had not been exalted, had not ascended yet, and so he, in this special union as the God-man had yet to send the Spirit as the anointed One. Jesus says, "Nevertheless I tell you the truth; It is expedient [*bearable and profitable*] for you that I go away: for if I go not away, the Comforter will not come unto you; but if I depart, I will send him unto you," (John 16:7). In John 14, Jesus promises the Comforter to come. Christ must ascend in fulfillment of all his covenant work to send the benefits of the covenant in the Spirit. When the Spirit is sent, the disciples, who do not yet fully understand all this, will be empowered for service. Among other things, empowerment is a gift from the Spirit. The disciples will do greater works (John 14:12). They will have knowledge imparted to them (14:20). They will be in a new and closer union with Christ through the Spirit (14:28). If Jesus does not go away, the Spirit cannot come in this manner, from the side of Christ, from the throne of the Son of Man.

In John 16 he takes up this continued line of thinking.

It is expedient, a notion and time to bear up in, for the Comforter shall come. "And when he is come, he will reprove the world of sin, and of righteousness, and of judgment," (John 16:8). This is a difficult verse to literally translate since the order of the words, apart from any theological interjection, can be somewhat unclear upon first read in the original languages. If translated literally, one would seem to understand that the Comforter who comes will reprove or convict *the whole world* of sin. How does he do that to the world? Does not the enmity of the world suppress the truth? How will they be convicted? Equally, if the verse is continued to be literally translated, how does the Comforter reprove the world of righteousness? Is not righteousness *righteous?* Why would the Comforter reprove the world of this, something they do not even possess? Can the world be righteous in any way apart from Christ?

Equally, the word "judgment" in the same way is somewhat confusing. The carnal heart is at enmity of God, unrighteous, suppressing the truth, and without proper judgment. The words are better suited to be translated as "he will show clearly and convict in" these things. This fits with what the Spirit does through the word. He shows clearly what sin is, and what unbelief is. He shows clearly that Christ was righteous and right in all he taught concerning the Father, and has ascended to God with the approval of the Father, and sends such imputed righteousness to humbled souls. He shows clearly that the ascended Son of Man, who is given all judgment, judges with justice against the darkness of the world, and the wiles of the prince of the world, restores the power of God in the world more extensively through the Gospel and the work of the Spirit.

So that his words remain clear, Jesus gives an explanation immediately following. "Of sin, because they believe not on me; Of righteousness, because I go to my Father, and ye see me no more; Of judgment, because the prince of this world is judged," (John 16:9-11). The world is wrong about sin. They do not trust the Lord's Anointed, and they revel in wickedness. They will be judged for their unbelief. The Spirit will convict them of such at the judgment, but even before. The world is wrong about Christ. They do not understand the sinless sacrifice of Christ, and they do not know him as the righteous Lamb of God, and they do not understand God's nature, and this is proved because Christ is going to the Father as the one who has satisfied God's righteousness. The Spirit will convict them of such at the judgment, but even before. The world is wrong about God's impending judgement. As a matter of fact, through Christ's work, coming death, resurrection and ascension, the prince of the world, the devil is even judged by way of Christ's exaltation and triumph. The Spirit will convict them of such at the judgment, but even before. At the Judgment seat of Christ, yes, all will bow to the justice of Christ, but how shall the world hear of such things *now?* How will the world be convicted by the Spirit now?

This exhortation to the disciples holds in it the preaching of the Gospel. The disciples will be endowed with the baptism of the Spirit to preach, and in this preaching the world will come to know the truth about sin, about Christ's righteous work, and the judgment of God. The mode and manner of this knowledge and conviction is the work of the Spirit on both those he regenerates, and those he condemns. Some have this preaching as a savor of life, some have it as a savor of death (2 Cor. 2:16). Both kinds of savors are the work of the Spirit. The preaching of the Gospel will go forth into the world, will arrest the world by conviction. Not all, but some. Calvin says, "When the Spirit is come, he will produce full conviction that, apart from Christ, sin reigns in the world."[1]

---

[1] Calvin, John, *Commentary on John*, Volume 2, John 16:8-15. http://m.ccel.org/ccel/calvin/calcom35.vi.ii.html.

Righteousness cannot be imparted to the soul that does not believe, and such a righteousness comes only from Christ after the soul has been humbled. Satan's grip on the world in darkness will be no longer, his reign in shrouding the truth is at an end, and Christ will rule and reign the hearts of men by the preaching of the word in the power of the Spirit who shall teach them all these things which will be extended into the world by the Gospel. Satan in this *has no power and stands condemned.* "And he said unto them, I beheld Satan as lightning fall from heaven. Behold, I give unto you power to tread on serpents and scorpions, and over all the power of the enemy: and nothing shall by any means hurt you," (Luke 10:18-19).

Jesus told the disciples, "I have yet many things to say unto you, but ye cannot bear them now," (John 16:12). Because of their sadness, Christ is not able to teach them *everything* that he would like them to have at this time. They are not able to bear it because of the speech about his departure. Christ is very careful not to break a bruised reed or quench the smoking flax. He will not instruct them at this time on certain inevitable truths, and does not want any of them to stumble. It is enough that he is going away, and it is comforting to know that he sends his Spirit to supply them with help. "Howbeit when he, the Spirit of truth, is come, he will guide you into all truth: for he shall not speak of himself; but whatsoever he shall hear, that shall he speak: and he will shew you things to come. He shall glorify me: for he shall receive of mine, and shall shew it unto you," (John 16:13-14). A particular work of the Spirit on regenerated individuals, is to lead them.

The Spirit drives men to Christ through the word in regeneration, the first act of illumination. After regeneration then they are converted, he then leads them into all truth, the further work of illumination. Jesus is saying to the disciples that the Spirit will cause you to know that truth comes from

God. My truth, which the Spirit will show you clearly, is illuminated to you as you look to the word. The Spirit reveals what he hears from God. Whatever he hears he speaks. He hears what the Christ says, what the word says, what God's word says, and these are all the same thing. The Spirit reveals things to come. Remember, the Spirit glorifies Christ, not himself. The Spirit glorifies Christ by receiving from Christ all that Christ will communicate, and the Spirit will show it to the disciples, will lead them into the truth of everything Christ had taught them from the word. *Things to come* does not refer to the cross or the resurrection here. Jesus has not yet ascended. After he ascends, the Spirit will come, and will teach what Christ communicates. The Spirit's job is to illuminate the minds of the disciples, to give them the tools and capability of knowing the truth, to show them how glorious and wonderful Jesus is, and all that he has accomplished in working before God as the anointed Messiah. The revelation which is delivered by Christ to the church, through the Holy Spirit, is divine revelation spoken by Christ, taught by Christ as the great exegete of the Father, inscripturated in the Bible for all time. In this, the Spirit will "tell you what he hears. He shall speak of what is coming. He hears it from me and repeats it to you. In this way he will reveal my glory." In this he will illuminate your mind that you might be able to understand through study of the word what Christ taught.

A side note, this work of the Spirit, divine illumination, is by no means new in the New Testament. It was very much taught in the Old Testament, and Jesus rebuked Nicodemus for not understanding that in John 3. "Teach me to do thy will; for thou art my God: thy spirit is good; lead me into the land of uprightness." (Psa. 143:10). "Open thou mine eyes, that I may behold wondrous things out of thy law," (Psa. 119:18). It is only furthered in the New

Testament in that the Spirit of God is sent from the exalted Christ to comfort his people out of his word as a result of his exaltation and departure from walking the earth and finishing his task as Covenant Mediator, as the new Testator of God's Covenant of Grace. He will not leave without sending that illuminating Comforter that will guide his established church into all truth. His work to exegete the Father continues through divine illumination which is a saving and sanctifying work of the Spirit sent from the throne of the Ancient of Days by the Son of Man.

The Spirit's work is to illuminate the bride of Christ to the beauty of the Gospel of Jesus Christ. Illumination falls under two main areas. General: which is divided into common illumination, restraining illumination, and convincing illumination as in relation to sin. Specific: converting and sanctifying illumination in believers.

Spiritual illumination is often thought of in a wrong way or applied wrongly. Spiritual illumination is not guessing at the text of the Bible, or feeling the text out, or making random comments about the text without understanding it. Biblical expertise doesn't just happen. One may, during their devotions, for example, be reading a text and wonder what it means. They might take a text of the Bible and guess at what the meaning of the text is. This is not divine illumination. Some people think that it is. "But the anointing which ye have received of him abideth in you, and ye need not that any man teach you," (1 John 2:27). They think that whatever feeling they have on a text is what the Spirit is teaching them about the text, and in this way, that is what the text means; as if human feeling about the Spirit imparts a true use of the Spirit's influence. They take in no account of what *studying* the text means. They are not engaged in *hermeneutics*.[2] They

---

[2] Hermeneutics is the science of divine interpretation which has specific rules and methods for understanding the text responsibly.

Chapter 6: Illuminated by the Spirit

are not interpreting the text. They are not necessarily uncovering the truth of the text. Simply because a person is converted doesn't mean they instantaneously, by osmosis, by being *zapped* by the Spirit, or think in some improper way that since they have the unction or touch of God, that whenever they read a text, whatever they think about *is right*. Where in the world does the Bible ever tell a Christian that?

Divine illumination is not a replacement for the work of the Gospel ministry by ministers. If one believes that by osmosis they go to a text and the Holy Spirit simply reveals, in some mysterious way, what a text says, or literally means, this would in fact do away with any need for the pastoral ministry.

Divine illumination is not about *guessing*. It is not about being so privileged that one is born from above that they suddenly have a privilege connection to a kind of mature faith and understanding about what the Bible means. Rather, the Spirit confirms what they learn about the Bible in a manner that all the promises of Christ are yes and amen to them. This does not negate learning, but rather strengthens it. Nor does divine illumination negate the pastoral ministry of preaching and teaching. If everyone is simply zapped into a full understanding, *why are you ever sitting in church?* Why do you come to hear the ministry of the word? Why does Scripture all throughout press the believer to go to the lips of the priest who have knowledge, or receive the preaching of the word as it is the word of God?[3] It is because people misunderstand the word and think illumination is somehow instantaneous knowledge. And when they do, they bring all kinds of trouble upon themselves as a result. Illumination does not furnish them with all the answers, the Spirit is the

---

[3] "For the priest's lips should keep knowledge, and they should seek the law at his mouth: for he is the messenger of the LORD of hosts," (Mal. 2:7).

means to the answers. He beckons the saints to consider, and ponder, and study, and exegete, and learn, and work through the word. And yet, there is a work of the Spirit in illumination that sets the truth of the text on the heart of the Christian. They may read Isaiah 53 as the Ethiopian Eunuch did, and when it is explained to them, because they are divinely illuminated to the truth by being born again, and they have the touch or unction of the Spirit on them, they agree with the truth of the word, for the Spirit bears witness in their hearts when they hear the truth proclaimed. If it were some kind of instantaneous zapping, then every english speaking Christian should be able to pick up a Hebrew Bible and Greek Bible and merely, *by divine illumination,* just read it and know it all; it is in fact the word of God isn't it? But what confused Christian would ever try that as a proof?

This is in practice what many Christians think. Just let me read the text, and whatever I *feel*, that's what it must mean. By way of side note, that is why pastoral ministry is so important where the minister has not only the divine illumination or equipping of the Spirit to understand and recognize the truth once it is brought out of a text, but, that they have the proper skills to draw out of the text what is being taught there. "...in which are some things hard to be understood, which they that are unlearned and unstable wrest, as they do also the other scriptures, unto their own destruction," (2 Peter 3:16). If it were simply a spiritual zapping of some kind, Peter is liar, for no one that is a Christian is unlearned or unstable for they would be unable to get the text wrong if the Spirit were in them if it is considered in that charismatic sense. (Reformed believers can also fall into charismatic chaos as well!)

The depravity of the mind is a great factor in understanding this. Scripture is clear that all the wicked, all those remaining in unbelief, those not righteous in God's sight, those under the grasp of the devil, the fall of Adam, original sin, and under the judgment of God, exist in a state of darkness. "The way of the wicked is as darkness: they know not at what they stumble," (Prov. 4:19). This is in opposition to the light. Light in Scripture is *truth*. God dwells in light that is unapproachable. But the Spirit illuminates this in a light the mind is able to bear. "The natural man receiveth not the things of the Spirit of God, for they are foolishness unto him; neither can he know them, because they are spiritually discerned." (1 Cor. 2:14.) Regenerated believers are exhorted by the Apostle Paul, "Ye were once darkness..." (Eph. 5:8.) This is the polar opposite, darkness verses light. All those under unbelief, who are ungodly and disobedient, are described as blind, those who do not know the ways of God. Paul says, "If our Gospel be hid, it is hid to them that are lost; in whom the god of this world hath blinded the minds of them which believe not, lest the light of the glorious Gospel of Christ, who is the image of God, should shine unto them." (2 Cor. 4:3-4; 1 Peter 2:9). "The Lord Jesus shall be revealed from heaven, in flaming fire, taking vengeance on them that know not God, and that obey not the Gospel," (2 Thess. 1:7-8). "Their minds were blinded. Even unto this day, when Moses is read, the veil is upon their heart. Nevertheless, when it shall turn to the Lord, the veil shall be taken away," (2 Cor. 3:14-16). "Yet the Lord hath not given you an heart to perceive, and eyes to see, and ears to hear unto this day," (Deut. 29:4). They are only delivered from this darkness when they are illuminated in their mind at conversion, or, as Jesus explained, born from above by the Spirit.

In conversion, people have their eyes opened. This is the first motion of illumination in them. They are turned from darkness to light. They are called out of darkness into marvelous light — to be delivered from the power of darkness, and translated into the kingdom of God's dear Son, (Acts

26:18; Col. 1:13). Such a conversion, Hebrews 10:32 says, is being enlightened. Samuel Hopkins said, "It appears here why this darkness is always spoken of in divine revelation as criminal. It is sinful in every degree of it, as it consists in the moral depravity of the heart."[4] Darkness is the place of the criminal, where they must be transformed by a renewing of the mind and illumination to the teachings of Christ. They are given the divine tools of ability to study rightly. When the mind is enlightened, it is brought *light* by the Spirit, and it is brought into the light. "Awake, thou that sleepest, and arise from the dead, and Christ shall give thee light," (Eph. 5:14). It is from Christ which is why it is called divine illumination. It is a supernatural illumination, a supernatural and divine light from the divine Christ. Puritan William Cooper said, "No man can love God truly, unless he knows God truly." "If any man love God, the same is known of him," (1 Cor. 8:3.) Therefore, examine what knowledge you have of God, especially what practical knowledge. It is clear, practical, Gospel-knowledge, to "know God" in Christ, this is saving, and brings "life eternal." (John 17:3.) This is knowledge that transforms; (2 Cor. 3:18;) this is a sanctifying knowledge; (Eph. 4:21, 22;) this is a justifying knowledge, or the knowledge of faith. (Isa. 53:11; Phil. 3:8–10.) This light and knowledge comes into the soul by the illumination of the Spirit of God, turning our darkness into light, and is the teaching of God, and "the anointing" of God, "teaching all things." (John 14:26; 1 John 2:20, 27).[5] Knowledge? *Knowing?* Not feeling or guessing?

The illumination of the Spirit is either ordinary or special. Illumination or enlightenment to God's revealed will in an ordinary way is not a gracious act of the Spirit when it is

---

[4] Hopkins, Samuel, *The Works of Samuel Hopkins*, Volume 1, (Boston, MA: Doctrinal Tract Society, 1854) 401.
[5] Nichols, James, *Puritan Sermons*, Vol. 3, (Wheaton, IL: Richard Owen Roberts, Publishers, 1986), 146.

generally spoken about. It is a general illumination. It is an ordinary illumination. There is a leading by the Spirit which extends to all creatures; it falls under providential government, which is still a kind and class of divine leading. All creatures, by God's divine power, in their beings, actions, and motions are ordered, governed, and ruled to the glory of the creator. They are all directed, moved in their being, by this Spirit in a general or ordinary sense. This means that they all come under his divine guidance and the kingship of God. All men, regenerate or unregenerate, "live and move and have their being in him," (Acts 17:28). In an ordinary providential way, God orders and regulates all their actions as the supreme and sovereign Lord of the created order. These depraved individuals work all their life to hinder this leading, and to suppress the truth of this leading. It is even apparent in creation itself, but they suppress it (Romans 1). There is in this, a kind of ordinary illumination, certain ordinary gifts, certain ordinary convictions, even certain ordinary restraints which unregenerate people can partake in. "And he hath put in his heart that he may teach, both he, and Aholiab, the son of Ahisamach, of the tribe of Dan. Them hath he filled with wisdom of heart, to work all manner of work, of the engraver, and of the cunning workman, and of the embroiderer, in blue, and in purple, in scarlet, and in fine linen, and of the weaver, even of them that do any work, and of those that devise cunning work," (Exod. 35:34-35). Artistic Ability is an ordinary working of the Spirit, a kind of illumination, which applies to the math wiz and the Mozarts of the world. Abimelech, "And God said unto him in a dream, Yea, I know that thou didst this in the integrity of thy heart; for I also withheld thee from sinning against me: therefore suffered I thee not to touch her." (Gen. 20:6). This fellow was a wicked king, but God restrained him in an ordinary manner of providentially governing his life for God's glorious purpose.

This is an ordinary kind of illumination or leading.

What should be said about Heb. 6:4-6? "For it is impossible for those who were once enlightened, and have tasted of the heavenly gift, and were made partakers of the Holy Ghost, And have tasted the good word of God, and the powers of the world to come, If they shall fall away, to renew them again unto repentance; seeing they crucify to themselves the Son of God afresh, and put him to an open shame." (Heb. 6:4-6). Those who are apostate, are *not* true believers. Yet, their faith, whatever it was, or is, is not the same as justifying faith. "But, beloved, we are persuaded better things of you, and things that accompany salvation, though we thus speak," (Heb. 6:9). Those actually saved and redeemed by Christ can never fall away as a result of Christ's work. Those in the first few verses are things not accompanying salvation, but things later that are better accompany those who believe. The reprobate can "be made partakers of the Holy Spirit" in an ordinary sense, to taste of the Spirit, without ever being converted. Matthew Mead in his work "Almost a Christian" talked about being almost a Christian, and still having the influence of the Spirit in some way in their life. They may still have initial acts of ordinary illumination and even ordinary conviction. *Judas did.* Esau *sought* the blessing with tears. Neither were converted. They can be illuminated and have an ordinary knowledge of the truth, "if not a practical and consoling, yet a theoretical and constraining" knowledge; like the demons do. They can "taste the good word of God." They taste this word by way of carnal sense, they taste *a feeling* with an outward experience but not an inner transformation. This idea is given to them as considered lost, as a profession of the truth rather than internally. There are principles, originally given by the Spirit, from ordinary illumination in the hearts of men, which may even extend and sit on some kind of moral and religious education. Do not kill. Do not lie.

Chapter 6: Illuminated by the Spirit

Do not commit adultery, and the like, all of which are pointers to God's divine Law written on the heart of all men.

Further, there can be a heathenish Mozart with the Spirit of God placing such a divine element of ability in him to write such amazing compositions of music. Artists can capture truth in painting. None of this can occur without the general use or operation of the Spirit on the hearts and souls of men. Men have *no power in this*. It is the Spirit's empowerment as he sees fit. Yet, none of this is grace, and such works of God's goodness should really lead such people to repentance.[6] But, how is one lead there? This is the special illumination the Spirit works through the word.

Special illumination in the first acts of regeneration and conversion; people are saved by this special act. There is only one gracious saving truth. The Apostle Paul says that all men whom God will have saved, "come to the knowledge of the truth," (1 Tim. 2:4). This truth is found in no other place, than the depository of the church of Christ in the word, ministered to souls by the Spirit of God in the word they hear preached. They gain this truth in the first act of illumination, because they have been anointed, because they have been indwelt, because they have been baptized and born from above. The church and the godly are, "the righteous nation, that keepeth the truth," (Isa. 16:2), as a result of all these things. Paul describes the Church as "the pillar and ground of truth," (1 Tim. 3:15). The Spirit by which the Church is lead and guided into the truth is called, "the Spirit of truth;" and it was promised by our Lord Jesus Christ that this Spirit should come and guide the Church "into all truth," (John 16:13). If then there can be no salvation without the knowledge of the truth, and no saving truth except for what is found in the church by God's providence and revelation in the illuminated

---

[6] See Romans 2.

word of God on the heart, it follows that there is no salvation outside of the Church; hold that thought for another time. This places those who do not like organized religion in a very sad state. There is no salvation outside the church. The pillar and ground of the truth is the place of the anointing, the place of illumination, because there is the preaching and teaching of the word found.

This initial illuminating work gives the believer a sense of and sorrow for sin, as committed against God, which are prerequisite of true repentance, which houses in it the element of divine illumination. Repentance consists in two parts; humiliation, and conversion. It is the casting down of the heart for sin in conversion, and the casting off of sin in the life of the believer. But neither of these can occur unless there is the initial act of divine illumination, a special act of grace through Christ by the power of the Spirit to enlighten the mind to the truth. Can a darkened heart repent "for uncleanness," επι τη ακαβαρσια, (2 Cor. 12:21,) from sin, with shame and hatred for sin? Can a darkened heart repent "from iniquity," απο κακιας, (Acts 8:22; Rev. 9:20,) and "from dead works." (Heb. 6:1.). They are dead, they are *not* somewhat alive. They exist in spiritual darkness, existing like spiritually dead corpses. They must have the initial illuminating power of the Spirit on their mind and heart in order to enact true repentance, humility, and be converted. They need a new heart and a new mind by way of the regenerating power of God in divine illumination.

Imagine a person in a cave, with no light, then beaming the sun into the cave. They won't even have Plato's shadows[7] without some illumination of light for them to see.

---

[7] In Plato's *Republic*, he writes of a "a cave." In his theory, the cave represents people who believe that knowledge comes from what we see and hear in the world – or, in other words, empirical evidence. The cave

In the Hebrew this is called נֹחַם *nocham*, "an irking of the soul;" and תְּשׁוּבָה *teshubbah*, "a turning from iniquity:" In the Greek it is μεταμελεια, *metamelia*, "after-grief;" and μετανοια, *metanoia*, "a turning of the mind."[8] Sometimes Scripture calls illuminating conversion *a humbling of one's self*. When Manasseh repented he is said to *humble* himself, (2 Chron. 33:12). This is repentance summed up as a whole, something which only can occur through the supernatural and divine light of illumination by the Spirit to the truth of the word. Under the Spirit's testimony of the Gospel, repentance for sin and from sin is described as "godly sorrow," which "worketh repentance," (2 Cor. 7:10), and there is found the light. In light of the coming of the fulness of the Gospel in covenant with God and through Jesus Christ, even Ezekiel says, "Then shall ye remember your own evil ways, and your doings that were not good, and shall loathe yourselves in your own sight for your iniquities and for your abominations," (Ezek. 36:31). "And I will put my Spirit within you, and cause you to walk in my statutes, and ye shall keep my judgments, and do them," (verse 27). This is the illuminating work of the Spirit of God.

How might we define special spiritual illumination? Spiritual illumination is the renovation of the heart and mind and the implanting of a new spiritual principle of wisdom now fit to see the divine beauty of the Gospel of Christ by the power of the Sovereign Spirit of God through the word. This is the first and initial act of it. Jonathan Edwards said this divine illumination is when the soul sees the sweet beauty of the thing (that is the Savior), and that it carries with it an

---

shows that believers of empirical knowledge are trapped in a cave of misunderstanding. The Shadows in the cave show the perceptions of those who believe empirical evidence ensures knowledge. But they are deceived because they never get out of the cave to see the sun exists.

[8] In Latin, it is *pœnitentia*, and *resipiscentia*; the one expressing the sense and sorrow of the soul; the other, the retrogradations and returns of it from sin.

impression left on the soul. "When the mind is sensible of the sweet beauty and amiableness of a thing, that implies a sensibleness of sweetness and delight in the presence of its idea. And this sensibleness of the amiableness or delightfulness of beauty carries in the very nature of it the sense of the heart, or an effect and impression the soul is the subject of, as a subject possessed of taste, inclination, and will."[9]

Illumination touches on the beauty of Christ, and his remedy against sin, (Acts 26:18). The cross, as disgusting a thing as it is, in this spiritual way is eminently beautiful. Why would a person carry a cross on a necklace or in an earring? It's a torture device. It's a cruel torture device. It is a most sweet and blessed idea to have the Christ upon it. It is a covenantal idea born of God. Such illumination gives a more clear and perfect insight into the mystery of Christ and Christianity, then any natural man could ever have in his own power, (1 Cor. 2:6-15).

Illumination softens the heart to love Christ (Luke 7:37). Illumination points the mind and heart heavenward, where Christ is seated at the right hand of God, like the star of the wise men were pointed to him in the stable, (John 6:45). It motions the soul to deny, do and suffer any thing for Christ.[10] In this way, illumination is termed spiritual understanding or spiritual wisdom, it is the word "sees" as Edwards said. The mind acknowledges the known truth of the word of God and understands its beauty, trusts in its beauty. There is no beauty without understanding. And there is no understanding by osmosis or magic. It allows the newly converted individual to make a distinction between something good and pleasing to God, and something evil and

---

[9] Edwards, Jonathan, *Religious Affections*, First Ed. (Worcester, MA: Henry Plantiga, 1851), 163-164.
[10] Phil. 3:7-8, *etc.*, *cf.* Acts 9:4-6; Heb. 10:32-34.

wicked. Phil. 1:10, "That you may discern things that differ one from another." 1 John 4:1, "Dearly beloved, believe not every spirit, but try the spirits whether they be of God." Try? Why not feel? Why not just be zapped. Why not just assume it so? 1 Thess. 5:21, "Try all things, and keep that which is good." It allows the mind to delight on things which pertain to holiness, which it was unable to do before, rather abhorring them. Now, Psa. 1:1, "But his delight is in the Law of God, and in that Law does he exercise himself day and night." Psa. 119:15, "I will meditate in your precepts, and consider your ways." There was a time when a darkened, dead, God hater, is turned to the light, who were once not enlightened, because they were "once darkness," (Eph. 5:8). They were, as Christ rightly judged of the Pharisees, by nature blind men, in regard of all the beauty of God's spiritual word, (2 Peter 1:9, Rev. 3:17). But converted, changed, renewed, illuminated upon in this first work of the Spirit, man is now capable of understanding the beauty attached to the Gospel of God because he has a new disposition, a new mind, a new heart; is a new creature.

This grace is from the Spirit, and at that point, men are changed into being *serious* Christians. It is the first element of initial sanctification. Conversion being the first step in the broader view of what it means to be separated to holiness. Divine illumination is such a powerful work of the Spirit, that a person who was a hater of God, an enemy to his divine law, is brought with understanding to love it, and to make it the leading guide and rule of the entirety *of his whole life.* And it is such a necessity to understand the things of God, that it takes Christ to die for it, and the power of the omnipotent Spirit to make it effectual. It is a work only God can do in opposition to the elements and darkness of unbelief.

After initial illumination there is ongoing illumination in the sanctified understanding of a believer. The saints throughout Scripture never tell God to make a new law or a new word easier to understand. There is no Scriptural warrant for dumbing down the truth, or making the truth easier to understand in this way. Certain truths cannot be born at certain times, which is understandable. "Ye cannot bear it..." But that in no way argues dumbing it down to tell them something now in a watered-down fashion. There is a great difference between Scripture having clarity (as Ezra gave the sense in his preaching so the people understood what he meant to say in Neh. 8:8) and people remaining in ignorance because they think the bible is a hard book to understand. It is not about rewriting the word, but having the eyes opened, illuminated, having *the tools* to understand his word. Is that alone not a great judgment against the church today? Never does God say *I will dumb the word down*, but rather, *I will elevate the mind in illuminating you to it that you might have the tools to study it well, as one approved.* Christ, not desiring his disciples, nor believers, to remain without spiritual insight, deposits the Spirit in them to lead them and teach them all truth. What does that tell you about ministers and ministries that dumb down the word? I tell you, God is never in those things he does not prescribe in his word. He sends his Spirit to enlighten his bride, and he sends his preachers to explain the word, that in turn, enlightened minds might understand what it says as it is explained to them. This is where knowledge and trust meet. They know it, and through illumination they trust that it is good and right. It may be called *a sanctifying persuasion*. This illumination of the Spirit on the word of God, in the preaching of the word, in the administration of the sacraments, in prayer, in devotions, in study, is a persuading of the truth of the word; who will be persuaded to the truth of the word that is illuminated to the word by the Spirit? All of them!

    Consider the internal testimony of the Spirit that one

is a Christian. The Holy Spirit is repeatedly promised and given to believers renewed and converted. They are regenerated, and they are confirmed and sealed with the Spirit *unto the day of redemption*. This gift of consolation, is from the Comforter, referred to in Eph. 1:13-14, and promised by Christ in our text. "In whom ye also trusted, after that ye heard the word of truth, the Gospel of your salvation: in whom also after that ye believed, ye were sealed with that holy Spirit of promise, Which is the earnest of our inheritance until the redemption of the purchased possession, unto the praise of his glory," (Eph. 1:13-14). "The Spirit itself beareth witness with our spirit, that we are the children of God," (Romans 8:16). Christ, through the word, communicates himself to his people, and the Spirit shines a divine and supernatural light on that word which bears witness to the truth of conversion, and eternal life. This is not a personal feeling. It is not a hunch or a guess. It is the active work of witness bearing, truth testimony, of that which God promises in Christ, pressed into the heart of the believer. It is understood with the mind as both true, and good. The sealing of the Spirit in conversion confers the believer an infallible assurance from the word; and this is the anointing. However, many people wonder why they don't "feel" this as strongly as they would like. They are actually chasing after something they will never grasp, as if it is some tangible thing that they can hold in their hand, that they do not have and need to get. Yet, it may be that years pass before the believer experiences an assurance from all this in a very deep way – which is why Paul calls it the full assurance of hope, understanding and faith (Col. 2:2; Heb. 6:11, 10:22).

A Christian's growth in attaining this assurance comes in stages, and this is because knowledge comes in stages. There is no instantaneous full assurance without any possibility of further growth without the word of God. A sealing at conversion, and a further growth of that seed of assurance as one matures by walking in the Spirit day by day (we haven't covered what that means yet) but it is how one cultivates that anointing. Such importance is laid upon this internal testimony of the Spirit, that one would be downright mad to seek something of the word without the work of the Spirit in the word. Light increases day by day. Submission to the word of God, for the service of Christ, is day by day. Submission is a daily walking of the Spirit, it is a daily increase of grace, it is a daily illumination of the Spirit that one is a son or daughter. He also works the mortification of sin and the renewing of life through divine illumination. The actual mortification of the old man and the quickening of life in the new man, revolves around a daily killing of sin, and a daily amendment of life only accomplished by the Spirit. As much as regeneration is illumination at the outset, this continued work of killing sin and living in service to godliness in Christ, is a daily renewal by spiritual illumination in the Spirit. And yet, is this a zapping? Is this a work of the Spirit apart from the means the Spirit uses in the word? No, he does all this through the word of God. What sins will be put off, and what new understanding will one come away with to serve God in reverence and godly fear? The image of God is restored in conversion, but it is cultivated in the illuminating grace of the Spirit through the word.

Christians are sanctifyingly persuaded by the Spirit to live rightly, to listen to all Christ said, and all Christ is, and to not merely be hearers of the word, but doers of it. Illumination brightens the road, the way of walking, but the Christian must strive to walk that road, they must know what the road looks like which they are to walk. Divine illumination has God as its author, in which he cures the blindness of the mind. The subjects of which concern Christ the Savior and the covenant and condescension of the Lord to save his people are bound up in this; they are subjects concerning the glory of God, subjects concerning the work of God through Christ in the power of the Spirit. How might one love God and live for God? The manner in which these things of Christ may be known is through the Spirit, through the word of God. They must be high and lofty things indeed if it takes the Spirit to demonstrate them in righteousness, holiness, justice, and right judgment. They must be high and lofty thoughts to consider all that the Christ has done.

The witness of the Spirit to the word in your life is a most important aspect to a godly walk. How are you as a believer certain that the Spirit witnesses to your spirit that you are a son or daughter of God? There are two important points to glean from that. First, by the power of illumination, a grace that you receive from the Spirit, which directs your mind upward to Christ, manifests itself in order to overcome all doubts about your spiritual state and about the truth of the word of Christ. This is the word is trusted. You trust the word. It does not mean that you understand it all. But it also doesn't mean that God wants you to only understand what you know now. He wants growth, and that continually. That occurs through the word by the illumination of the Spirit.

Second, there is an agreement between the testimony of the Spirit of God and our spirits. There is a spiritual harmony between the word of Christ, and our acknowledgement of that truth, to be certain and true, and this is because you are illuminated, and you are anointed. Your assurance is always confirmed by the testimony of the word, of your conscience, and, of the Spirit's illumination all working together as one. The undisputable word of God lays down certain marks of true grace, and witnesses these signs in you to be divine evidence of your conversion; this is the fruit of conversion and belief. It is fruit deriving from the Spirit in good works. Then your own spirit bears witness to the truth that these marks are true, and they are in all believers. Then

God adds the witness of his own Spirit enabling you to more fully know all these graces which are freely given to us of God. And now, "what doubts can remain?"

Through the Spirit, it is certain that by the word and conscience a believer may infallibly prove the testimony of the Spirit to be true. The Puritan Richard Fairclough said,

> "The graces of God's Spirit imprinted on the heart, the eye of conscience open in examination and observation, and the light of the Spirit as the sunshine,—these three concurring together, and all of them agreeing with the word, which is the standing rule of judgment, by which all the others are regulated and ordered; I say, from here arises a demonstrative, undoubted, and infallible certainty; and this concurrence being possible, it is therefore possible for a believer to attain to an assured knowledge that he is [spiritually illuminated by divine grace, and a son or daughter of the mighty high God]."[11]

I am hard pressed to find anyone who has said that better. In this way you turn to have a zeal for the truth. You labor after it. You do that in sincerity. You have new minds, divinely illuminated, the light of Christ's countenance shining brightly on them by the Spirit. You look to be sanctified, "in simplicity and godly sincerity, not in fleshly wisdom," (2 Cor. 1:12). You look to be obedient to the truth (John 18:37; Rom. 2:8; 1 Cor. 13:7; Gal. 3:1). You look to walk in it. You look to be sanctified in it (John 17:19). As the Spirit has divinely illuminated you in this through the word, you look to be more like Christ, and conformed into his image, by the Spirit, who directs you in the ways for this to take place. *The way* is God's way. There is no

---

[11] Nichols, James, *Puritan Sermons*, Vol. 6, (Wheaton, IL: Richard Owen Roberts, Publishers, 1981) 406.

other way then, than through the word.

We are, through the word, made like God and made partakers of the divine nature (2 Peter 1:4). Peter van Mastricht said, "[Through the word] we receive the favor of the triune God: the Father, who is the God of truth (Psa. 31:5); the Son, who is truth itself (John 14:6), from which the truth is called the truth of Christ (2 Cor. 11:10), the Holy Spirit, who is called the Spirit of truth (John 14:17; 15:26; 16:13), who leads his own into all truth (John 16:13; Psa. 143:10), because of which truth is called a fruit of the Spirit (Eph. 5:9)."[12] This is not by magic or osmosis, not by zapping, or by striving after some phantom idea that you are lacking something as a Christian that must be spiritually "felt" in a certain way; or in contrast that you are somehow now above and beyond study of the word and simply know what It all means by some feeling. We demonstrate to the church, to God, to ourselves, that we prove to be true and living members of the church, the pillar and ground of the truth (1 Tim. 3:15; 4:3; John 18:37), through the word, through the promises, and yet, through confirmation in the Spirit, through anointing, through indwelling, through baptizing, through a victorious life guided by a divine illumination to that word.

Whose word is to be read and studied? God's word: and so, who better to know the word of God than the Spirit of God? The foundation of our spiritual preservation in Christ lies in spiritual light, from supernatural illumination, to discern the beauty of the Gospel. John Owen said, "When the glory of the wisdom and grace of God, of the love and grace of Christ, of the power of the Holy Ghost herein, is made manifest unto us, we shall despise all the paintings of this invention, Dagon will fall before the ark; and all these things

---

[12] Van Mastricht, Peter, *Theoretical-Practical Theology*, Volume 2, (Grand Rapids, MI: Reformation Heritage Books, 2019) 291.

do gloriously shine forth and manifest themselves unto believers in this mysterious way of purging all our sins by the blood of Christ."[13] There is never, in you, or ought never to be in you a leaning on your own thoughts and ideas when reading or studying the word, or hearing the word; one does not guess at the word. Good preachers don't preach sermons about themselves or their ideas. They are parrots. They are heralding God's mind because they have been a workman approved rightly dividing the truth. You cannot lean on your own understanding. Men of the greatest intellectual capacities have been men of the greatest mistakes and some of the most devilish of errors. This goes back to a wrong understanding of divine illumination. When a person searches through the mysteries of godliness, and into the mysteries of the Gospel, they have to be sensible that they have need to be illuminated by the Spirit above for success.

You might be thinking right now, "I don't see how this necessarily becomes practical to me personally." I see I have this divine illumination, but how does that work into my daily life? Do I merely guess at what the word means, or believe that because I am a Christian, he will give me some zapping understanding that I did not know or study about before? Did not Jesus Christ promise that the promised Spirit would guide you in a right judgment, and to teach you his ways for the purpose of being a Comforter? The Scriptures are hard to understand, and Peter tells us that unstable people twist them to their own destruction. But Christ promises to you the necessity of the Spirit of illumination, and that is coupled with the work of the minister to explain the Scriptures in such a way as they are not confusing. Divine illumination is the pathway to understanding the bible; it is not a knowledge in and of itself. It is an illumination to be able to understand

---

[13] Nichols, James. *Puritan Sermons*, Vol. 3, (Wheaton, IL: Richard Owen Roberts, Publishers, 1981) 247-248.

what is preached and studied.

Want to live for God? For Christ? You must understand the word. Want to understand the word? You must be spiritually illuminated to the word, first, and then, daily pray for that illumination to grow, that you may study well to know God. There is no more practical manner of living than this before God. But do not expect to pray for illumination without doing any work or study in the word. Many people are told just that – to be zapped, and then what happens when they pray for it and it doesn't happen? Pray for understanding and pray for divine illumination, but couple those with your work to understand the word. Pray for illumination, but further illumination comes through work set together in good hermeneutics. These employ principles of rightly interpreting Scripture.

Now understand me, I concur wholeheartedly that the ploughboy can pick up a copy of the bible and read it and be converted by it. The *Spirit* can do that; let me give you a very simple example.

"Seek ye the LORD while he may be found, call ye upon him while he is near," (Isa. 55:6).

"I cried unto thee; save me, and I shall keep thy testimonies," (Psa. 119:146).

"This is the work of God, that ye believe on him whom he hath sent," (John 6:29).

"Repent, and be baptized every one of you in the name of Jesus Christ for the remission of sins, and ye shall receive the gift of the Holy Ghost," (Acts 2:38).

"For whosoever shall call upon the name of the Lord shall be saved," (Rom. 10:13).

The ploughboy says, "I don't know what all that means, but I seek you Lord, I cry to you to save me through Jesus, I repent of my sins, I call upon you to be saved." And so, *he can be saved.* The Spirit bears witness with his spirit that these things are true to him and apply to him, though he might not understand them fully. He is divinely illuminated to their truth by the Spirit bearing that testimony, though he is no scholar; but divine illumination is *not* understanding it all; it is merely the tools of a new nature and a new mind ravished with spiritual light that shines on the truth that one might concur and agree with it. Use the prayer of the psalmist, which is a most important Scripture relating to the practical nature of all this. "Open thou mine eyes, that I may behold wondrous things out of thy law," (Psa. 119:18). He means "regard or perceive or see," further, see *more.* You see here that David doesn't pray to give him something *new* for him to understand. He prays that God would illuminate him to the truth *already set down.* But how many times does he, as the psalmist, say, show me, teach me, help me, open your word up to me as I meditate, study, look to, seek, read, learn? It is almost *innumerable.*

You will never understand the truth of God unless you rely on his Spirit to open his word to you. It is, in fact, his word; but this in no way negates your study of it. And just because you think you have something from the word does not necessarily mean you have it all right. This is why God does not say *study, and leave it at that,* but study in such a way as to be approved as you are illuminated by the Spirit with the tools to make a good study of the word. The Bereans of Acts did not, as they were now believers, stop studying; they studied daily to see if what the preacher said was true (Acts 17:11). "We see little in the word till we come to be more deeply acquainted with it: and then, Psa. 119:18, "Open mine eyes, that I may see wonders in thy law," then we come to discern depths, and such wisdom as we never thought of. The word is an ocean, without bottom and banks."[14]

Christian, pray this way:

> "Father, let your Holy Spirit work in me the beauty of the Gospel of your Son; lead me in the truth of your word, cause me to search it out, learn what it means, rightly divide the word, and preserve me, that I never swerve from it, to any error or any false worship. And let your Spirit open my eyes more and more, to see the wondrous things of your law, and open my lips to them (Psa. 119:18, 51:15), that my mouth may daily defend your truth, and set forth your praise as I learn what it means, and as I rest in its truth by trust. Increase in me those good gifts, which of your mercy you have already bestowed on me, and give me a patient spirit, a chaste heart, a contented mind, pure affections, wise behavior, and all other graces which you see to be necessary for me to govern my heart in reverence for Christ, in godly fear, (Psa. 19:14), and in the illumination of your Spirit. Guide all of my life in your favor; that whether I live or die, I may live and die to you, who are my God and my Redeemer, Jesus Christ."

For, the Spirit's work is to illuminate the bride of Christ to the beauty of the Gospel of Jesus Christ, and that includes you.

The next chapter will be dealing with the idea of being *filled* with the Spirit.

---

[14] Manton, *Works*, Vol. 4, 130.

Chapter 7:
Filled with the Spirit

"And be not drunk with wine, wherein is excess; but be filled with the Spirit," (Eph. 5:18).

In Ephesians 5 we find Paul's concluding exhortations to the Ephesian church. This spans from verses 3-20. Because the days are evil, verse 16, they are to walk as those wise, verse 17, having already been exhorted to walk rightly, verse 15, and they are doing this walking in the summation of walking wisely, not being fools, not being unwise, and understanding the will of the Lord *to redeem the time*. Professing Christians, who have walked with the Lord for many years, may have a great amount of knowledge, but oftentimes relatively little wisdom; Paul exhorts them to rightly use *knowledge applied* – or *wisdom*. They are filled with all kinds of knowledge, and they forget that knowledge puffs up. But Paul here, requires they walk circumspectly, *i.e. wisely*. How it ought to be the prayer of the church at large that professing believers act and live with all manner of wisdom. Wisdom is in fact the right application of knowledge.

Interestingly, these verses are set in the context of *worship*. "Speaking to yourselves in *psalms and hymns and spiritual songs, singing and making melody* in your heart to the Lord; giving thanks always for all things unto God and the Father in the name of our Lord Jesus Christ; Submitting yourselves *one to another* in the fear of God," (Eph. 5:19-21). This also brings into the question as why *wine* is described in verse 18. How would wine be part of the worship service? Could it be like in excess of the Lord's Supper in Corinth thinking that some freeing intoxication would draw one more openly and receptive to the things of God? Drinking wine in worship to gain communion with God may have been a practice among certain religious groups of that time, certain heretical sects. This is not what God requires. Yet, this was in excess, which is what Paul is writing against – excessiveness in the wrong things and in the wrong way. He certainly dealt with that at Corinth, for many came not to eat of the supper, but to get drunk (1 Cor. 11). Wine was *in the church*, but its excess and abuse was seen in using it in the wrong way.

In verse 18 Paul says, "and (especially) be not drunk with wine." Καὶ μὴ μεθύσκεσθε οἴνῳ, ἐν ᾧ ἐστὶν ἀσωτία, ἀλλὰ πληροῦσθε ἐν πνεύματι, (Eph. 5:18). The word here μεθύσκεσθε (*maythuskow*) means to drink as to be intoxicated, to be dull in the senses; in other words, to be tipsy is inconsistent with the mindset of a Christian. Excess in the world, in those things of no profit, give the Christian over to sin. To be drunk with wine is sin. It does not say "do not drink wine." It does say not to be tipsy, effected, drunk, by way of excess. This excess is described as ἀσωτία (*asotia*) meaning having an abandoned, dissolute life. Drunkenness is a work of darkness, it is acting foolishly, and it leads everyone who yields to it to act unwisely in a dissolute life. Find an unwise Christian in general, and one may *liken* them to a drunken man.

Paul is pointing here to social circles of the church, which argues not solitude in this verse, not Christians at home, but Christians in worship, where prodigal "riotous living" ruins everything and ought never to occur among the faithful. Worldly people find temporal refreshing in worldly things. The person who does not act foolishly, does not walk unwise, redeems the time, is the one who will not seek refreshment from the excess of the intoxicating power of wine, but, instead, will find refreshment, filling, from the Holy Spirit.

πληροῦσθε ἐν πνεύματι (Eph. 5:18), "be filled with the

Spirit." In drunkenness, one gives themselves up to a destructive course of life. They are not merely tipsy, but they are *filled up* with wine, completely under its influence. It captivates their mind, it really darkens it, and it then makes the heart "merry" in a manner in which the mind cannot control with sharpness, precision and Christian obedience. The faculties are impaired, and the life then loose. Those who are filled with the Spirit are under the total involvement or utter filling up the soul when the Spirit motions all their thoughts, feelings, words, and actions to glorify the living Christ. What good would this do a Christian on their own, only alone, and apart from the body? – hold that thought for a moment.

"He was full of the Holy Ghost," (Luke 4:1); Jesus was full. Stephen "was full of faith and of the Holy Ghost," (Acts 6:5). Barnabas as well, "was a good man, and full of the Holy Ghost and of faith," (Acts 11:24). Interestingly, these descriptions are from other people writing about them. Being full of the Holy Ghost, being filled with the Spirit is discernable by others. The opposite of this, being unwise is also discernable. It is especially so if one is given to the excess of drunkenness. The Christian's life-giving source, the place where rivers of living water, not wine, flow from him, is to be found in the filling up of the Spirit of God. As David said, "my cup runneth over," (Psa. 23:5). God fills and overflows the cup of the Spirit in the believer. Where there is excess of wine in drunkenness creating a debauched life, so in opposition the Holy Spirit produces joy which expresses itself in psalms, hymns, and songs; worship. It is not my intention to link this and expound on the corporate assembly in singing psalms here. The point tied to this idea of corporate singing, though, is set in the context of being *filled up* with the Spirit. If one is filled with the Spirit in the assembly, filled up, they exhort one another in the singing of psalms and hymns and songs. See, the "kingdom of God is not meat and drink; but righteousness, and peace, and joy *in the Holy Ghost,"* (Rom. 14:17). It is to be a fullness of singing, filled with joy in the Spirit.

To be "filled" is found a number of times in Scripture, where these are but a few instances: "And the child grew, and waxed strong in spirit, filled with wisdom," (Luke 2:40). "Who appeared in glory, and spake of his decease which he should accomplish [*fulfilled*] at Jerusalem," (Luke 9:31). "And they were all filled with the Holy Ghost, and began to speak with other tongues, as the Spirit gave them utterance," (Acts 2:4). Filling among the corporate body for service is particularly attached to preaching here. "Then Peter, filled with the Holy Ghost," (Acts 4:8). Same here, "And when they had prayed, the place was shaken where they were assembled together; and they were all filled with the Holy Ghost, and they spake the word of God with boldness," (Acts 4:31). And here, "...that thou mightest receive thy sight, and be filled with the Holy Ghost," (Acts 9:17). Conversion is here, "Then Saul, (who also is called Paul,) filled with the Holy Ghost, set his eyes on him," (Acts 13:9). Elymas blinded, yet first discerned by Paul in power, where, "the disciples were filled with joy, and with the Holy Ghost," (Acts 13:52). And, "Which is his body, the fulness of him that filleth all in all," (Eph. 1:23). "Being filled with the fruits of righteousness, which are by Jesus Christ, unto the glory and praise of God," (Phil. 1:11). And so Christians are to be, "filled with the Spirit," (Eph. 5:18).

Interestingly, though Paul is telling these Ephesians to be filled with the Spirit, the Spirit is not like a bottle of wine. The Spirit is the one who does the filling. The believer does not grab the Spirit off the shelf, and take a swig, so to speak. The Spirit fills them for the service and life they live before the face of God. But they are certainly to seek it and look to be filled up by the Spirit.

Christians should be cultivating the making of melody in the heart to the Lord. They ought to be seasoned with thanksgiving in the community of the faithful. They ought to submit themselves to one another in the fear of the Lord and in humility – this is *opposite* to being unwise. This joyous Spirit-filled life of corporate worship will eclipse, completely, the carnal delights which worldly men set so much of their existence on. How do believers in the corporate community of the church, make the most of their time, walk wisely, not unwisely, circumspectly, not in a drunken stupor, to glorify the Lord? They are filled with the Spirit and this filling, and this further filling, this *added* filling, is exemplified by their worship together, not their drunkenness together by wine. It operates in being wise, with the right application of knowledge, not unwise, by sin. Here, believers can be filled with the Spirit. In contrast, then to drunkenness with wine, believers are to be so filled with the Spirit, that they are *drunk* with the Spirit; Paul doesn't say it "that way" but *that's what he means*. They will in fact, sing to one another by making melody in their heart to the Lord in the fullness of excess in the Spirit.

All true believers should labor to be filled with an abundance of the Spirit. What does it mean to be *filled* with the Spirit? It means to be either filled *with* the Spirit of God, or can also mean to be filled with an *influence* of the Spirit of God. People drunk with wine are influenced with wine. Unwise people are influenced by ignorance in wrongly applying the truth to daily life. Circumspectly walking before God in the Spirit is opposite to this, for it is a seeking of being filled up. Filled is first to be converted by the Spirit, baptized in him. There is no filling if the vessel has not been made suitable for the Spirit to reside there. Filled means, then, the Spirit continually sets believers apart as holy. The Spirit produces fruit in those who do what God commands. This is killing sin and living righteously.

Filled means a leading into truth, the promises of Christ, spiritual persuasion, or divine illumination. The Spirit leads his people into all truth confirming that truth and comforting them by it. The fullness of the knowledge of the Gospel. And he helps them to be so wise in this that it comes out in assembly singing.

Filled means the Spirit comforts the believer and increases assurance. Rom 15:13, "Now the God of hope fill you with all joy and peace in believing, that ye may abound in hope through the power of the Holy Ghost." Acts 13:52, "The disciples were filled with joy and with the Holy Ghost." The fountain of joy and the Holy Spirit are given as the same thing. Filled with Joy and filled with the Holy Spirit are synonymous. Consider it, then, in the opposite. To not have the Spirit is to not have any of the effects of the Spirit. Romans 8:9, "Now if any man have not the Spirit of Christ, he is none of his." 1 Cor. 12:3 says, "No man can say that Jesus is the Lord, but by the Holy Ghost." "But Peter said, Ananias, why hath Satan filled thine heart to lie to the Holy Ghost, and to keep back part of the price of the land?" (Acts 5:3).

To not be filled with the Spirit, is to be open to be filled with the world, flesh and devil. Paul even says in Eph. 4:27, "Neither give place to the devil." He speaks to *Christians* here. Even though the Holy Spirit has taken up residence in the believer, indwelling him, changing him, bearing fruit in him, Satan still desires to overtake that heart, and again, rule in its place. If one is filled with wine, if they are intoxicated with losing their mind and senses and faculties, how easy will the devil come to them? Hoe easily will they be influenced by wickedness? This is not wise. If one is filled with the Spirit, under the influence of the Spirit, then such an overthrow is impossible. Temptations may come, but the regenerate, baptized, indwelt, anointed, enlightened Christian is wielding his sword in a way to keep off the attack. He cannot do this if he is drunk with wine. He cannot do it if he is unwise. If one is not filled with the Spirit, there is room for something else. Wine, ignorance, sin, it doesn't necessarily need to be *wine*. It could be any form of *self*, any form that exercises a lack of Christian wisdom in self-love that throws off the works of the Spirit in their life.

The filling of the Holy Spirit is a direct result of Christ's merit which he works in every believer. Christ, the Anointed Messiah, had the Spirit imparted to him without measure. "For he whom God hath sent speaketh the words of God: for God giveth not the Spirit by measure unto him," (John 3:34). "How God anointed Jesus of Nazareth with the Holy Ghost and with power," (Acts 10:38). For what reason? It was for service to God in covenant. Such a filling rests *solely on the merit of Christ*. Titus 3:5-6, "And the renewing of the Holy Ghost, which he hath shed on us abundantly through Jesus Christ our Saviour." Thomas Manton said, "If we neglect the benefits in part or in whole, we slight the price. His intent was that we might have abundance of his Spirit."[1] What does this mean "in abundance," but that Christians are utterly filled with the power of the Spirit? He who has the Spirit without measure, gives the Spirit in measure because he has an infinite supply. Christ was sealed with the Spirit without measure, so each believer is sealed with the Spirit in a proper measure sufficient to God's purpose for them. He gives this to his body. This *Meschiach*, which is the Hebrew term for the Anointed One, is the One specially chosen and ordained, blessed by the Spirit without measure, with unction, with power, for God's covenanted divine work. If this Anointed Savior has the Spirit without measure, then he is very able to dispense that measure to every believer suitable for service to them in the

---

[1] Manton, *Works*, Volume 19, 102.

Chapter 7: Filled with the Spirit

bounds of his mystical body.

The fullness of the Spirit comes from Christ. Christ regenerates, baptizes, indwells, anoints, illuminates, fills *with* his Spirit. All of it rests on what Christ accomplished, and the benefits of his life, death, resurrection and present intercession. Penitent believers take hold of Christ and his benefits by faith. The Spirit is now sent from the side of Christ as the comforter to progress in the believer a constant movement toward drawing near to God, and being made more holy. Christ has an abundant measure from God to work in his office as the mediator. In like manner he has an abundance of the Spirit as a discharge of his office, which turns to an abundant fulness of the Spirit, to be filled with the Spirit, for his people. There is no supply that can run out from the infinite God who sends the infinite Spirit to dwell in the hearts of his people. Unlike the limited bottle of wine, there is enough of the Spirit of God to go around. He will fill his people, always with a never-ending supply. God did not give Christ only a little of the Spirit and his power, but rather, poured the Spirit out on him without any tightfistedness. He was full of the Spirit. He is able to fill others with the Spirit. And because Jesus Christ is God, there is a suitableness of his nature that could allow for such a fulness of the Spirit without measure. His divinity upheld his humanity in such a way that his humanity could operate by being "anointed with the oil of gladness above his fellows," (Heb. 1:9). Believers, then, receive of *his* fullness (John 1:16). Stephen Charnock said, "The Spirit was not given as a treasure to be preserved in a cabinet, but as a fountain to send forth fresh streams for a supply."[2] It's not like a bottle of wine in a cabinet stowed away. In this way, not only is Jesus Savior, but he is a *capable* Savior, and a Savior that holds a supply of grace for every need big or small for the

---

[2] Charnock, *Works*, Volume 4, 405.

believer who desires to be filled up; increasing most in joy and comfort, and for the good of the whole body. He has, in this way, full power given to him over all things in his church because of his perfect and complete and finished work on the cross. He satisfies God's divine justice, fulfills all the requirements of the covenant, and bestows all its benefits to his people so that they may live victoriously in abundance of the power of the Spirit.

Christians are not only touched (anointed), by the Spirit, but *filled.* Jesus' benefits are a deep well by which the Spirit is compared to a fountain springing up in the believer. Isaiah 54:3, "I will pour water upon him that is thirsty, and floods upon the dry ground; I will pour my Spirit upon thy seed, and my blessing upon thy offspring." John 4:10 says, "If thou knewest the gift of God, and who it is that saith to thee, Give me to drink, thou wouldst have asked of him, and he would have given thee living water." Verse 14 continues, "The water that I shall give him shall be in him a well of water springing up unto everlasting life." God has made everlasting promises in Christ which surround the abundance of blessedness, in that everlasting covenant between himself and the righteous. He promises to be their God forever, and to bestow an abundance of endless blessedness on them now and in the world to come. John 8:28. "I give unto them eternal life," (and see John 4:14). This living water, this baptism of the Spirit welling up in them for not only salvation, but great assurance, and endless supply, is eternal. Is this not something to *sing* about? Drunks in a tavern sing. What of the corporate assembly of the mystical body filled with the Spirit? What will they sing about?

This water is the grace of the Spirit, glorifying the work of Christ in the soul, which in turn, if rightly sought in the word of God, will spring up in joy, and cultivate a sealing result in making melody in the heart, because they are filled up with the influences of the Spirit. In this Christians are not looking for drops, but streams flowing out of them for all eternity. In filling Christians up, the Spirit motions in believers the fruit of Christ's work. It is called vivification – making further life refined in them. He implants grace in the believer, and the seeds of such righteous fruit, but there is still a maturing process that must take place. One implantation is enough for salvation, but not enough for continued sanctification. In other words, the principal started, is not merely a start, but it invokes a whole race and a finishing of the race. There is an initial filling of the Spirit, and then there is a striving to be continually filled up and overjoyed in the Spirit. Eph. 3:16 says, "That he would grant you according to the riches of his glory, to be strengthened with might, by his Spirit, in the inner man." This is to *seek* to be filled more and more with the influences of the Spirit daily.

How can such seeds of grace, fruit, righteousness, holiness, be cultivated? This is what Paul is getting at. There are higher pleasures men should be taken up with, namely, the joy of faith and a delight in holiness. Wine can never satisfy such things. It deadens the senses in excess. It causes them to *forget*. The Spirit enlightens to remember. In the Spirit there is no excess, as it is in drunkenness. The Scriptures never tell a Christian that they can be filled too much with the Spirit. Or that they should only be filled up to a certain amount. They are encouraged and commanded and directed to be filled eminently, continually and without a cap. Ceasing something, stopping something, anything, is always tied to sin; to stop this or that, which is another aspect of the Spirit's influence on the life of the believer called the mortification of sin, or killing sin; stopping sin. Mortification is to strive against temptation which is set down as riotous living, for to mimic riotous living is to act unwisely. It is to take up the disposition of a drunk in comparison to being filled with the Spirit. The sensual pleasure which men find in wine entices them to be drunk with it in excess. 1 Peter 4:3 says, "When we walked in lasciviousness, lusts, excess of wine, revellings, banquetings, and abominable idolatries." Instead, the Ephesian church is directed to make melody in their heart, being filled with the Spirit, singing to one another, exemplifying their fullness; for it is discernable.

When Christians have a filling of the Spirit, they express their thankfulness and joy in psalms, hymns and praises; songs to one another and to God. Redeeming the time, and the glory of God are one and the same, which means, in these the Christian is to kill sin, and walk in the fruit of the Spirit of joy and thankfulness. If Christians serve the living Christ, if they are fit for acceptable service in worship, with thankfulness and joy, filled with the Spirit, then they are constantly at odds with anything that will detract from that path. Yet, how is this done, and where do they get it? The thief on the cross had the shortest converted life of anyone in Scripture, still, he certainly exemplified this. He had a short life, but an effective, Spirit-filled life. One can *see* his change even while hanging on a cross (Luke 23:43).

Methuselah, the longest human life, had to deal with spiritual growth for 969 years, and the man didn't even have a bible he could hold (Gen. 5:27). Imagine living so long and looking to be filled with the fulness of God day by day over a *millennium?*

How can believers fill themselves with the Spirit? First, to be filled with the Spirit is an act of the Spirit. In regeneration, the Spirit gives birth to spirit (John 3:3-5). Then having fruit in the Christian life, it is in fact, *fruit of the Spirit.* "For the fruit of the Spirit is in all goodness and righteousness and truth," (Eph. 5:9). Interestingly, the bible doesn't call it fruits, but *fruit* of the Spirit. The entirety of the spiritual blessing in Christ in the Spirit is the Spirit's fruit. Believers have the whole fruit of the Spirit (we will talk more about that in a later chapter). Yet there is more to this fruit than merely having it, but exercising it and causing it to grow further, and to do it wisely. "For this cause we also, since the day we heard it, do not cease to pray for you, and to desire that ye might be filled with the knowledge of his will in all wisdom and spiritual understanding," (Col. 1:9). Only God can bestow the Spirit, and the further filling of the Spirit.

Second, to *have* the Spirit is not the same as being *filled* with the Spirit. There is a careful use of the *Means of Grace* in the life of a believer to cultivate the measure of the Spirit one obtains in practical daily living. Titus 3:6, "Which he hath shed on us abundantly through Jesus Christ our Saviour." Whatever the Spirit does, it is in Christ's name, and by his work. And Christ desires his people to live in an abundance of the Spirit, with a victorious life. "...abundant in mercy to all those who call upon You." (Psa. 86:5). "...abundant redemption." (Psa. 130:7). "It shall blossom abundantly, and rejoice even with joy and singing," (Isa. 35:2). "...delight themselves in the abundance of peace," (Psa. 37:11). "...and will reveal unto them the abundance of peace and truth," (Jer. 33:6). "...much more they which receive abundance of grace and of the gift of righteousness shall reign in life by one, Jesus Christ," (Rom. 5:17). But to have the Spirit, to be baptized and indwelt and the like, is not the same as to be continually cultivating the filling up of the Spirit by way of being influenced by the Spirit. Keep the similarity to wine. One bottle of wine will run out. The drunk must go get more to continue his sin. One who is filled up with the Spirit, must build upon that spiritual influence to grow in grace and the knowledge of Christ, and then to be wise in its exercise. They have the Spirit. They have an abundance of the Spirit. But they must also deal with the way spiritual influences work on their soul. They must not let the influences be pushed out or get old or get stale or get them to sleep in them. They must cultivate the work of the Christ in them through the Spirit through the word, through all the means of grace.

Third, the abundance of the benefits of Christ in the Spirit, and the victory of the Christian life is lived out in the knowledge of the Gospel. John 17:17, "Sanctify them through thy truth; thy word is truth." Be filled by the truth, be sanctified by the truth, be filled with the Spirit of Truth by working in the truth of the word. 2 Peter 1:4, "Whereby are given unto us exceeding great and precious promises, that by these ye might be partakers of the divine nature." James 1:18, "Of his own will begat he us with the word of truth." The Spirit and the word are vitally connected in this way, and there is no filling up of the abundance of the Spirit, or any kind of victorious living, without knowledge of the word, and the right application of the word to the life of the believer; and what will happen if the Christian only learns one thing? If one truth is known, is there more to know? At first the one truth seems like a mountain. The Christian seems so filled up by the Spirit by it that they can hardly contain themselves and they can't wait to break out in song with the corporate body about it. Look what he has learned about this week, and so he meditates on it, it sticks in his mind, and he applies it to himself walking in the light of the word. But, what of the next week?
And the week after? Will such a person rest content to have a little of the Spirit, only a few things known? Will they rest content to have a little knowledge and a little wisdom? What will happen to what they have if they do not cultivate what they know? The life which believers have because of the work of Christ, is abundant life; it cannot be had with little. "I am come that they might have life, and that they might have it more abundantly," (John 10:10). The Lord had shed forth the Spirit abundantly. All the graces and influences of the Spirit

in the Gospel are the very riches of Christ, riches of his grace, riches of the mystery of godliness, riches of his glory, and all this is spoken about the work of the Spirit, the abundance of the Spirit, which believers obtain and cultivate from the very life of the Anointed Savior. They are filled, and filled, and filled, and filled. With what? Spiritual Strength and Stamina – how? Through the word! With the confirmation of the Spirit on that word. It works comfort. It works joy. It works thanksgiving. Like being born again *again* by the doctrines of grace. They not only know something, but it is applied to them, and they are filled up by it.

Assurance of the Spirit's work or not is a matter of filling. What will the Christian do the next time they come together in the corporate assembly? Do they feel dry? What will they be filled with during the week that prepares them to burst out in joy in the corporate assembly singing psalms and hymns and songs? What about the one who says, "I must do my duty whatever it is no matter what." Is this joy? Or is this pushing through a spiritual task? Is that the same as being filled? Oftentimes drunks drink to forget. But the Christian is filled to rejoice, to remember. The more they get the more they have joy. The more joy the more filling. The more filling, the more thanksgiving. The *more* is Christ. They must use all the means of grace to do this. What are these means? Prayer. Reading the word. Godly meditation. Teaching their children and such. So how might one define being filled with the Spirit? It is either being filled with more of the influence of grace, or being filled with more of the Spirit's gifts for service. They are practically worked out in this way. They are not drunk with wine, but filled by the Spirit to serve God in the way Christ so requires; with zeal and with devotion to him.

If Christians neglect being filled up by the Spirit through the word during the week, what will they have to offer the church in their gifts and graces on the day they are commanded to sing? It is to get more of the presence of the Spirit into the heart.

One might object and say, "But preacher, didn't you say we are indwelt with the Spirit? How might we gain more of him? Isn't he the infinite Spirit in us?" True, the Christian has the Spirit, but consider this as one would say, "I will open the window shade to let the sun into the house." The rays of the sun warm the house. But shades can be closed. Finite beings cannot contain the infinite Spirit of God. But they can contain his influences and work in the soul. Scripture does not speak to the church in a way in which God himself resides inside the actual body (bones, blood, muscles, flesh) of the Christian where they can be cut open in their skin and God leaks out. They are described as a dwelling, a dwelling effect and work in the soul; like the rays of God's sunshine beaming into the heart and residing there through Gospel influences for all time in a spiritual sense. They are a place of spiritual residence; an indwelling presence of the Spirit where he works and motions the believers to godliness through his influence.

Now, the Christian must cultivate the influences of the Spirit over their fallen mind and hearts. They are converted, but they know they are inadequate in everything. They rely on the Spirit of Christ, the merit of Christ, for all their graces, for all their joy. It must be cultivated and increased through faith in believing the word, which the Spirit presses into their heart. He knows that he must abound in holy inclinations, and where are these found, and how are they moved within the heart? They are found in the word and they are motioned by the Spirit. These Christians, then, are under his influence as they are in the word of Christ.

How much of the Spirit is enough? What will only a little bit of the Spirit do to you as a Christian? Little will not comfort; what will you do with little drops of water? John

15:11, "These things have I spoken unto you, that my joy might remain in you, and that your joy might be full." Little drops will not stop the world, flesh and devil. Heb. 6:4-6, "For it is impossible for those that were once enlightened, and have tasted of the heavenly gift, and were made partakers of the Holy Ghost, and have tasted of the good word of God, and the powers of the world to come; if they fall away." A taste will not do. A little of the Spirit will not do. Thomas Brooks, in His *Precious Remedies Against Satan's Devices* said,

> "If you would not be taken with any of Satan's devices, then labour to be filled with the Spirit. The Spirit of the Lord is a Spirit of light and power; and what can a soul do without light and power 'against spiritual wickedness in high places'? Eph. vi. 12. It is not enough that you have the Spirit, but you must be filled with the Spirit, or else Satan, that evil spirit, will be too hard for you, and his plots will prosper against you. [That is a sweet word of the apostle, 'Be filled with the Spirit, Eph. v. 18; i.e. labour for abundance of the Spirit. He that thinks he hath enough of the Holy Spirit, will quickly find himself vanquished by the evil spirit. Satan hath his snares to take you in prosperity and adversity, in health and sickness, in strength and weakness, when you are alone and when you are in company, when you come on to spiritual duties and when you come off from spiritual duties, and if you are not filled with the Spirit, Satan will be too hard and too crafty for you, and will easily and frequently take you in his snares, and make a prey of you in spite of your souls. Therefore labour more to have your hearts filled with the Spirit than to have your heads filled with notions, your shops with wares, your chests with silver, or your bags with gold; so shall you escape the

snares of this fowler, and triumph over all his plots, etc.³

It is the abundance of the Spirit that conforms the life into the image of Christ. It is the abundance of the Spirit which motivates you to holiness. William Dell said, "And according to the measure of the Spirit in each duty, is the measure of power in the duty. If there be none of the Spirit in a man's duties, there is no power at all in them, but only weakness and deadness, and coldness, and unprofitableness. If a little of the Spirit, there is a little power; if abundance of the Spirit, there is great power; and that duty that is most spiritual, is the most powerful."⁴ Oliver Heywood said it this way, "the essence and abundance of life are both from him."⁵ "If ye then be risen with Christ, seek those things which are above where Christ sitteth on the right hand of God. Set your affection on things above, not on things on the earth. For ye are dead, and your life is hid with Christ in God. When Christ, who is our life, shall appear, then shall ye also appear with him in glory." (Col. 3:1-4). What does the apostle say next? "Mortify therefore your members which are upon the earth," (Col. 3:5). This is to be seeking the abundant life, seeking it in Christ, that holiness might abound. Or, to "be filled with the Spirit," (Eph. 5:18). How? Through the word, through its understanding and incorporation into your life.

Strive for being "filled;" the abundance of the Spirit of Grace in full measure. Do you regularly talk like this or think like this? When you ask for a drink, do you ask for a drop? Go into Starbucks, and you direct them to not put so much ice so

---

[3] Brooks, Thomas, <u>Precious Remedies Against Satan's Devices</u>, *The Complete Works of Thomas Brooks*, (Vol. 1) 159.
[4] Dell, William, *The Works of William Dell*, (New York: Joseph Sharpless, ND) 53.
[5] Heywood, Oliver, *The Whole Works of Oliver Heywood*, Vol. 2, (London: R. Baynes, 1825) 31.

that you get more of the drink. You want that coffee filled up. You want to enjoy it to its fullest; and that's simply a drink. Do you believe you have the abundance of the Spirit? Do you walk in the abundance of the Spirit as a victorious Christian? Paul would ask you, from this passage, two things, then: how wise are you to put godliness into practice, and how outwardly discernable do others see of such works? "I am come that they might have life, and that they might have it more abundantly," (John 10:10). Life and the Spirit in this way are the same thing, and are gotten in the same way – through the word. Do you believe what Jesus says as the great baptizer of the Holy Spirit and of the godly zeal of Spirit-fire? Do you have rivers of living water flowing from you? Is this the way you characterize your life, or describe yourself? You have many that use these terms and words in a flippant and unbiblical way, TV preachers and the like, who think that some kind of worked up ecstatic experience is what constitutes the filling of the Spirit. They will tell you to *open yourself up to the Spirit*, whatever *that* means, and allow him to ozmatically zap you and fill you up. They are dead wrong, because *they* are spiritualy dead, and do not understand the first thing about the abundant life of Christ in the Spirit. They see it as a gimmick. They do not see its ties to Christ, nor to the Gospel, nor to the illumination of the Spirit in truth of the word. This is because to *feel and experience* is much easier than to know and grow in wisdom.

    Where do you get this abundance of the Spirit, this filling up? Abundance of the Spirit is tied to your intake of the knowledge of Christ and its application to the soul. Your life shines most gloriously when the riches of the mystery of godliness of the Gospel of Christ are more gloriously revealed to your heart and mind. You discover Christ, his grace, mercy, love, glory, person, work, death, and such; all various facets that you are to contemplate. More Christ, more knowledge of

Christ, more experiential time with him in the truth, more Spirit bearing witness with your Spirit about the truth of the word, and the reality of your vital connection to Jesus, and all the godliness that affords the practical outworking of that, not in your own mind, but even discernable to others. More Spirit, more truth, and more truth and Spirit, more practical victory in both living righteously and casting off sin, with all its temptations. You will know what to do, you will know how to do it, and you will be confirmed by the Spirit to do it, and you will indeed be endowed with power, for power comes from the Spirit through the word. More casting off, more walking in the Spirit, more abundance, more holiness; and *holiness leads to happiness*. And happy are those who are assured in Christ for all that Christ has done for them, and all that Christ gives them in the Spirit.

This means you live your life in Christ, but not only that you live, but that you are spirited, invigorated, motivated, in your life by the word through the Spirit wisely; circumspectly. Spirited living, is not simply alive in the Spirit, but that you are active in walking in the Spirit, and how will you know how to walk and where to walk but by the word and applying that word rightly in all the situations and providences God bestows upon you. Either you are given a storehouse of grace to use and cultivate and grow, or, you are comforted in the difficulties of using and cultivating and growing in grace. Thomas Manton said, "This lively living is mainly seen in the two necessary graces of the soul to which the Gospel is sometimes reduced, and they are faith and love. These are the graces wherein life consists; and as these are acted and excited to God, so we are lively, and when these decay we are dead."[6] These are the marks of a biblical disciple, living in faith, and living in love.

---

[6] Manton, *Works*, Vol. 6, 435.

Chapter 7: Filled with the Spirit

How will you attain being filled with the Spirit? Knowing that the saint is not in control of the infinite, all powerful, Spirit of Christ, there still are certain promises annexed to this idea of being filled, that reside in your hands. No one will ever be able to say, "I didn't have the fullness of the Spirit because Jesus didn't give me more of the Spirit." Christ is there ready to dispense to those who ask, seek and knock, those who seek first the kingdom of heaven. Do you see that he says to you, ask, seek, knock,[7] *etc.* Open the door and I'll come in to you. I'll have supper with you.[8] That's to the church.

There are two Scriptural ways to be filled. Prayer, "But ye shall receive power, after that the Holy Ghost is come upon you," (Acts 1:8). How did they obtain this power and abundance of the Spirit? "These all continued with one accord in prayer and supplication," (Acts 1:14). Mutual, complimentary prayer. They continued praying for more of the Spirit. But that is not all they prayed for.

The use of the word is extremely important, 2 Peter 1:4, "Whereby are given unto us exceeding great and precious promises, that by these ye might be par takers of the divine nature." This is divine illumination from the word in the promises of God and his Gospel. Is being filled in this way, abundantly, odd or strange in obtaining it? They [point of reference *they*] continued together in one accord in prayer. Such things are *given unto us* [point of reference] *the preaching of the word*, the promises of the word, given to us. When the word does not take center stage, when prayer does not take center stage, there will be no filling of the Spirit in abundant life. "And they were all filled with the Holy Ghost,"

---

[7] Luke 11:9.
[8] "Behold, I stand at the door, and knock: if any man hear my voice, and open the door, I will come in to him, and will sup with him, and he with me," (Rev. 3:20).

(Acts 2:4). Christ sent the Spirit, and they were all filled. Not partially, or a little filled! Very much filled. The spiritual vigor of any church can easily be seen in two things – prayer in one accord, and central ministry of the word to the soul. Your church has no prayer meeting? What? No biblical preaching of the word? What? To lack one or the other, a church cannot even call itself Christian, much less, Spirit-filled. Do you really think, in looking at church history, that God pours out the abundance of his Spirit, for the filling up of the church, for its strengthening, anywhere else other than those in prayer in one accord and by knowledge of the word of Christ rightly applied? Revival of that kind never occurs without the centrality of preaching the one true Gospel, or without corporate prayer. One preacher said he was, "particularly insisting very much in public prayer and preaching," during revival.[9] A great many professing churches fail here, have no power, do not live abundantly in the ways I've described. But they have so many people. They have such a big building. They are on TV. They have many ministries. But are they really Spirit-filled? It is because they think that being filled, or being illuminated or being anointed or being baptized is some mere experiential occurrence that occurs without any prior work in the word of God or its right application. And they are *very wrong* in this. We are to be filled with the Spirit so that even our worship would prosper in singing psalms and hymns and songs to one another. As a conclusion to this chapter, listen to Jonathan Edwards again as a final remark on this:

> "Certainly it becomes us, who profess the religion of Christ, to take notice of such astonishing exercises of his power and mercy, and give him the glory which is due, when he begins to accomplish any of his promises

---

[9] Edwards, Jonathan, *Jonathan Edwards on Revival* (electronic ed.; Simpsonville SC: Christian Classics Foundation) 146.

Chapter 7: Filled with the Spirit

concerning the latter days: and it gives us further encouragement to pray, and wait, and hope for the like display of his power in the midst of us [to be filled with the Spirit]. The hand of God is not shortened that it cannot save, but we have reason to fear that our iniquities, our coldness in religion, and the general carnality of our spirits, have raised a wall of separation between God and us: and we may add, the pride and perverse humor of infidelity, degeneracy, and apostasy from the Christian faith, which have of late years broken out amongst us, seem to have provoked the Spirit of Christ to absent himself much from our nation. "Return, O Lord, and visit thy churches, and revive and shine your own work in the midst of us."[10]

The next chapter will deal with being *spiritually empowered* by the Spirit.

---

[10] Ibid, page 3.

Chapter 8: Empowered by the Spirit

"Now the God of hope fill you with all joy and peace in believing, that ye may abound in hope, through the power of the Holy Ghost." (Rom. 15:13).

Before considering Romans 15:13, take a moment to think through the following outline of the book, to know where this verse falls in the grand scheme of Paul's theological argumentation. Briefly, Paul covers the topic of justification in chapter 1-5; of sanctification in chapters 6-8; of predestination in chapters 9-11; and of good works in chapters 12-16. This 15th chapter of Romans is set under what might be considered supplementary material. It houses in it some conclusions to his arguments of the inclusion of the Gentiles in the hope of Christ. It focuses on good works as a result of being born again.

In chapter 15, Paul teaches that Christ became a servant to demonstrate the truth of God (verse 8). He confirmed all the promises made to the patriarchs by fulfilling everything that God had promised as a servant of the Covenant of Grace. In this, not only had Christ come to the lost house of Israel, but also that the Gentiles would be included, so there is one fold, and one Shepherd. An intriguing thought for a Jew was that the Gentiles can glorify God for the mercy he has shown to them. In this way Christ is said to have a double purpose in becoming a servant of the Jews: 1) to confirm the promises that God made in the Old Testament and 2) that the Gentiles would in turn glorify the salvation of the Lord.

The Gentiles are countlessly mentioned through the Old Testament as those *included* by Christ's work. Just look at the praise of nations, Gentiles, in the psalms.[1] Keep in mind, *the Old Testament* is what Paul is teaching here. Romans has no substance without the Old Testament, and all the promises made in Christ are found there. It was not, as the Jews thought, that they were the only nation to be saved unless someone was somehow proselyted in to be Jewish, but God's eternal and everlasting covenant show his one and only Son, born a Jew, would in turn gather in the Gentiles, in reconciling those of every nation under the sun. Paul quotes in chapter 15, "Therefore I will give thanks unto thee, O LORD, among the heathen, and I will sing praises unto thy name," (2 Sam. 22:50; Psalm 18:49, *cf.* Rom. 15:9). David vowed to praise God *among* the Gentiles, to sing in honor of his name. Jesus rebukes the elders of Israel for not gathering in *the Gentiles*, where Israel was to be the instrument through whom God's redemptive work would extend.[2] Then Paul quotes, "Rejoice, O ye nations, with his people," (Deut. 32:43). Nations? Then Paul quotes, "O praise the LORD, all ye nations: praise him, all ye people." (Psa. 117:1). All nations were always part of God's plan of salvation? Yes. Then he quotes Isaiah 11:10, "And in that day there shall be a root of Jesse, which shall stand for an ensign of the people; to it shall the Gentiles seek: and his rest shall be glorious." So, Christ, the Messiah, comes from David's line, and will rule the nations, (not just Israel) and on him the Gentiles will rest all their hopes and all people will praise God. Then comes Romans 15:13.

Romans 15:13, "Now the God of hope fill you with all joy and peace in believing, that ye may abound in hope, through the power of the Holy Ghost." "Now the God of hope," this leads Paul to pray to the God of all hope, because there is no hope apart from Jesus Christ. Christ is the source of all hope. Power in the Spirit and hope are intrinsically

---

[1] Psalm 22:27, 57:9, 67:4, 72:11, 117:1, *etc.*
[2] Matthew 23:37.

linked. Christ's work in the *Covenant of Redemption*, worked out in the *Covenant of Grace*, in the full power of the Spirit, conquered all obstacles to bring his sheep, believers, true and lasting hope.

What is the work of hope in a person? It is to wait for and expect the accomplishment of all the promises of God. Martin Luther said, "Faith beholding the word's intention is the main property of hope."[3] It is the eager expectation of God to fulfill as he promised to do in a patient faith. These Romans were to abound in this hope, and pray to this God of hope. They should be thinking, I expect him, and in deliverance expect a reward with him, and this expectation of "hope will never make ashamed," (Romans 5:5).

What is the substance of this hope? The promises of God. Where are these promises found? In *the Old Testament*. For this reason the apostle is so serious that the believing Romans, "might be made to abound in hope," (Romans 15:13), which is the meaning of the phrase. Praying to this God of hope, hope in promises, hope in the Old Testament, hope in expectation of all fulfillment, they are to expect a filling up of joy and peace. Filling implies degrees. Not all are filled in the same degree. That surrounds the use of the means of grace, for Paul explains that filling is of hope in joy and peace through believing. Some believe more and some believe less; it matters little what church might be used as an example. Some Christians just don't know the Old Testament promises very well at all. They think the bible consists only as a New Testament and Psalms for them. Paul is teaching them the Old Testament in Romans. Their believing these promises, these hopes, will determine their power. What they know translates to how they act practically. Christ is the one who fills his people with all joy and peace. In joy and peace is found

---

[3] Quoted in Nathaniel Vincent's "A Covert from the Storm," (Coconut Creek, FL: Puritan Publications, 2012) 44.

the Spirit. In joy and peace is found power. Joy and peace come through believing. Christ is the one who gives them an abundant life. Joy and peace are part of abundant life. "But the fruit of the Spirit is joy, peace," (Gal. 5:22). "For the kingdom of God is not meat and drink; but righteousness, and peace, and joy in the Holy Ghost," (Rom. 14:17). Christ is the fountain of joy. What makes people joyful? Is it that an easy life is somehow a happy life? Was Christ's life easy? Yet, for the joy set before him he endured the cross (Heb. 12:2). The cross was by *no means* easy.

Happiness often equates to the negation of trials, or the accumulation of some amount of wealth or possessions to ease the burden of difficult living. But God's will, according to the Apostle, is that the God of hope fill the Roman Christians up with joy. It is there that true power is found. True exuberant joy can only be found from God's eternal election in Christ as a believer who has been justified, sanctified, with the hope of being glorified. Is this not Romans chapter 5, chapter 8 and such? Paul is arguing that the God of hope, who is prayerfully solicited, works joy in his people through the promises he has given them so they may see Christ more clearly by the Spirit. Their perception of Christ in this way translates into joy. Prayer and the word translate to joy, to power, to the filling of the Spirit.

Christ is the fountain of peace. "Therefore being justified by faith, we have peace with God through our Lord Jesus Christ," (Rom. 5:1). Enmity turns to peace. One who is hell-bound is saved and changed and sanctified and filled with joy and has an abundance of hope leading to peace, not only for the Jews but also the Gentiles. Weak brothers, strong brothers, *this is not the point,* it is the cultivation of hope with a desire to be filled with more joy and peace. This all stems from Christ's work, and his sending of the Spirit. Such joy and peace flow from believing, for, "in believing, that ye may abound in hope." Not a *mere hopefulness* will do, one must *abound* in hope. This occurs through belief in what Christ has done as the suffering servant, the lion of the tribe of Judah, he who gathers in the heathen into one fold with one Shepherd. Belief in Christ, belief in his work, belief which is not mere assent to something, but that one sees it not only as good but true, so that it cultivates joy and peace in a believer. All this hinges in what is to be believed, and what is found in the word of God. This is the voice of Christ to his people. And this joy and peace in Christ, flowing from understanding the word, is "through the power of the Holy Ghost," (Rom. 15:13).

Such things flow from the Spirit who is both the communicator of joy and peace from Christ to the believer. Paul desires that the Romans would pray that God would fill them up by believing in the hope of the Gospel, daily, continually. Such a believing would cultivate both joy and peace in the hope settled by the covenant in Christ. God provides hope as these Christians believe the truth of the Gospel and the work of Christ, and in turn they are filled up with joy and peace, and this is done in the power of the Holy Ghost. It emphasizes here a continuing trust in God through Christ by the power of the Spirit. Such an experience of overflowing hope is made possible by the power of the Holy Spirit, which power is in the Christian. These Roman Christians cannot muster up any hope themselves. The Christian life is founded on Christ's empowering presence which is to say it is through the sending of the Comforter, who brings joy and peace. The Roman Christians are being taught, that the only way to access this power, is to be filled up with joy and filled up with peace, which breeds this hope, and it is all by believing.

What do they believe? What? *Not feel?* Their belief is certainly something that will create a feeling, but belief is first. Paul was not at Pentecost when the Spirit was poured out on the Jews. He was not in the upper room. Paul was not in Cornelius' house when Peter was preaching to the Gentiles and the holy Spirit fell there, that the Gentiles would be included in the salvation of the Messiah. Yet, he has a very vivid description, as a matter of fact, all through his epistles on the Spirit, and the Spirit's work and fruit in the life of the believer. How did he know about this "power" in the Spirit? It was said of him, that after his conversion, "Brother Saul, the Lord, even Jesus, that appeared unto thee in the way as thou camest, hath sent me, that thou mightest receive thy sight, and be filled with the Holy Ghost," (Acts 9:17). When he was to be sent out to preach, after taking a good many years to study the Lord Jesus Christ, he is said to be "separated" and sent forth by "the Holy Ghost" to the task of preaching (Acts 13:2). Paul knew the power of the holy Spirit; but how did he know this? Because he knew that *every* Christian is empowered by Christ through the Spirit if they are believers which produces joy and peace in them, and sets them apart to serve the Christ because they believe the promises of God. The Old Testament is filled with passages about the power of the Spirit. "But truly I am full of power by the spirit of the LORD, and of judgment, and of might, to declare unto Jacob his transgression, and to Israel his sin," (Micah 3:8). "Then he answered and spake unto me, saying, This is the word of the LORD unto Zerubbabel, saying, Not by might, nor by power, but by my spirit, saith the LORD of hosts," (Zech. 4:6); *i.e.* by my Spirit's power. They are to pray to God for his continued filling, so that joy and peace might ensue through the Holy Spirit. They do this by believing in the Gospel of Christ every day for daily living always relying on the Holy Spirit. They even pray to the God of hope for it and that they would come to a greater understanding of it through the Holy Spirit. They do it for sustenance, for spiritual food, the hope that is being worked in them to grow stronger in believing the promises of God in

Christ in the power of the Holy Spirit.

Paul never speaks about the power of the Holy Spirit detached from believing, or the word of God. Power is not contained in some giving up of the senses and feeling one's way through an experience. He is not saying that the Holy Spirit zaps the Roman Christians into peace and hope. He tells them that they must be always believing, always praying for the filling, believing the promises of God, believing the God of hope, that they may gain comfort, that they may gain peace, that they may have the power of the Spirit working in them, for a specific purpose. But what is it, what is this purpose, actually? Let's consider first this doctrine and then tie it all together.

All born again believers partake of the supernatural, spiritual, and divine power of the Holy Spirit communicated to them in Jesus Christ by God to reverse the fall. All elect believers have the power of the Spirit in various degrees. Most Christian people, have no idea what the phrase "the power of the Spirit" is, much less to live in it, and the charismatic community thinks they have a monopoly on this due to a faulty theological view of the Spirit. In Paul's argument, hope is not a natural fabrication in man's own mind. In thinking about the Christian faith, hope is not natural to him at all in this way. Hope is the fruit of the Spirit through faith in his Son. Hope is born of the Spirit, and enhanced by believing the promises. Joy is born of the Spirit, and enhanced by believing the promises. Peace is born of the Spirit, and enhanced by believing the promises. It is very interesting that such promises for the Apostle were *the promises found in the Old Testament.* Can a New Testament Christian have hope and peace without understanding these promises?

Now, it is assumed, at this point, in the Apostle's argumentation, in considering the work of the Spirit on the Christian, that the professing Christian is the elect of God, born again by the Spirit. This is part of the argument that Paul is making here in Romans. Those who were once of the world, chapter 1, who were dead in sin, falling short of God's perfect standard of the Law, enemies of the Gospel, chapters 2-3, who have been changed by the Spirit like father Abraham and justified by the second Adam, chapters 4 and 5, have been brought into the love of God, demonstrated by the work of the Anointed Messiah, who then sanctifies them, chapters 6-7, in which all this rests on the power and righteousness of God's holy and perfect plan to save his people by ordained grace, chapter 8, in which these elected believers are grafted into the covenant, into the same substance as father Abraham was, chapters 9-11, to serve God as living sacrifices both in the world and to God, chapters 12-13, not squabbling about good works as making one weak or strong over another, chapter 14, but elect believers looking to be filled up with hope, through joy and peace, by the power of the Holy Spirit. Those in this redeemed situation are elected of God, chosen in Christ, made partakes of the beloved to such a holy extent that in chapter 8, Paul calls them justified, even, glorified. That is how certain and wonderful this hope is in Christ – the Apostle can tell Christian believers they have the hope of being glorified in heaven, as if they are glorified even now. Such an exhortation is a great means of assurance.

These elect believers partake of a supernatural power in the Spirit. Now this supernatural power is not *a charismatic zapping.* It is directly related to Christ, the Gospel, hope, joy and peace in believing. If a person does not believe, there is no hope. Salvation is set in the realm of supernatural hope. It requires, then, that salvation for elect Christians, born again, growing in hope, joy and peace, being filled with the fullness of Christ, is supernatural. Man, in this, is appointed for a supernatural culmination in heaven as the bride of Christ in the age to come. He must have given to him, transforming him, working in him, working on him, a supernatural means for reaching that goal. He cannot muster this up on his own. It is never merely about the here and now, it is about the now which reaches into the not yet (Heb. 11:10). Filling up now, service now, hope now, joy now, peace now, for preparing *for the not yet to come.* And while waiting for this not yet fullness of the coming of the Kingdom, the now has certain supernatural graces that stem from Christ in the power of the Spirit. Know that such a supernatural salvation in Christ has never been, is or shall be natural to a man. It is above man. It is in theology bestowed on man as an alien righteousness from Christ applied by the Spirit (Rom. 4:24). In this the elect find repentance, pardon, mercy, grace, all the supernatural benefits of Jesus to their soul. This is why the Apostle Peter can say, "Whereby are given unto us exceeding great and precious promises: that by these ye might be partakers of the divine nature," (2 Peter 1:4).

Still linked to this supernatural bestowal of the divine nature of God working in and through the elect believer, there are great and precious promises to be believed. Where are these promises found? Hold that thought for a moment. That which is supernatural surpasses human reason and is communicated to elect believers by God in the new light of grace in the power of the Holy Spirit, those enlightened. It has bound up in it, the covenantal work of God sending the Christ, as its author and object, and communicates the truth of God through this supernatural light because the Spirit shines the light of truth on the Messiah.

As a side note here, supernatural power in the Spirit, for the church today, is not like the supernatural miracles of the church in times past; nor is it like magic or hocus pocus. The Spirit's power in working certain miracles, in attesting to the Savior by the work of the apostles in the initial spread of the Gospel, is a heightening of natural means by a super-

Chapter 8: Empowered by the Spirit

natural, or super added work of God on them for the propagation of the Gospel. Philip, for example, after speaking with the Ethiopian Eunuch was translated to another place by the power of the Spirit. He could have walked by natural means, but the Spirit heightened the work by moving him more quickly, instantaneously, from one place to another (Acts 8:39). Peter healed the crippled beggar, where the beggar was, above nature, supernaturally worked on to receive a healing that nature would not give, but God could (Acts 3:6-7). Such a supernatural power in this way is not exercised by men, but by the Spirit. Peter had no power, rather, the Spirit used the word of Christ to work on the beggar in a miraculous, or supernatural manner, again, for the propagation and attestation of the Christ as the Messiah. What would someone merely being healed of disease really care about healing in that way if they ultimately knew they would spend eternity in hell? Miracles attest to the word of God, and were used by the Apostles in the early church for the purpose of validating the preached word, and Jesus as the Christ. This same Spirit empowers the elect today. But Christians often do not understand how to tap into this power, which is eminently spiritual in nature. They think it is a supernatural *zapping* kind of power. "I want to heal. I want to at least speak in other tongues, I want to do a miracle like Jesus did," *etc.* They are somewhat distant to it because they think that it is a foreign power that they must somehow seek or gain in some *ecstatic experience.*

All Christians partake of the spiritual and supernatural; at least they should be. Something is spiritual in nature when it is offered by the Spirit of God to the human mind in such a way that it can apprehend, and enjoy, based on knowledge and in spiritual power. It cannot be handled like a hammer. It cannot be played with like a toy. It is, again, not of human creation, nor of personal invention, and it cannot be subjectively worked up in a person. It is the Spirit, working some grace on the mind, believed on by faith. In the context of Romans 15, *spiritual* is more properly seen as that which the Holy Spirit works on the mind of man from the word of God. From believing, there is hope in Christ, joy in Christ, and peace in Christ in various degrees in various stages of discipleship. Such hope, joy and peace is to be constantly prayed for, that it might be continually filled up. It is a cultivation and exercise, not gaining something they do not have or possess.

The born-again Christian has all the influences of the power of the Spirit in them *right now.* The question is how will they *unlock* that power, that joy, that peace, and cultivate its goodness in their life? A spiritual man, in contrast to a natural man, in the way that the doctrine has been stated, is that one has been worked on by the Holy Spirit, and one has not. "Which things also we speak, not in the words which man's wisdom teacheth, but which the Holy Ghost teacheth; comparing spiritual things with spiritual," (1 Cor. 2:13). One has this power, and one does not have this power. One is born again, and one is left in their original sin.

Christians literally partake of the divine nature in all this (2 Peter 1:4). Divine as it relates to God is that which is most excellent according to his perfection and attributes. God is the first and best of beings, and anything that he communicates to men about his being is divine, or even as it is studied is called "divinity." Men of old were called divines, not because they were divine, but that they taught God's communicated word to others in a way consistent with the truth. For an elect believer to partake of the divine, is to have the supernatural work of the Spirit indwelling them in a spiritual way, and communicating to them some truth surrounding the attributes and character of God. Again, "Whereby are given unto us exceeding great and precious promises: that by these ye might be partakers of the divine nature," (2 Peter 1:4). As Paul then says, "Now the God of hope fill you with all joy and peace in believing, that ye may abound in hope, through the power of the Holy Ghost," (Rom. 15:13). These are the same ideas stated in different ways. Filled, in believing, through the power of the Holy Spirit. The Greek ἐν here can mean *in, by or through.* It also has a number of New Testament references meaning *under the influence of.* And so here it would be under the influence of the Spirit by believing. After being born again, and having this indwelling influence, this communication of the divine influences on the soul by the Spirit (which occurs through the word of God), to further understand the word is to further be built up and strengthened in the divine nature.

Today's perverse generation seeks after a sign. This is what might be called a charismatic *experience.* That's not what Paul is teaching. Husbands and wives after they are married learn about one another through subsequent years and spending time together. Elect believers joined to the divine nature, indwelt by the Spirit, the place where the Son and Father make their dwelling with them in their soul, nurture that relationship by knowing more about them and communing in fellowship. This is done by continued believing, in the power of the Holy Spirit, by the word.

Do Christians *have* the power of the Holy Spirit? Many think "power" the idea of power in this light, as being zapped somehow, *apart from knowing.* Hope is produced in the mind by the agency and power of the Spirit of God. Power is daily living in hope. Hope is assurance. Assurance rests on knowledge. Knowledge comes from believing. Believing comes from the promises. God communicates this hope but he gives it through the Holy Spirit. In the work of redemption, this is the special station of the of the Holy Spirit – to teach, to communicate truth, to testify of the truth, to shine the light of Christ all over the word for the elect believer who looks to the word for hope, joy and peace in Christ. To gain any measure of this, to cultivate any degree of this, must be understood, Calvin said, that this growth in Christ, this believing, this filling, this joy and peace and hope, is "inseparably connected with the power of the Holy Spirit in inwardly enlightening the mind, and stimulating it."[4] The Spirit excites, motivates, fuels, accelerates, invigorates the mind of the elect believer which is a direct correlation to the power of the Spirit. The Spirit stimulates the mind when they read the word or apply it. The Bible is a tangible object, and has pages and letters and paragraphs and such but the meaning behind the words is supernatural, spiritual, and divine, stimulated only by the Spirit of God to produce hope, joy and peace in Christ. See all these people all over the world looking to fill up their boring lives by some ecstatic experience they think they can have with God apart from believing the promises of Christ?

    Holy Spirit power is communicated to elect believers in Christ by God. The God of hope is the author of all hope in his people. If the world looks to have hope in something, without the hope of God, it is a false hope, it is a devilish hope. It is not grounded on the truth, it is not grounded on God, it is not grounded in the Spirit, it does not communicate the hope of Christ; much less joy or peace. Any hope that any Christian might receive, or even cultivate in their walk, is worked in them by the power of the Spirit of God himself and communicates to them truths they read about and understand in the bible. The Spirit does not merely zap people with nothing. He helps them *to believe the truth*. In that truth is power to vanquish evil of every kind. Any joy, peace or hope that can be searched out and found in Jesus Christ, is a gift of

---

[4] Calvin, John, *Institutes of the Christian Religion*, Vol. 3, (Edinburgh: The Calvin Translation Society, 1845) 309.

Chapter 8: Empowered by the Spirit

God, a gift of his Spirit, and in it is true power. Man has no ability to conjure up any joy, peace or hope of his own accord because of the fall. All the promises and declarations of Scripture would fail in producing joy and peace in the mind of a sinner, if the supernatural, spiritual and divine Spirit did not stimulate their mind in this. The fall ruins everything. It ruins man. It curses him. It sets him at enmity against the living God. It sends him to hell for all eternity. And all their actual sins, on top of the fall that produces those sins, aggravates the situation to such an extent that God must punish it forever. Sin is a horrible evil. So then, what is this Holy Spirit power? It is the Spirit-given ability to reverse the fall by applying and exercising Christ's work to the soul. If the Christian acquires any hope, joy and peace, such influences should be ascribed altogether to God's work through the word. Any work attributed to the Spirit of God without the word of God attached to it is false. In such things, people are not looking for hope, joy and peace, but some kind of "experience." Christians experience power, but they do it through God's constituted means which is a direct reversal of the fall on them – in this way being conformed to the image of Christ. *That* is spiritual power.

In the fall of man, and by the curse of God, the image of God in man was totally corrupted. God, through Christ, through the Spirit, reverses the fall. He regenerates – that's a reversal of the fall. He baptizes with Christ's work on the redeemed sinner – that's a reversal of the fall. He indwells the soul with his influence towards holiness – that's a reversal of the fall. He enlightens the dark mind – that's a reversal of the fall. He gives them hope, joy and peace through the word to conform the Christian daily to Christ, to mortify sin, to bring life – that's a reversal of the fall. Real power is not charismatic hocus pocus. Real power is not some sideshow slaying in the Spirit and falling down in some ecstatic experience which does not rely on reversing the fall of Adam. Every word, every action, every miracle, everything that Christ did, was a reversal of the fall. Now it would be nice if that reversal was complete and instantaneous in being made perfect upon conversion. It is certainly complete in *promise*, but in degrees in *fulfillment*. It is in degrees, day by day, as the Christian rests on that reversing power over the fall.

  The Christian has *degrees* of filling. With the directive for being filled, this implies that there are degrees of joy and peace in the minds and hearts of Christians. They all have the same Spirit and they are all part of the same reversal of the darkness. Christians all receive Christ the redeemer by the power of the Holy Spirit, who unites us to Christ. But the communication of hope, joy and peace is *relative* to their understanding of the word, their feeding on Christ in all his ordinances, in the power of the Spirit. Some may have a degree of this who do not necessarily *flourish* in it. Others may have a degree that is extensive and the Spirit uses such individuals more extensively as a result. In and of itself, it is a great privilege to be filled with them, but further hope, joy and peace from Christ, is a work of stimulating the mind and exercise one's self in the power of the Spirit. If there are different degrees of hope, joy and peace, is it not very important, then, to pray, as Paul exhorts, to look intensely to the Spirit for the fullest communication of those blessings. In believing and being filled up with any supernatural, spiritual and divine blessings, these are communicated by the Spirit through faith, and in the amount of faith based on what one has and exercises. Does a person have faith as big as a mustard seed? Big or small, to what degree it is in the mind, and so stimulated by the Spirit in a believer, so is their walk, and so is the power of the Spirit present in them to work that reversal of the fall – *that* is the power of the Spirit.

  You should be encouraged to have abundant life in the

power of the Spirit. Are you? Do you operate in the power of the Spirit to see the fall reversed in your life? Did you think power was the *power of a super hero?* These "Spirit-filled" revivals in countries all over the world where thousands of people come to see some charismatic evangelist push people over, or give them a "personal word of prophecy," or some supernatural experience because they are trying to escape, even for a little while, their poverty or their affliction, *is not of God's power.* There is no godly power there. After the fact, the people go back to their adultery. Their lying. Their murder. Their coveting. Their envying, and are not the better for seeing such a display of *showmanship.* Or, they try to live in the light of something that has no power to overcome the fall of man, and this turns to nothing beneficial. "O faithless and perverse generation," (Matt. 17:17). Jesus says such people have no faith; no setting of the self on the word. "An evil and adulterous generation seeketh after a sign; and there shall no sign be given to it, but the sign of the prophet Jonas," (Matt. 12:39). Jesus said no signs will be given but the resurrection. But people all over the world sure do seek after signs. Jesus warns such people. "Not every one that saith unto me, Lord, Lord, shall enter into the kingdom of heaven; but he that doeth the will of my Father which is in heaven. Many will say to me in that day, Lord, Lord, have we not prophesied in thy name? and in thy name have cast out devils? and in thy name done many wonderful works? [*charismatica*] And then will I profess unto them, I never knew you: depart from me, ye that work iniquity," (Matt. 7:21-23). *Law-less-ness* – without the law, without the word, without the power of the Spirit to reverse the fall. No hope, no power because no believing in the truth, no power to cancel out sin.

All born again believers partake of this supernatural, spiritual and divine power. But to what extent? Maybe you thought to yourself, "I never really knew what that was because I always thought it was some kind of zapping experience that I'm not familiar with, or that hasn't happened to me." It's not a zapping, it's a thought-provoking work. How will you have high, thought provoking contemplations about Jesus Christ and how will the Spirit use those thoughts to empower you to reverse the fall in your life? He's given you power. Christ did everything by the power of the Spirit in connection with the word, and he had the Spirit without measure, and he was the living word, and he did all so that you could live in the power of the Spirit every day to reverse that terrible curse. If it were all about some zapping electricity from the fingertips, wouldn't one of the best places for Christ to demonstrate this have been in the wilderness, against the devil? But you are to believe, continue to believe, pray for more belief, pray for more hope, joy and peace in Christ. Jesus was given that Spirit without measure for you, "For he whom God hath sent speaketh the words of God: for God giveth not the Spirit by measure unto him," (John 3:34). And Christ said so many times, "The Scriptures say," "It is written..." God "declares..." "truly, truly..." *etc.* The relationship between Christ's work and your salvation is of chief importance here because Christ, the Spirit and the word are all tied into one. The fundamental idea that the Messiah should be anointed with the Spirit and come in the power of the Spirit was consistent with what the Jews understood in that day. This was the coming of the Son of Man to vanquish the fall; to reverse it. *That is where there is power.*

God is not interested in propagating side show events. He wants to see *the fall reversed in people.* So, Christ works as the Mediator of God's elect (Isaiah 42:1; 1 Peter 1:19-20; John 3:16; 1 Timothy 2:5; John 17:6; Psalm 22:30; Isaiah 53:10; Ephesians 1:4). He at that time had the supernatural power to step beyond the natural order. This is why we call things he did *supernatural.* He could, by the immeasurable power of the

Chapter 8: Empowered by the Spirit

Spirit, change water into wine, or walk on the water if he so desired, raise the dead, heal diseases, and such. Again, every miracle ushered in the fullness of the Kingdom that is "upon you" and "coming" in its fullfilment; a reversal of the fall; it's very overthrow. As Mediator he fulfills the law perfectly, where Adam transgressed that law in the garden. He works all those works, upholds the whole law, everything, perfectly in the Spirit to reverse the effects of the fall, *for you.*

Jesus had so much of the Spirit when he walked on the earth, that he could discernably tell when power had gone out of him. "And a woman having an issue of blood twelve years, which had spent all her living upon physicians, neither could be healed of any, Came behind him, and touched the border of his garment: and immediately her issue of blood stanched. And Jesus said, Who touched me?" (Luke 8:43-45). Imagine living so sensitively in the power of the Spirit to reverse the nature of the fall, to such an immeasurable extent, that when someone else merely touched you, you felt the power leave you. Jesus was not a sinner, holy and perfect, but he was so sensitive to the effects of the fall on others that a mere touch caused that sensitively to be experienced. Jesus lived, walked and worked in the power of the Spirit, so you could live in the power of the Spirit by faith in him, by believing. He wants to see you live in power, in the reversal of the fall in your life.

In this power of Christ, the believer rests on Christ's work by faith, by belief. They believe and rest on the holiness of Christ's manhood (Philippians 2:7; Hebrews 2:14, 16-17, 4:15; Psalm 45:7; John 3:34; see Isaiah 61:1; Luke 4:18; Hebrews 1:8-9). Christ's fulfillment of the Law (Galatians 4:4). His accursed death (Matthew 26:67-68, 27:27-50). His Burial (Mark 15:24, 37; Philippians 2:8). His bondage in the grave for a time (Matthew 27:60; Acts 2:24, 27; 13:29, 37; Romans 6:9). His glorious resurrection (Matthew 27:60; Acts 2:24, 27, 13:29, 37; Romans 6:9). His ascension (Luke 24:39; John 20:25, 27).

His enthronement at the right hand of God (Acts 2:34, 5:31, 7:55; Romans 8:34; Ephesians 1:20). And His current high priestly intercession (Romans 8:34) where he sends his Spirit in power to dwell in the elect believer. The work of the Holy Spirit is extremely important in the fulfillment of the covenant of grace made and completed for you in this way. Christ is not interested in merely allowing you to perform miraculous acts. What good would that do *your eternal salvation?* How would that save you? No, he is looking for a bride without spot or wrinkle who is, to use the phrase loosely, miraculous in their belief, and miraculous in their holiness before him. He wants to see sin vanquished in you. The Spirit gave Christ the body in which to work, by the decree of the Father, and Christ came under the submission of human flesh to accomplish that end for you. Without the work of the Spirit in this way, there would have been no body to fulfill the work given to Christ, nor any spiritual power as enacted by the Holy Spirit. Jesus is said to go out into the wilderness to deal with temptation, "full of the Holy Spirit and power," in that regard.

    Christ conquered the devil by the word, "it is written." And when He returns from the temptation and the devil flees, Christ is said, in Luke 4:14, to return "in the power of the Spirit to Galilee." And as a living fountain he flows out to all his people giving them power in the Spirit through the same word. But there is a catch. Though this flowing from Christ moves in you as a believer, it is not a continual flow apart from his ordained means of grace. Spiritual power is not untied from the word. Reversing the fall is not tied to mere subjective feeling. The ease of walking up on some charismatic stage to be touched by some false prophet to be slain in the Spirit is easy. *You just walk up.* There is no *power* there, it's a show. Christ is not about shows. He is about real spiritual power that can subdue the influences of original sin and wickedness by godly belief, which produces faith, hope and joy and will cultivate love to God. In a world as fallen as this world is, that's where real power lies; that's what Paul was teaching the Roman Christians.

Cultivating spiritual discipline in the Spirit is a work you need to *engage* in. To do anything in the Spirit is to do it in the light and power of the Spirit. You can never do anything in the dark. You must walk in the light (1 John 1:8-9). God is light and in him there is no darkness at all. Light is truth. You partake of the supernatural, spiritual and divine power of the Spirit through being immersed in the truth. To do anything, to pray, to look for hope, to look for joy, to look for peace is all done in the light, which is the word and power (*the stimulus*) of the Spirit. "For God hath not given us the spirit of fear; but of power, and of love, and of a sound mind," (2 Tim. 1:7). Not *a sound feeling*. It is done only by born again *believing*. What can the spirit of unbelief do in a Christian? *O ye of little faith.* "And all things, whatsoever ye shall ask in prayer, believing, ye shall receive," (Matt. 21:22), "and be not faithless, but believing," (John 20:27), "that believing ye might have life through his name," (John 20:31). What kind of life? Eternal life, abundant life, victorious life in the Spirit. "Now the God of hope fill you with all joy and peace in believing, that ye may abound in hope, through the power of the Holy Ghost," (Rom. 15:13). Abound, to exceed in measure. Some hope? Some joy? Some peace? No, no, *abounding hope, joy and peace*. Did you think God would just change your emotions to abound in it without the word just to make you *feel* a certain way? Feelings are very fickle, and they come and go. Belief in the promises is so much different, light years away from just feeling something. Belief can vanquish the fall as one works such belief in trust and hope and joy in Christ.

Do you exceed in measure in Christ in the power of the Spirit believing? Do you see its difficulty and why so many people and so many denominations rely on a subjective experience? It's hard to know and believe and cultivate real joy. It's not hard to walk up on a stage with hands lifted high and fall over. It's not hard to tap into some subjective experience to speak in a babbling tongue, or laugh for a while in the Spirit, as so many today believe. But *hermeneutics* is hard. And that leads to *knowing*. And that leads to *believing*. And that leads to the Spirit's *power* because *only that crushes sin*. And only that leads to hope. And only that leads to joy. For all *that* leads to Christ. Anything else is merely a devilish darkness and deception.

Believing, *faith*, is the way to receive all God's truths into our minds, to know them, and to be stimulated by the Spirit in them, enlightened, so that in our hearts we might hold fast to them; conformed from darkness to light. We are to rest on them for our justification. Rest on them for our eternal salvation. Speak about them to confess and profess them in Christ. And we are to live by them in our whole man, to live the rest of our life in the power of the Spirit so that we may live by faith in the Son of God, who loved us, and gave himself for us (*cf.* 1 Peter 3:22; John 1:11-12; Hab. 2:5; John 17:3; Rom. 10:10; Gal. 2:20).

Living in the power of the Spirit is about believing and acting to reverse the fall in your daily walk. First, sin quenches the power of the Spirit in us; sin is a retreating back to the fall. We should be thoroughly aware that we must fight against breaking the commandments of God and we ought to be at war with bringing reproach on Christ when we sin. We transgress the Law of God, as James comprehensively says, "For whosoever shall keep the whole law, and yet offend in one point, he is guilty of all," (James 2:10). All sin is diametrically opposed to the entirety of God's revealed will. To sin is not living in the power of the Spirit, but rejecting that power; that grieves the Spirit. Scripture repeatedly directs us to mortify (or kill) the deeds of the flesh, not quench the Spirit; that's squelching sanctification. Romans 6:12 says, "Let not sin therefore reign in your mortal body, that ye should obey it in the lusts thereof." We should not allow the carnal delights to rule us, but rather, we ought to kill all of them by the power of the Spirit. Romans 13:14 says, "But put ye on the Lord Jesus Christ, and make not provision for the flesh, to fulfill the lusts thereof." No provision, or instance, should be given to reviving the fall in us.

Secondly, you have to remember who you are and what you are. You do not belong to yourselves, but to Christ, if you are a Christian. 1 Corinthians 6:19-20, "What? know ye not that your body is the temple of the Holy Ghost which is in you, which ye have of God, and ye are not your own? For ye are bought with a price: therefore glorify God in your body, and in your spirit, which are God's." Since we are the tabernacles of the Trinity (yes, the Father, Son, and Spirit all indwell in us as to their affect of holiness in our spirits, John 14:23) we ought to conduct these vessels honorable and in accordance with supreme piety and holiness.

Thirdly, you should be *very* devotional in your life towards God in four ways. First, there should be a constant filling of the mind with the influences of the Spirit through Scripture. Spirit power, abundant life, comes tied to the word. Christopher Love said, "Be skillful in the word of righteousness, and this will be a great means to keep the flesh from prevailing over the Spirit. As Christ did to the devil, so must you do to the devil and *your flesh*. Call with the written word against the work of the devil in your own heart. Be so skillful in the word of God that there may be no temptation to offer itself to you but you may drop an argument out of the word against it."[5] *That's* power.

---

[5] Love, Christopher, *The Works of Christopher Love*, Volume 1, (Morgan, PA: Soli Deo Gloria, 1997) 171.

Secondly, you should besiege heaven with a holy fervor praying without ceasing (1 Thessalonians 5:17). To be filled up abounding with hope, joy and peace is to pray for it. Your prayers should be put to use in praying skillfully in the power of the Spirit. We are even encouraged and commanded, "But ye, beloved, building up yourselves on your most holy faith, praying in the Holy Ghost," (Jude 1:20). We will talk about that later.

Third, you should meditate on the Scriptures and work them into your soul. Psalm 1:2 states, "But his delight is in the law of the LORD; and in his law doth he meditate day and night." What you have read should hang in your minds all day long, and you should feed on it through meditation of the word.

Fourth, Scripture memorization is essential. What may a warrior fight with but his sword? If the power of the Spirit is tied to the word, if the power of the Spirit is tied to hope, joy and peace in Christ, memorize the word. Without having the word on your tongue, wickedness has a better chance of overcoming your thoughts. 2 Corinthians 7:1, "Having therefore these promises, dearly beloved, let us cleanse ourselves from all filthiness of the flesh and spirit, perfecting holiness in the fear of God." Know the promises of God by memory and they will be the sword which decapitates the head of any sin in the spiritual battle for your soul.

All born again believers partake of the supernatural, spiritual, and divine power of the Holy Spirit communicated to them in Jesus Christ by God to reverse the fall.

The next chapter will cover, as annexed to this one, being *led* by the Spirit.

Chapter 9: Led by the Spirit

"For as many as are led by the Spirit of God, they are the sons of God," (Rom. 8:14).

Romans deals with the righteousness of God both in lieu of the fall, and in lieu of God's covenant and saving activity through Christ. The results of salvation, of justification, has certain consequences to believers in contrast to those who remain at enmity with God, and who reap the wages of sin. These believers are in a blessed condition, having been rescued from darkness by the righteousness of Christ, that which is merited by Christ's work, and imputed to believers. As Adam's sin was credited or imputed to the account of all men, so Christ's righteousness is credited or imputed to redeemed believers in the work of the Spirit; there the reversal of the fall is the power of the Spirit that Paul speaks about.

The Spirit applies all the benefits of Christ to believers, and these believers demonstrate a holiness that is no longer merely bound to the Law of God, but in the righteousness of Christ. In 8:13, the apostle places walking contrary to the Spirit as death. "For if ye live after the flesh, ye shall die," (Rom. 8:13). If you do what Adam did in the garden, *dying ye shall die*, yes, *you will die*. Much of what the Apostle Paul is speaking about here revolves around sin and its mortification as a demonstration of justification, not its cause, in those converted to Christ. He has paved the road to election, and the glorification of God by showing off the bride of Christ in the holiness of their new life, their abundant life. "...but if ye through the Spirit do mortify the deeds of the body, ye shall live," (Rom. 8:13b). If one lives after the flesh, the natural man, he will only find death and hell; those are the wages of sin. Condemnation and wrath for the infinite sin or propagating the works of the fall against the prescription of God's nature. If one mortifies the deeds of the body, if they are engaged in mortification of sin, if they live in the power of the Spirit to vanquish the fall and reverse it, they shall live. Putting to death sin, throwing off sin, casting off sin in the way God prescribes, is a demonstration of conversion, and the power of the Spirit.

The drunk can look at his family and see the affects of alcohol on his family, and so stop drinking. But that is not what Paul is speaking about. This is not really casting off sin. This is not really the power of the Spirit to reverse the fall. That is not the way sons and daughters of the most high God see their sin. They look at sin in light of God's truth and Christ's glory.

In verse 14 there is a commentary or conclusion on what verse 13 says, though also a commentary or description of verse 9. "But ye are not in the flesh, but in the Spirit," (Rom. 8:9). "For as many as are led by the Spirit are sons of God." This "sons" is taken for the whole family of God, both sons and daughters. It is a high and most exalted relationship that such people have with the most high God. They are in a relationship where God marks them as sons and daughters. God has enemies. He marks many people as enemies, he marks most people as his enemies. They are carnal, natural men and women who are not led by the Spirit. "For to be carnally minded is death," (Rom. 8:6). They are designated enemies, at enmity with God (verse 6). They are at war with God, and they are in a war with him that they cannot possibly win, though that does not stop them from trying to in their flesh. This commentary or description of these who are sons and daughters have a particular quality about them. They are *led* by the Spirit, meaning, to lead, bring, or even to carry a person.

Chapter 9: Led by the Spirit

Some divines here look to this leading as actually being "acted" by the Spirit, pushed by the Spirit, so to speak. In English, this is more easily rendered *led* or *brought* by the Spirit. Paul is showing, in a rather excited way, that as many as are led by the Spirit are sons of God; which is an exciting statement. The Spirit and his work in the believer is used as a reference point in defining what it means to be a Christian, in fact, sonship itself rests on the Spirit's work in this way. The Spirit applies all of Christ's work and merit to the believer, and without the Spirit, there are no sons nor daughters in this way. In contrast to this Spirit created sonship, is the Jews who thought that sonship was found in the natural man keeping the law. If you are a son or daughter of father Abraham, you keep the law. What they missed, is that because of the fall, no one can keep the law as God so requires. God requires *perfection*. They had certain good intentions, so to speak, but without any ability to do so. So, sonship had to move, at the inauguration of the Covenant of Grace (that's in Genesis 3), from keeping the law, to the Spirit's work in first leading people out of darkness by a spiritual birth, then a leading by illumination to the word of God. And if one believes *that*, they are, like father Abraham, justified by faith, and truly, led by the Spirit as sons and daughters (Rom. 4:2; Gal. 3:8; James 2:21).

The Spirit of God leads sons and daughters to walk in a victorious manner of life to glorify Christ. This leading of the Spirit can be taken biblically in two ways, extraordinary or ordinary. It does not matter which testament one looks in, the work of the Spirit is the same in this way, either extraordinary or ordinary.

Extraordinary leading was worked by the Spirit at certain times and various places with specific people in redemptive history for very precise purposes in God's purpose to unfold his truth of redemption to his church. This was the working of extraordinary miracles, as with Moses. "When Pharaoh shall speak unto you, saying, Shew a miracle for you: then thou shalt say unto Aaron, Take thy rod, and cast it before Pharaoh, and it shall become a serpent," (Exod. 7:9). This was also with Elijah when he called fire from heaven, "And Elijah answered and said to the captain of fifty, If I be a man of God, then let fire come down from heaven, and consume thee and thy fifty. And there came down fire from heaven, and consumed him and his fifty," (2 Kings 1:10). This was as with the Apostles such as Peter, "Then Peter said, Silver and gold have I none; but such as I have give I thee: In the name of Jesus Christ of Nazareth rise up and walk," (Acts 3:6). This is also as it was with extraordinary events, with Jonah and extraordinary circumstances. "Now the LORD had prepared a great fish to swallow up Jonah. And Jonah was in the belly of the fish three days and three nights," (Jonah 1:17). Or as with Philip and the Eunuch, "And when they were come up out of the water, the Spirit of the Lord caught away Philip, that the eunuch saw him no more: and he went on his way rejoicing," (Acts 8:39). Even in 2 Peter 1:21 is seen the *extraordinary* writing and transmission of the Scriptures. "For the prophecy came not in old time by the will of man: but holy men of God spake as they were moved by the Holy Ghost," (2 Peter 1:21). These all can be seen as a form of leading or bringing or carrying of the Spirit. But these are *extraordinary*.

Miracles recorded in Scripture were intended as a mark of divine revelation from the Spirit before the written word, they in turn form part of this revelation. One can read about all of those in the Bible, in their various stages and appearances. They attested to and confirmed the message of the prophets and apostles, even the early demonstration of the Spirit in his miraculous work of translating Philip for the expressed purpose of preaching and explaining the Gospel.

Chapter 9: Led by the Spirit

They are no longer in exercise in the current age of the church. For miracles are extraordinary displays of God's covenant Sovereignty to support the church before the completion of the written word. They were used to display the inauguration of the kingdom of heaven and validate the preaching of religious truth before the completion of the written word. But now the church has the completed canon of the written word. Now, the church is led by the Spirit in ordinary means because they have everything that God desires to say to them in the written word. Now, *God has spoken* in Christ, and in the word.

Ordinary works in redemption are those things which apply to the church in all ages, until the consummation of all things in heaven. Though redemption by Jesus Christ is by no means ordinary in its understanding, for it is a reversal of the fall, it is by way of the progression of redemptive history, the ordinary working and means of the Spirit in leading Christ's church. It is the ordinary means by which the Spirit applies the work of Christ to the church to lead it as Christ so desires.

The first ordinary means of the Spirit's leading is at conversion. John 3:3, the Old Testament idea of being "born again" by the Spirit, from above, which Jesus instructs Nicodemus that he should understand and know such things (verse 10). At the time of regeneration, the Spirit gives birth to an enlightened soul. The soul now has the ability in being illuminated, to understand the Spirit's leading that soul to Christ. This is in fact the place where the Spirit leads, to Christ, by the word. This first ordinary leading is done once. Before, the mind was not led by the Spirit, and it was in fact in rebellion against God. It was hostile to God, at enmity with God, rebelling against God at every turn, with every thought. But the Spirit, in implanting that habit of faith in the soul, now enables the soul to be led by things that the soul previously hated. Now, the world loves sin and wickedness, but anyone converted by the Spirit, through the word, being born from above, they have a new principle in them that causes them to love the word, an causes them to want to love the word. That soul desires, then, to be continually led by the Spirit from even the first motions of the Spirit in the soul. This does not mean they are instantly scholars, but that new powerful principle drives them to hear the voice of the Shepherd so that they can reverse all the ruinous work of the fall that has infected them.

Here, the soul receives all the benefits of the everlasting covenant in Christ by the Spirit. The entirety of the Spiritual Blessing that Christ has so merited by his death and resurrection, and now so lavishes on the soul by way of his word, in his present intercession of sending this powerful Spirit to lead them. Wilhelmus a' Brakel says, "As one would lead an ignorant person along the way he must go, the Holy Spirit leads them in a way which they have not known (Isa. 42:16). He shows them this way, saying, "This is the way, walk ye in it," (Isa. 30:21). He inclines their will, making them willing to walk in this way. He encourages them, repeatedly stirring them up to walk in this way. Time and again he gives new strength. "He giveth power to the faint; and to them that have no might He increaseth strength," (Isa. 40:29). Thus, in His light they travel through darkness."[1]

The second ordinary means of the Spirit's leading is in sanctification, and this is where I will spend some time in the point at hand. What does it mean to be led by the Spirit as sons and daughters? Having been illuminated by the Spirit to the work of Christ and his *Good News* in conversion, the sons and daughters of Christ are guided by him through his Spirit. We have not talked about *walking* in the Spirit yet, but know, that the guidance of the Spirit is given so that sons and

---

[1] à Brakel, Wilhelmus, *The Christian's Reasonable Service*, Vol. 1, (Morgan, PA: Soli Deo Gloria Publications, 1992) 185.

daughters know how to walk in the Spirit, live in the Spirit, to know how they are to live to God. There is power in living to God. There is power there, in the Spirit. There is power in being led by the Spirit to reverse the fall. He is a leading agent in redemption. "For thou art my rock and my fortress; therefore for thy name's sake lead me, and guide me," (Psa. 31:3). "And the LORD shall guide thee continually, and satisfy thy soul in drought, and make fat thy bones: and thou shalt be like a watered garden, and like a spring of water, whose waters fail not," (Isa. 58:11). "Lead me, O LORD, in thy righteousness because of mine enemies; make thy way straight before my face," (Psa. 5:8). Where does he lead or guide them to? The Spirit shines a light on Jesus Christ; he guides them into the work and merit of Christ, and into the everlasting arms of the Father. He does not shine a light on himself, but on Christ. Thomas Jacombe said, "[The Spirit's leading,] all may be reduced to these two things,—truth and holiness."[2] To be led into the truth, to exercise this truth, to see the power of the Spirit in vanquishing the fall, to be made more holy both in killing sin and putting on righteous living pointing to Jesus. "Howbeit when he, the Spirit of truth, is come, he will guide you into all truth: for he shall not speak of himself; but whatsoever he shall hear, that shall he speak: and he will shew you things to come," (John 16:13). "For the fruit of the Spirit is in all goodness and righteousness and truth," (Eph. 5:9). "For if ye live after the flesh, ye shall die: but if ye through the Spirit do mortify the deeds of the body, ye shall live," (Rom. 8:13). Mortification is that road to holiness that Paul was speaking about defined as living to God; killing the fall in people. The whole of the Christian faith can be summed up as living to God, by reversing the fall. Sons and daughters

---

[2] Nichols, James, *Puritan Sermons,* Vol. 3, (Wheaton, IL: Richard Owen Roberts, Publishers, 1981) The Leading of the Holy Spirit Opened, Thomas Jacombe, 593.

are led in such a way as to live to God, to magnify the glory of Christ. By the truth into holiness by the Spirit's leading. How are they guided or led by the Spirit?

The skill of living to God through Christ by the power of the Spirit in victorious living, is not a natural power. This has been pointed out in previous chapters. It is not something that a son or daughter can muster on their own. It is not even something which they can by necessity be taught from the outset, but as being born from above shows, they are *made* by the Spirit to be guided in a very particular manner. Human beings have no power to muster their own strength in this. Those who muster their own strength, as Jeremiah says, are cursed for they trust in themselves instead of being led by the Spirit. Living to God for the glory of Christ in the fall-reversing power of the Spirit is an acquired ability, given by the Spirit. But to direct this newly acquired ability in their spiritual birth, they must have a rule, or standard or objective course to follow. What shall they follow to be led? What will they look to? It cannot be a course that a mere man creates. That would be something of their own making. Nor can it be something which rests on a feeling or subjective idea. Again, that would be of their own making. It would be a leading of themselves. And this will not do.

This leading of the Spirit must be a course that God prescribes, that Christ communicates to the pardoned soul, and that the Spirit facilitates. This rule, this course, is the word of God, or Scripture. The word of God is the rule by which the Spirit leads and guides. God was pleased to reveal himself and to declare his will to his church in truth. "God shall send forth his mercy and his truth," (Psa. 57:3). "Which things also we speak, not in the words which man's wisdom teacheth, but which the Holy Ghost teacheth; comparing spiritual things with spiritual," (1 Cor. 2:13). And in doing this, for the preservation of the church and its comfort, and the propagation of the truth of the Gospel of Christ's everlasting covenant, to commit the truth of God to the written word.

There was a time when the word was not written, and so God many times spoke to our forefathers in diverse ways, as Hebrews said. But the perfect has come, Christ has declared the Father, and Christians have everything that pertains to life and godliness in the Bible, as the Apostle Peter says. It is there they are led to and from, for that leads them to and from Christ. This makes the Holy Scriptures quite necessary to demonstrate the truth of the Gospel, and to uphold all sons and daughters. "All scripture is given by inspiration of God, and is profitable for doctrine, for reproof, for correction, for instruction in righteousness: That the man of God may be perfect, thoroughly furnished unto all good works," (2 Tim. 3:16-17). "Thy word is a lamp unto my feet, and a light unto my path," (Psa. 119:105). Such a light and lamp, and the path that is set down as a course is tied inseparably to the leading of the Spirit.

This kind of biblical leading in and of itself, cancels out, the whole idea of "God spoke to me in a vision" or such things, in this ordinary time of the church. Shall the vision, or dream, or thoughts of such people, such that claim some supernatural feeling, *override* the Bible? They would say certainly it won't and couldn't. Then if that is the case, the church only needs the word of God rightly set down by preaching, and the leading of the Spirit in that word to understand it. They have no need, if they have the word, to have anything else but the word led by the Spirit. That is where Christ is found. He is found nowhere else.

If the words of a so-called prophet here or there are not to be over and above the written word, they are in fact useless. One simply needs to be led by the word. They are to know the word, and rely on it; but they don't like that kind of thinking because that takes authority from them, *specialness from them*, and makes the Christian walk hard; because now it is by knowledge of the word rightly divided. The Spirit always guides by the word, according to the word, for Christ is found not in men's imagination, but in the word rightly divided.

Christ is the Living word. "In the beginning was the word, and the word was with God, and the word was God," (John 1:1). "Let the word of Christ dwell in you richly in all wisdom," (Col. 3:16). That supernatural and divine light is not a subjectively created feeling, but an objectively relatable understanding, that then, further, causes sons and daughters guided by his power to be quite emotional about what they understand to be true, and all that in a good way. People can be emotional, if the word of God is rightly impressing truth on their mind by the Spirit, by all means be guided by the words to an emotional state. Is this not joy? Is this not peace? If they are being led by the Spirit, God uses those truths to make them happy. These are happy, joyful emotions. God created human beings *with* emotions. They are simply to use them rightly. Emotions do not come first, they come after the truth is understood. Such a leading of the Spirit is always by the word in supernatural fall reversing power. Can the Spirit not be powerful in this way to the son or daughter of Christ to reverse the fall in leading them to the truth? They must conform to it. In all his illumination, can such be so ordinary that it lacks power? The corruption of sin must be very great for believers to need supernatural help, by the Spirit to understand it, to be led by it, to overcome the fall. It is the epitome of power, every time they are led by the Spirit.

The Spirit leads inwardly, by a secret motion on the heart attesting to the word. He motions the soul to follow what he impresses on them as true in the word that they have studied. He inclines them, presses them, even, as many of the old preachers used to say, woos them, to bend their wills to his word. A favorite verse on this, sorely neglected I might add, (I don't think I've ever heard a contemporary preacher preach a message on this verse in any Reformed church I've ever attended), "And I will put my spirit within you, and cause you to walk in my statutes, and ye shall keep my judgments, and do them," (Ezek. 36:27). This is the Spirit's leading. He *causes* them *to do* by his powerful Spirit that reverses the fall. But, when the Spirit directs or leads in this way, the Christian is not forced against his will. Sons and daughters do not kick and scream against the Spirit; consider that for a moment. They are pliable to the Spirit's leading because they have been made that way by regeneration and enlightening. "Thy people shall be willing in the day of thy power," (Psa. 110:3). Thomas Manton says of this, "You have a grant, and an offer of mercy from God, and then he inclines and moves his [sons and daughters] [you] to make a right choice."[3] Willing followers of the Lord Jesus are *made willing*, caused to do what the truth says, by the prompting of the Spirit. It is not simply "just all words on a page." There is a vital element of supernatural power that is exercised in them daily. Do Christians, generally speaking, even know it's there?

Sons and daughters yield themselves willingly to be guided by the Spirit towards the divine prescription of everlasting happiness in Christ. Sometimes, it may not be pleasant. "My brethren, count it all joy when ye fall into divers temptations; Knowing this, that the trying of your faith worketh patience," (James 1:2-3). Yet, "For the LORD shall comfort Zion: he will comfort all her waste places; and he will make her wilderness like Eden, and her desert like the garden of the LORD; joy and gladness shall be found therein, thanksgiving, and the voice of melody," (Isa. 51:3). So he leads them into truth, that they may, in power, reverse the fall, and

---

[3] Manton, *Works*, Volume 9, 269.

become more holy.

The Spirit leads them into holiness. This is the direct context of mortification on Romans 8. Mortification, to kill sin. To fight against the fall. To be conformed to Christ. To be like him. To *live to God* like Christ lived. Not to walk in the flesh, not to walk to be approved of God, they are already approved, they are already saved, but they are led and guided by the Spirit. Conformed to Christ, is the end and object of all leading, for that not only glorifies God greatly in the life of a son or daughter, but it brings them happiness, for holiness leads to everlasting happiness. The Spirit of God goes before them and leads them in the way by a demonstration of the truth and prompts them to exercise the truth to be holy. He does so gently, and with grace and comfort, but, with supernatural strength and power. He must lead them against corruption: the world the flesh and the devil are out to pull them off this light of truth and way of holiness. They willingly submit themselves in this to the guidance and leading of the Spirit.

Are you led by the Spirit, or just think you are because you get warm and fuzzy thinking about God? Someone asks you, are you led by the Spirit? How? What do you tell them? I ask that of you now. How do you know if you are led by the Spirit? "I'm giving it my best guess." What? No! You are *commanded* to be led by the Spirit. Can you guess at that? Are you weighing all things by the word of God? This is the same as asking how you might know if you live victoriously in Jesus Christ. Do you do this in every way? Don't merely limit this in some uber-spiritual means. Don't merely place this thought of being led in churchly things, it's far bigger than that. Consider what it means to be led in the *wrong way*.

Most people are feeling and emotionally oriented. They are led by what they feel is right. Those confused on how the Spirit actually leads, will tell you, "yes I'm led by the

Chapter 9: Led by the Spirit

Spirit." You say "how?" They say, "you have to be in tune with the Spirit?" What does *that* mean? "In tune, you have to feel his presence, you have to be connected to him, sensitive to him." What does *that* mean? "You know, feel that spiritual power flowing through you and guiding you." No, I don't know what you mean, what does that *feel* like? They answer, "It's Holy Spirit Power!" But *what does that mean?* They have no idea; they might as well use language from Star Wars about the force; which is really all a Buddhist idea – feel it flowing through you. They are more influenced by George Lucas and Hollywood than Scripture. They don't know how to answer what it is because they don't know what it is, because it is a fabrication of something they subjectively "force" on themselves. They think guessing is leading and leading is guessing in some way. They have nothing in this. Supernatural leading is not a fleshly excitement. It is not goosebumps. Do a search in your bible, use your concordance for the word "goosebumps." It doesn't exist. Do a search on *feeling, feels, feel, feeleth.* They all surround things like feeling the hairy arm of Jacob's deception against his father, or Samson feeling the pillars of the Philistines to push them over. The only place those words apply to this situation is when Paul says they are "past feeling" or in his explanation, they have a seared conscience where he is instructing Timothy on those who are lost (Eph. 4:19). There is no supernatural feeling command in that way; it is foreign to the Bible. There is no supernatural feeling oriented leading of the Spirit in *anything.* There is *always* a supernatural understanding commanded.

You might feel a certain way after you have been led by the Spirit in a certain manner. But you are not led by feeling. You are led by supernatural wisdom. At this point, though, you should be able to answer that question, "are you led by the Spirit," with a *yes or no.* Everything that I've been talking about surrounding Romans 8, lends itself to the answer. You might say, "It tells me *to be* led, but I don't know *if* I am led." What is the Spirit doing in your life? He is there to lead you into all truth, to make you willing to follow it, and to produce in you the fruit of a holy life based on the truth of the Gospel to reverse the fall, in that, there is power and leading. Is that you? There is no living a victorious life in the Spirit without that; but that is being led by the Spirit. Are you so attached to the life-line of the word of God which so clearly presents the work of Christ that you can say you are led by the Spirit? We are naturally backwards in our walk, very slow of heart, lethargic in spiritual things, and fail to do anything that is good. We know that Christ is our all, all we do is because of his principle of life in us. We can do nothing without him. But, when the Spirit's power passes over your mind and moves and motions your heart to do his will to reverse the fall, and when he makes you willing to do it by the word, and you strive to do it, there you find the victorious Christian.

You might say, "I try in this, but I fail." But pray the prayer of Augustine, "Lord command what you will, but grant to me what you command." This is a very good prayer to pray, being stitched to the power of the Spirit and his guidance to walk after the Lord Jesus, focusing on the power of Christ, and being covered by his blood, motioned by the Spirit in supernatural power to vanquish the fall in us.

What can you do to be led by the Spirit? You have to see that the Spirit precisely guides you as God prescribes the course. I cannot tell you this enough: God is never in things he does not prescribe *no matter how sincere you might be*. Many professing Christians think that, and I'm quoting, "praying for an hour," "God will do great things." Where does the word of God say that, as if God can be manipulated by time? That's witchcraft; trying to manipulate God by extended prayer by the mere act of prayer. So, if you pray 59 minutes, well, you missed it? If you prayed 30 minutes, well, you're not even close? Read the prayers of the saints. How impactful has Psalm 23 been? How long is *that?* If they are not praying in the Spirit (whatever *that* means), according to the word, what good will it do them to try and emotionally excite themselves apart from the means by which the Spirit leads? People like this often try to be led by their own feelings; they equate goosebumps with the Spirit. There are no bible verses for this; nothing that rests on manipulation of emotions. "I have taught thee in the way of wisdom; I have led thee in right paths," (Prov. 4:11). Where is that found? It is found in wisdom, *Wisdom crying out for all to hear her.* Is there one example, in all of Scripture, that says, lead me by my emotional state and give me goosebumps to prove it? No, "As many as are led by the Spirit of God, they are the sons of God."

    The idea of sonship gets canceled out when people are led by something other than the Spirit leading by the word. Goosebumps are not a confirmation of the Spirit. The Spirit leads in being born again, leads to make you sons and daughters, then brings forth and produces fruit, motioned by his power, directed by the word; the mind informs the intellect as the Spirit stirs up thoughts about Christ the word. The Spirit stirs up thoughts about the fall, and in such exercises of grace, the fall is reversed to a degree. There is power, and there is leading. Those who are led this way are sons and daughters of the Father. Those who are not, are not. They are not led by the Spirit. You must be led in things that God prescribes. "Oh, but I do Christian things," you say. "Do I have to be so fanatical about the word of God and about the course God has laid out in that way? Isn't everything to some extent graded on a curve?" No. The glory of heaven, your eternal happiness in Christ, your spiritual power against the forces of darkness, against sin, are on the line. "For it is not a vain thing for you; because it is your life," (Deut. 32:47). Do you think about the leading of the Spirit, to be sons or daughters, as that which is your life? You must be willing to be led by God in the things he prescribes. So many people look to complying with the Christian faith to do what *they think* is enough of it. Is this the way the Savior thought?

Imagine if Christ performed only so much, but was not zealous for *all* God's covenantal requirements. What would be left for you to do? If Jesus died only for some of your sins, imagine how terrible that would play out. The Spirit is not about leading sons and daughters to be conformed to Christ's image in some things, things in "part," in partial things, but in *all* things, though, by degrees. The Spirit does not lead you all at once. You would in fact most likely go insane if you knew all your sins, all of them, all at once, in their depth. Your heavenly Father detests all your sins, but he knows you are too fragile as to break a bruised reed or quench a smoking flax. He leads you by degrees. Sanctification is necessarily that way. But if you are not willing to be led by the Spirit, or don't like what the Spirit says in the written word which leads you, or don't bother to commit yourself in the written word to be led, what will that show? Does that show one is a son or daughter of king Jesus? Does it show the initial leading of the Spirit in salvation? Does it show the continued leading of the Spirit into truth and holiness? How are you greater in religion this week than last week? Do you pray for the Spirit to lead you in this?

Maybe all this is a relatively new concept and so you resolve to start praying about it. Our next chapter deals with that, praying not only for the leading of the Spirit, but praying in the Spirit; and what does that mean? Is that all chills and goosebumps too? No, it is not.

And why do *any* of this? The reason, the proper leading of the Spirit *demonstrates* sonship. To be a son or daughter necessarily presses you to demonstrate this grace in your life. But you do it not merely selfishly, to gain more of the

Savior, to be more conformed to him, but as you do all things, you do it for the glory of God. "For thou art my rock and my fortress; therefore for thy name's sake lead me, and guide me," (Psa. 31:3). For God's name sake you do it.

Consider a further dimension of motioning by the Spirit's leading. It is not that the Spirit pinches you to go and open the bible and find out what God has said about whatever the situation you are in might be. But, what you have stored in your head, that has translated down into your heart, and is part of this conforming image of Christ, is what the Spirit also motions and leads you in. It is still by the word, because the word is in your head. But it is a motioning of the Spirit in you, in and by the word, that you do certain duties or avoid certain sins. You used to be a drunk, and you drive past a liquor store. You sense, don't even go into the parking lot. Why? "The earth shall reel to and fro like a drunkard, and shall be removed like a cottage; and the transgression thereof shall be heavy upon it; and it shall fall, and not rise again," (Isa. 24:20). There the Spirit works on your knowledge of excess, and presses you and motions you not even to go in, or near it. You either listen, or you don't. You are either led, or not. You used to be a murderer, a vicious tempered man or woman, and find it so very easy to fly off the handle. You begin having a conversation with someone and a verse about the "spirit of meekness" those "contrite" those "esteeming others better than themselves, comes to mind. It is not by accident you have those thoughts. The Spirit motions you to remember the word and recall what it says as good sons and daughters. This is the motioning of the Spirit. But what if there is nothing up in those little grey cells of your mind? What will he remind you if little or nothing is there? Thomas Jacombe says very astutely on this,

> "So as to act just as he would have you act, to move just as he would have you move, to keep pace with him

step by step in all his holy motions. What Israel did to the cloud,—"At the commandment of the Lord they journeyed, and at the commandment of the Lord they pitched: as long as the cloud abode upon the tabernacle, they rested in their tents. And when the cloud was taken up in the morning, then they journeyed: whether it was by day or by night that the cloud was taken up, they journeyed," (Num. 9:18, 21,)—that we should do to the Holy Spirit, in the exact ordering of all our motions by and according to his guidance. This should be the aim and endeavour of every one of us," ["though, through weakness and infirmity, we cannot actually and universally come up to it."][4]

Then as the Spirit teaches you to follow him and be guided by him to glorify Christ at every turn, so, you desire to more fully do it. Your desire for the word, produces in you a more willing spirit. The more you know, the more you do. The more you do, the more fully you are led by the Spirit. The more you are led, the more power you have, and the more power you have, the more the fall is reversed in you and holiness results. "But my servant Caleb, because he had another spirit with him, and hath followed me fully, him will I bring into the land whereinto he went; and his seed shall possess it," (Num. 14:24). You resolve to say, I will fear God, and eschew evil as Job. I will be led wherever you desire me to go.

Side note: but if you do not follow him, he will motion you less and less until he leaves you to yourself. And what can you do in your own power? Remember, vexing, grieving, resisting the Spirit? Will the Spirit always strive with you in daily sanctification if you continually put him off? What does

---

[4] Ibid, *Puritan Sermons*, Vol. 3, 605–606.

he do? He leads you by the word, and the wise application of that word to your life. He keeps pressing you in a course, and you wisely apply the word to that course. You consider everything that needs to be considered, so that you have a right application of the word to your life. That might be spiritual, or it might be practical. But that is how he leads. What does God need to do to press you to trust him. What does he need to do when people miss apply the word to their life and miss the will of God because they are thinking carnally instead of spiritually?

You've heard the story of the man on the house where God sends him three means of escaping the flooding waters. The man carnally thinks God will save the house. But God sent a helicopter and a couple of boats to save *him*. And he sits there atop the house not paying any mind to the deliverance; he has felt differently, in contrast to what God has objectively shown him. When the word of God isn't applied rightly, or if you are carnally trying to mold into something a thing that God doesn't even want you to consider, you will hinder your sanctification. We have lots of helps for the remedy to this. The word, minister's advice, godly friends, and such. In the midst of counselor's plans are firmly established. So, when they are led, and led rightly, those who are led by the Spirit have a great assurance that they are sons and daughters of God, they are led by him.

The Spirit of God leads sons and daughters to be led in a *victorious* manner of life to glorify Christ, in all things. You are not out for your own glory, but for the glory of Christ. *In all things*. You are led by the Spirit and striving after the Spirit in a desire that God would not be ashamed to be called your God. You see, all these ideas work hand in hand to have a whole overview of how the Spirit works in you as a Christian. All if it is for leading you closer to Christ, and doing his will. You want abundant life in Christ? Understand that the Spirit regenerates you, indwells you, anoints you, illuminates you, fills you, empowers you, leads you ... and as we will see in the next chapter, the Spirit places these in a practical framework of *good works*, the first is *praying in the Spirit*.

Chapter 10: Praying in the Spirit

"But ye, beloved, building up yourselves on your most holy faith, praying in the Holy Ghost," (Jude 1:20).

The letter of Jude is a general epistle concerning the besiege of false doctrine in the church, and the need to overcome it, to stand firm, and fight for the truth. The writer's name, Jude, comes from Judah, possibly Thaddaeus, or typically Judas. His office is written as, "A servant of Jesus Christ," which is in direct relation to his Apostleship; it is the Apostle Jude. "Judas (not Iscariot) said to Him, "Lord, how is it that You will manifest Yourself to us, and not to the world?" Jesus answered and said to him, "If anyone loves Me, he will keep My word; and My Father will love him, and We will come to him and make Our home with him," (John 14:22-23). He is also designated "the brother of James." Again, this is differentiated in Scripture from Judas Iscariot. He is Judas the apostle, the author of this epistle, which the Scriptures describe as an apostle, and in personal relation to James. Matthew 13:55, ""Is not this the carpenter's son? is not his mother called Mary? and his brethren, James, and Joses, and Simon, and Judas?" (*cf.* Mark 6:3). He does not assume some superiority simply because he has some family relationship to the Lord Christ, as a brother. Instead, he submits himself under the apostleship of Christ, by calling James his brother, and himself a servant to the Christ.

This one chapter epistle, a general epistle, is addressed to all believers in the Gospel. Jude speaks against false teachers who had begun to creep into the Christian church propagating dangerous teachings scattering them throughout the church. They attempted to lower Christianity into a merely nominal belief and outward profession of the Gospel. They denied the obligations of personal holiness. They taught their disciples to live in sinful courses, at the same time flattering them with the hope of eternal life. One cannot, though, have it both ways. One cannot be a saint on Sunday and live like the devil the rest of the week. The vile character of these seducers is demonstrated by the apostle. Their sentence is denounced by the apostle. The epistle concludes with warnings, admonitions, and counsels to believers in opposition to them. This is where the 20th verse is found, with a very interesting phrase attached to it.

Verse 20, "But ye, beloved, building up yourselves on your most holy faith," What is the "faith." It can be many things from Scripture. Mere doctrine? "The devils believe," (James 2:19). Fleeting faith? "...who believe for a while and in time of temptation fall away," (Luke 8:13). Justifying faith, which is biblical and relies on the promises of Christ, for salvation and remission of sin by Christ's imputed righteousness. "But to him who does not work but believes on Him who justifies the ungodly, his faith is accounted for righteousness," (Rom. 4:5). There is in Scripture examples of a profession of the faith. "Your faith is spoken of throughout the world," (Rom. 1:8). But, here in Jude it is for the great body of the doctrine of faith, or the whole body of truth to be believed for eternal life and salvation in Jesus Christ. It is the entire body of Christian doctrine believed and given "once delivered," that Christians are to uphold against any heretical doctrine or adversaries that rise up against such truth (verse 3). Jude has already talked about this faith, and explained this faith in contrast to the false doctrine of false teachers. Only this "body of faith" leads to eternal life. Only the entirety of this singular truth delivered once by Christ through the Spirit is the rule of faith. This faith is what is to be believed and applied throughout the history of the Christian church. Jesus

Christ imparts to all believers, all the spiritual blessings that he is filled with, and withholds nothing from his sons and daughters to lead them in the power of the indwelling Spirit, from any that have union with him, in this body of doctrine, which will work in them a reversal of the fall. The faith which had been delivered to the church can be nothing but the system of doctrines contained in divine revelation.

Consider who this faith is given to, "beloved." It is not given to everyone, but to the saints, those *loved of God.* That in and of itself is a most sublime doctrine to consider. Faith given to the loved of God; all those God loves he bestows this body of doctrine to be believed. Such a faith is "entrusted to the saints" like a family heirloom, for they are God's beloved and favorites, the apple of his eye (Deut. 32:10; Zech. 2:8). They, through the bequeathing of the testament of Christ's everlasting covenant, have been singled out to be infected with the faith delivered to the saints, and then, to be infectious to others who may very well be snatched from the fire and saved. They are to build themselves up in this most holy faith. He makes a difference between unholy false teachers he already spoke about previously and those who have the holy faith. This *holy faith* is intrinsically linked to the Holy Spirit, who carried holy men to write down God's holy inspired word. Such beloved people are to participate in construction. *Building themselves up.* They are builders. This faith, which they are to build up in themselves, works holiness in their heart and throughout their life. It is not instantaneously given in its complete perfection in this light, it is to be built up. This argues that it is not fully built and must be built. They are laborers. Christ commended the wisdom of all those that "built his house upon a rock," (Matt. 7:24). He also rebuked those who "built his house upon the sand," (ver. 26). The beloved of God know the difference. And when they are substantiating this building, building it up, of which they are a part, what do they do? One of those things is "praying in the Holy Ghost," (Jude 1:20).

First, consider that prayer is only made to God. It is basic Christian duty to pray to the Almighty God. God alone is to be served by the Spirit endowed and enlightened Christian, because God alone is to be worshipped and served in the capacity that God has set down and required, through the Mediator. There is a certain way or manner of acceptable prayer to God. Jesus said, "After this manner therefore pray ye," (Matt. 6:9). Scripture has specifics in the method. Now, hold that thought, and consider instead, the manner of praying. Prayer is assumed, praying in the Holy Spirit is commanded. Prayer is to be made to God *only* in the Holy Spirit. Praying in the Holy Spirit is not different from praying. There are not regular *prayers*, and then a *special praying in the Spirit*. When the *beloved* pray, when they are built up in this faith of doctrine and truth, they pray in the Spirit, they are commanded to pray in the Spirit. If a Christian prays, he prays in the Spirit according to that manner every time he prays. There is no prayer, ever, outside of the Spirit, that is acceptable to Christ. To pray wrongly, without the Holy Ghost, without praying in the Holy Ghost, is to pray the hypocrite's prayer. As it is the office of Christ to intercede with God for his people, so it's the office of the Spirit to intercede in believers. William Strong said, "The prayers that go up to God, come down from God."[1] What does *that* mean? That is quintessentially what the Apostle Jude is teaching. *Ideally*, it is what he is teaching. *The 1647 Westminster Shorter Catechism* asks in question 98, "What is prayer? Answer. Prayer is an offering up of our desires unto God [a], for things agreeable to his will [b], in the name of Christ [c],

---

[1] Strong, William, *The Saint's Communion with God*, (Crossville, TN: Puritan Publications, 2015) 130.

with confession of our sins [d], and thankful acknowledgement of his mercies. [e] in the power of the Holy Spirit."[2] In the Larger Catechism they ask in question 182, "How doth the Spirit help us to pray? Answer: We not knowing: What to pray for as we ought, the Spirit helps our infirmities, by enabling us to understand both for whom, and: What, and: How prayer is to be made; and by working and quickening in our hearts (although not in all persons, nor at all times, in the same measure those apprehensions, affections, and graces which are requisite for the right performance of that duty." Prayer is done, then, and required, in a very specific manner. It is so specific, that without accomplishing this it is not prayer. Some people may even be alarmed at that. They might think, "I don't know if I've ever prayed if this is the case? I don't know if I have prayed in the Holy Spirit." They are commanded to pray in the Holy Spirit. They are to pray with his help, as he is in them. And they are to pray in the Spirit of Christ, the Spirit of Faith (2 Cor. 4:13). The Spirit intercedes in these Christians to send their prayers to the great High Priest in heaven, with acceptance, "Through Christ we have access by one Spirit unto the Father," (Eph. 2:18). If these Christians listen to Jude, they pray in the Spirit by faith and will not falter in it. They pray in the Spirit, with great confidence that all their prayers will gain victory in Christ; abundant life will result. It is praying "without doubting," (1 Tim. 2:8). It is faith which rests on the word, motioned by the Spirit, sent to the Father, through the Christ, for "Whatsoever ye shall ask the Father in my name, he will give it you," (John 14:13; 16:23). And so it is done also, in his Spirit.

Acceptable prayer can only be made to God in the Holy Spirit and under the blood of Christ. The manner in which Jude sets this very simple statement down is to prove

---

[2] [a]. Psa. 10:17; 62:8; Matt. 7:7-8, [b]. 1 John 5:14, [c]. John 16:23-24, [d]. Psa. 32:5-6; Dan. 9:4-19; 1 John 1:9, [e]. Psa. 103:1-5; 136; Phil. 4:6.

and show that without the Spirit, one cannot pray. There is no praying without the Spirit. Without the Spirit, a person cannot pray. They must be regenerate, or born again. The Sovereign God of the universe is in utter control of all aspects of his universe and immutably wills whatsoever his good pleasure desires to be done. All conceived human beings as a result of the fall in Adam have been totally corrupted in their mind, emotions, will and body, and by this corruption have had Adam's sin imputed to them, called original sin. This original sin is, in and of itself, enough to send this mass of fallen people to hell for all eternity, whereas God would be completely just to do so having to punish sin in a righteous judgment. As a result of this corruption, men's wills are now bound to evil and only free to choose what they desire, which is sin, evil and wickedness in all their actual sins which work out from this original sin. But, God has elected, from eternity, in Jesus Christ, a certain number of people to be his saints, predestinated by his good pleasure, to glorify him in heaven, by nothing they did or could do. The rest of mankind God leaves as a mass of ruin to suffer under his just judgment and glorify him in his justice in hell. God sent his one and only Son into the world to be a sacrifice for the sins of his elect people, and that Christ would be their vicarious sacrifice imputing to them his righteousness and removing from them the damnable curse of their corruption. In this way Christ dies only for those whom he elected to eternal life to eternally secure them in the free gift of his grace. He delivers them out of the world, out of corruption and bondage to sin, and *he* is the Savior. God the Father draws in the sinner through the Gospel, and must regenerate the sinner by the power of the Holy Spirit, the fall reversing power, which is irresistibly enacted on the corrupted soul to change it from a state of wickedness to a state of newness in Christ. This change renders the soul capable of righteous belief, faith, which is also a gift given by

Chapter 10: Praying in the Spirit

God, to the saving of the soul by faith, repentance and to justification by the blood of Christ. Those who are predestined, called, *born gain* [internally regenerated,] have belief by faith, are justified, are then sanctified and receive all the benefits of Christ's work by the power of the Holy Spirit to further their sanctification in reversing the fall, until they reach glory and are made perfect. They persevere in Christ and are preserved by God to be raised up in the last day as the bride of Christ, where there is no possibility of losing their salvation if they have truly received the gift of grace through the power of the Spirit. In this, only believers have this precious gift of Christ, and Christ sends them this gift wrapped in the Holy Spirit. He is the seal of Christ's redemption.[3] What does all this have to do with praying in the Spirit?

The Spirit is the one who enlivens people to pray, "Thy will be done." When they pray, they pray in fall-reversing power of the Spirit every single time they go to the throne of grace. And this is only accomplished in and by the Spirit of Prayer. Those who are unregenerate, lost and in the world, cannot pray as God instructs; their prayers are never acceptable. "The sacrifice of the wicked is an abomination to the LORD: but the prayer of the upright is his delight," (Prov. 15:8). "...even his prayer shall be abomination," (Prov. 28:9). Why is this? It is because they do not have the Spirit, they are not covered by the blood of Christ. It does not matter how many times the wicked pray, prayer is impossible without the Spirit. Publicans and tax collectors may forever go to the temple and pray side by side, but the publican alone left justified (Luke 18:14).

One might say, "what about conversion? Don't wicked sinners pray first in order to be converted, and doesn't God

---

[3] See John 3:1-10, 16; Romans 8-9; Ephesians 1:5, 11, 2:1ff; Prov. 16:4, *etc.*

honor that prayer?" No, and no. The Spirit first changes their heart, regenerates them, indwells them, baptizes them, supplies grace to them, and then they pray because now they pray in the Spirit, now they have the tools to pray, because the Spirit attends those prayers and delivers them to God covered in the blood of Christ's work and merit.[4] Those without the Spirit, in their natural condition in Adam, cannot pray in any way that is pleasing to God. That does not mean God gives them a pass not to pray. They are required to keep the law of God perfectly. It just means that though they are required to fulfill all the stipulations of the covenant of works to God as a fallen sinner, they cannot do it. The wicked really do not call on God, they call on a material hope when they pray. They have no mind to holiness or the glorification of Christ. They think, "I hope that my friend is cured from cancer. I hope that my family is not destroyed by my sin of [fill in the blank]. I hope that God will do something I like for me in my life." That is not praying. No prayer detached from the word of God and from the Spirit's motion in that word, is ever acceptable. It is thievery, because they attempt something bypassing God's ordained means, as if they have the ability to outwit God into doing something they want. How many Christians do that when they pray?

    The lost engage in a kind of devilish trickery even if they do not know they are doing it when they try to pray carnally. If a man is not regenerate, not saved, then, he does not have the Spirit of Prayer. He is a complete stranger to everything that Christ ministers in his work of redemption. And even if he is instructed on how to pray in the Spirit, in Christ, he will not do that. He cannot do it. William Jenkyn said, "The wicked howl upon their beds, not pray in the Spirit;

---

[4] This was Jesus' argument to Nicodemus in John 3.

they may say a prayer, not pray a prayer. They are but like Balaam, into whose mouth God put a word, without any heat of love or zeal in his soul."[5] The converted Christian has the entire spiritual blessing of Christ in them, which includes the Spirit, but, they continually need his motions, fire, strength, and help. Even after a Christian is born again, he still needs the work of the Spirit. What did Jesus say about what Christians can do or not do? "Without me ye can do nothing." And Christ does all things in the Christian by his Spirit. Can the Christian pray without Christ or the Spirit? They cannot, and so, how is it that they are commanded to do this?

How do Christians pray in the Holy Spirit? It is to pray according to his word. As the Spirit teaches Christians to pray, they pray and ask for things according to the will of God. These things are those which Christ said, "Thy will be done." "And this is the confidence that we have in him, that, if we ask any thing according to his will, he heareth us:" (1 John 5:14). What if they pray about things not according to his will? Well, he does not hear them. This is likened to saying he doesn't *honor* that, because it is not according to his word, and his word is what God honors. God always honors his word. Prayer is never contrary to the word, above the word, or beside the word.

Praying according to the word of God, praying in the Spirit, utterly cancels out the abominable practice of speaking in charismatic babbling tongues. That practice is not tied to the word, nor is it tied even to intelligible speech. That kind of foolery is not praying in the Spirit regardless of what anyone wants to call it. Praying in the Spirit is the exact opposite to that act. Babbling is devilish because anything that pulls Christians from the Christ of the word is of the devil. Not even the actual gift of speaking in tongues, speaking

---

[5] Jenkyn, William, *An Exposition Upon the Epistle of Jude*, (Edinburgh: James Nisbet & Co., 1865) 234.

in *a known language*, in the early church, was any kind of this form of babbling in some ecstatic nothingness. "I will pray with the spirit, and I will pray with the understanding also," (1 Cor. 14:15). Want to understand tongues in the early church? Speak in Korean for Korean people by the Spirit's power, and then interpret the Korean language by the power of the Spirit instantaneously for their benefit in the act of preaching during the service to explain the will of God to the people. No apostle *ever* babbled. No Christian, praying in the Spirit, *ever* babbled.

So, when the Christian asks anything according to the will of God, as taught by the Spirit, it is accepted by God as God's will, because it is God's will. Even that which they pray is God's will, because it is God's word applied in some situation. One prays that God would send harvesters out in the harvest. He might even name people in the harvest, knowing that God may send harvesters out to reap them, or that it is only by the Spirit that people are converted. Where does one find what the will of God is? This is why one might pray for the hurricane to dissipate, for it would be horrible for people to be killed in such a disaster, but the prayer is according to *God's will*. This is why "thy will be done"[6] has two applications. In knowing the will of God, and hoping for the will of God. God's will is found in the Bible, and the need for practical applications of it are found there as well. Knowledge of Scripture fuels prayer. The Bible teaches Christians to live life in Christ to the fullest with an eye to looking toward the heavenly Jerusalem, the city made without hands. God says, "Eat, O friends; drink, yea, drink abundantly, O beloved," (Song of Songs 5:1). Drink abundantly from God. "Let your soul delight itself in fatness," (Isa. 55:2), the fatness of the word. And in this, Christians have found a great deal of

---

[6] See Exod. 8:10; Psalm 119:9; Luke 11:2; Matthew 6:10, 26:22.

difficulty in praying without a form or strategy at first, much less having a time of study, or godly contemplation of the word.

When Christians are not used to some type of set form, devotions will seem to become a strange and difficult work to them. Praying will be difficult. Meditating on the word will be difficult. But, strategies are so helpful in this. But the moment such a hard work becomes delightful, they will have a hard time parting with that spiritual and Christ-centered delight. The word fuels those acts. Their prayers must be fueled by the word, and understanding of that word. Prayers are useless unless they are fueled by the word, which is praying in the Spirit. It is no wonder why so many have a difficult time in personal prayer because they do not know, not only how to pray, but what the language of prayer should sound like because they are unfamiliar with the word. If one does not read, study and meditate on the word, prayer will be very hard.

Leading by the Spirit is by the word. Leading by the Spirit *in prayer* is by the word. Consider even the Lord's Prayer would be misunderstood, as Christ directs how Christians are to pray in that prayer, and what petitions there are there, and what they should focus on and apply to themselves, well, how will they do this without understanding what the Lord's Prayer *means?* The fuel of prayer is the word understood. How will they misunderstand the Lord's Prayer, if they are not familiar with the basis of the Lord's Prayer? What is its basis? It is the Psalms rolled up and compiled together. Hold that thought for a moment.

Christians pray in the Spirit also in *the way* they pray. This is not about speaking in unintelligible babbling tongues. It is not in that way, but the way to pray is considered as Christians are stirred by the Spirit to pray according to his will according to his word. They should be praying with importunity. "...praying exceedingly," (1 Thess. 3:10). "Pray without ceasing," (1 Thess. 5:17). Jesus likens his disciples to pray like the widow who went to the unjust judge who granted her petition because she went again and again to him without ceasing *with her petition*; did she babble before the judge? Or, did she bring a well thought out petition before the judge? And if an unjust judge will grant the petition, what will *God* grant to a Christian who prays in the Spirit in line with the word?

Christians should also be praying in the Spirit with watchfulness. "Take ye heed, watch and pray," (Mark 13:33). These are coupled together. Watching puts the Christian on praying. Not, *babble in prayer*. No need to watch anything in *babbling*. "Watch ye and pray, lest ye enter into temptation," (Mark 14:38). It guards even against temptation if prayed rightly. They should be praying in the Spirit with fervency. "Let us lift up our heart with our hands unto God in the heavens," (Lam. 3:41). "The effectual fervent prayer of a righteous man availeth much," (James 5:16). It is made effectual by the word and the Spirit. One of the symbols of the Holy Spirit in Scripture is fire. When the disciples had the Spirit come on them in prayer, he touched their heads, with a tongue of fire, (Acts 2:2). The power of praying and speaking the word, power in the Spirit, from praying in the Spirit. Cold prayers always freeze before they reach heaven. A prayer will only go as far as the person praying it in the Spirit. As zealous as they are, as fervent, is as fervent as their prayers will be. How zealous and fervent, considered in and of itself, is the word? It has the power to divide bone and marrow, soul and spirit if such a thing could be done. And this is the fuel of prayer.

Prayer is described by many things in Scripture all which revolve around words of action: knocking, seeking, striving and wrestling. I love the word "wrestling. "And Jacob was left alone; and there wrestled a man with him until the breaking of the day," (Gen. 32:24). Did you think it was just a wrestling match? A World Wrestling Federation sporting event? Jacob was just rolling around in the dirt wrestling on the ground? What good would be simply rolling around in the dust and mud? "Yea, he had power over the angel, and prevailed: he wept, *and made supplication unto him:* he found him in Bethel, and there he spake with us," (Hos. 12:4). Jacob *wrestled and prayed* to the Angel of the Lord in the dust, wrestled in prayer, with tears. "...that ye strive together (agonize and wrestle with me in your prayers to God for me," (Rom. 15:30). "...yet because of his importunity he will rise and give him as many as he needeth. And I say unto you, Ask, and it shall be given you; seek, and ye shall find; knock, and it shall be opened unto you," (Luke 11:8-9). Wrestling, fervency, striving, agonizing, in praying. What would a sporting event have done merely in wrestling in the dirt for Jacob? And so, the angel touched the socket of Jacob when he was wrestling in supplication all night, and on his knees, and in prayer, and in striving, and in wrestling, where, then, he couldn't hold himself up in prayer being physically encumbered because the mere touch of the Angel of the Lord *wrent* his hip out of place. Why not his nose? Or his arm? Well, I believe, because *the Spirit holds him up in prayer.* Want to wrestle with God well in prayer, the Spirit must hold up the Christian. His own strength will not do, not even in his kneeling, not his own strength.

    How will a Christian know if these prayers are heard? Prayer is an arrow, the point of the arrow is the promises of God, and the feathers of the arrow are the Spirit. He makes it to hit its mark. But, he is also the bow, and the strength and aim behind the bow. He that truly prays, prays *in the Spirit.* Prayer is likened to incense. "Let my prayer be set forth before thee as incense; and the lifting up of my hands as the evening sacrifice," (Psa. 141:2). For incense to rise, what must be done but that it is burned to the precise rule of God's worship; and there must be fire on it. Such should be done with a genuine disposition to bring all requests to God, through Christ in the power of the Spirit; they should be fiery prayers. This means to pray with a pure heart in holiness. The Spirit is designated as "a Spirit of holiness," (Romans 1:4). He is a Spirit of holiness to change Christians and purify them so they will more be conformed into the image of Jesus Christ. Even in public prayer meetings it is said that men everywhere pray, "Lifting up holy hands," (1 Tim. 2:8).

God not only answers prayer, but in essence, through the Spirit, he makes their prayers what they are. God commands that his people pray in the Spirit, and helps them to pray in the duty. He gives them the very ability to perform it.

There are four qualities to consider in praying in the Spirit. First is motion. Christians must be sensible to the motions of the Spirit to prayer and in prayer. When the Spirit motions to prayer, he will give help and strength and guidance in prayer by the word. Everyone "should have an ear to hear what the Spirit says," (Revelation 3:22). This motioning is linked to quenching and grieving the Spirit, which Christians must avoid. When the Spirit says, "this is not the way to holiness," they are to escape it. When the Spirit says "do not do this abominable thing that God hates," they must prevent it. When the Spirit says "this is the way, walk in it," (Isaiah 30:31) they must do what God requires. "If my people, which are called by my name, shall humble themselves, and pray, and seek my face, and turn from their wicked ways; then will I hear from heaven, and will forgive their sin, and will heal their land," (2 Chron. 7:14). Holiness and prayer in this way are linked together. They are motioned to pray by the Spirit in their regular devotional time, in regular Christian services, and yet, there are also times when the Spirit motions them in some frowning providence, or some special need or time of, even, say, revival. "At midnight I will arise, to give thanks unto thee, because of the righteous judgments," (Psalm 119:62). Such an odd time, midnight (??), the breaking forth of the new day; where fresh mercies are new every morning.

Second, help. "Likewise the Spirit also helpeth our infirmities: for we know not what we should pray for as we ought: but the Spirit itself maketh intercession for us with groanings which cannot be uttered," (Rom. 8:26). The word *help* means to lay hold of. The Spirit causes the praying Christian to lay hold of heaven, lay hold of Christ, lay hold of the Father, through the word. By that Spirit they cry Abba Father. "Give heed to me, and answer me; I am restless in my complaint and am surely distracted," (Psa. 55:2). The Spirit helps by pressing the Christian to consider their prayers in light of the word. There is found...

Third, strength. The third is strength in the Spirit. "But ye are not in the flesh, but in the Spirit, if so be that the Spirit of God dwell in you. Now if any man have not the Spirit of Christ, he is none of his," (Rom. 8:9). "...to be strengthened with power through His Spirit," (Eph. 3:16). This is fall reversing power. Prayers that encapsulate this power are prayers that harness the word of God. "In that day shall the LORD of hosts be for a crown of glory, and for a diadem of beauty, unto the residue of his people, and for strength to them," (Isa. 28:5-6). God provides strength in this. That is where strength and power lie.

The fourth is guiding. "And I will pour upon the house of David, and upon the inhabitants of Jerusalem, the spirit of grace and of supplications," (Zech. 12:10). "Praying always with all prayer and supplication in the Spirit, and watching thereunto with all perseverance and supplication for all saints," (Eph. 6:18). "But when He, the Spirit of truth, comes,

He will guide you into all the truth; for He will not speak on His own initiative, but whatever He hears, He will speak; and He will disclose to you what is to come. "He shall glorify Me; for He shall take of Mine, and shall disclose it to you," (John 16:13-14). All this guiding and power and the Spirit-worked motioning is done through the word. Acceptable prayer is only in the Spirit through the word. Acceptable prayer can only be made to God in the Holy Spirit and under the blood of Christ.

Do you practice a present, effectual and continual praying in the Spirit? It must be done at present. Pray without ceasing (verse 17), presently so. 1 Thess. 5:17 is an extremely easy verse since it is only comprised of two words. "Pray incessantly." Relentlessly, persistently, nonstop. It cannot mean that the Thessalonian church was to pray continuously doing nothing other than pray. This would be impossible. One must eat, sleep, hear the word preached, sing, *etc.* What Paul is doing is reproving the general neglect of prayer in the church. Prayer is not negotiable for you. Prayer is not to be sporadic for you. Prayer is like breathing to the congregation, it is to be done incessantly. Praying, this way, incessantly, like breathing, by the word, is in the Holy Ghost. The church is to have a continual attitude toward prayer in unity in the Spirit. It is, in fact, a necessary duty. It is a sanctifying duty. "...nothing is to be refused if it is received with thanksgiving; for it is sanctified by the word of God and prayer," (1 Tim. 4:4-5). This is fall reversing prayer, and fall-reversing power.

It is to be effectual. If one prays to Christ, this is the way of prayer; there are no other means to pray other than in the Spirit through the power of the Spirit, through the power of the Christ, under the blood of Christ, that are acceptable to God. You must pray in the name of Christ even if you used the best expressions and greatest theological thoughts, for without Christ and his Spirit, there is no real praying. There is no sent Spirit to pray without the sender of the Spirit. The Father, Son and Spirit all have a hand in the prayer of the saint if done rightly. To the Father, in the name of the Son, by the power of the Spirit. It also has to be in the Spirit. "The effectual fervent prayer of a righteous man availeth much," (James 5:16), meaning the entreaty of that man prevails. It only prevails in the name of Christ by the power of the Spirit if it is according to the word. You don't pray for a billion dollars to the Father, in the name of Christ, in the power of the Spirit. Or, maybe you do! But is that, realistically, according to the word? To be provided for certainly is. To neither be poor or rich as Proverbs tell us, certainly is; you see there is the prayer, to have what you need. There must be wisdom in the way such prayers are framed. That too, is praying in the Spirit with wisdom.

This praying is to be continual. Praying in the Spirit is cultivated by continual use. It is kept by following the Spirit's motions through the word. His presence is to be cultivated. Every time you pray, you do so knowing you are praying in the Spirit. What can keep the Spirit away when you pray? What you must develop is understanding that he is always there, and you must tap into that power, by using the word. Jenkyn said, "If the Spirit be gone, thy best friend is gone. It was David's prayer, "Take not thy Holy Spirit from me." Without the Spirit, thou art like lockless Samson, as another man; poor, weak Samson, when the Lord was departed!"[7] The Spirit of God teaches you what you are to pray in the word. Do you take advantage of this? He teaches you that it is your responsibility to study the word, to understand the word, and to know what his will is in the word. Sometimes, "We know not what we should pray for as we ought, but the Spirit maketh intercession for the saints, according to the will of

---

[7] Ibid, 344.

God," (Romans 8:27). The Spirit makes those groans to the Father. You don't make those groans. He does. You pray, you strive, you wrestle with a hip out of joint, not able to hold yourself up, you do a poor job of it you think, but the Spirit is interceding with those requests making them all perfect in Christ and his blood so that the Father will accept them because they are the communications of the Spirit to him.

Lastly, the Spirit is the only one that can make prayer sanctifying, and so, he is the only one that you must rely on to make it powerful. He can remove things that hinder you through knowing better how and what you should pray. The Spirit encourages you to pray. The Spirit enables all the work of the Gospel in you so that you can pray well. He makes you humble. He increases your faith to pray in accordance with what God sets down in the word. He makes you to come boldly in Christ for salvation. He makes you patient under the answers that are received, or not, or even in the time of waiting. He is the one who leads you by the hand to Jesus Christ, who is the only Mediator between you and God. You have access to the Father, by the Spirit, and through the Son, (Ephesians 2:18) and all of that according to God's will, from the word. Christ is the only way to the Father, and his work covers all your infirmities and sins to make you acceptable.
You then, rely on Christ's intercession, the sending of the Spirit, and praying according to Christ's will, so God hears you. This, the Spirit practically works in you who believe. This is praying in the Spirit.

The next chapter will be on the practical nature of the *fruit of the Spirit* in our daily walk and life.

Chapter 11:
The Fruit of the Spirit

"But the fruit of the Spirit is love, joy, peace, longsuffering, gentleness, goodness, faith, meekness, temperance: against such there is no law," (Gal. 5:22).

In the epistle to the Galatians, the writer, the Apostle Paul, writes to call the church at Galatia back to the Gospel which they had at the first received from his preaching. In Acts 15:1 there is recorded by Luke, Judaizing trouble at Antioch, "certain men coming down from Judea." Troubled about the meaning of what justification is, they were now looking to go back to the law. What is on the line is the eternal Gospel, heralded by Paul as a result of God's eternal covenant through Christ, the only means of salvation or justification for that matter. It is the unchangeable Gospel of justification by the free grace of God, through faith in Christ by the power of the Spirit. Such a Gospel cannot be had by the works of the Law. It cannot be twisted into a work of the Law. Fallen humanity has no ability to work for abundant life. Fallen humanity cannot live victoriously in the Spirit without the Spirit working this one true Gospel into their lives. Such a Gospel is set in his overarching principle in 1:8-9. "But though we, or an angel from heaven, preach any other Gospel unto you than that which we have preached unto you, let him be accursed. As we said before, so say I now again, If any man preach any other Gospel unto you than that ye have received, let him be accursed," (Gal. 1:8-9). Such are not slapped on the wrist and sent to their room. Preaching a *Gospel of works* will send people to hell. They are eternally accursed. Those who do not receive the faith once delivered to the saints are accursed (I know we have covered this once or twice, but it is eminently important in the grand scheme of this study to keep Gospel content pure and unmixed).

The true Gospel not only saves through Christ alone by faith to justification, but it also produces from that justification a righteous fruit in the lives of those that have been saved (see Paul's arguments in Romans 3-5). It is not merely about what professing Christians say, but much about what professing Christians then do (James 1-2). Justification, then rightly understood, leads to a proper sanctification that produces fruit in contrast to the works of the flesh. Works of the flesh hold all kinds of wickedness in them. But when the Spirit arrests the sinner, and changes the sinner into a son or daughter of the most High God, only then there is spiritual fruit. Good trees, well, they produce good fruit. And what is this fruit? "But the fruit of the Spirit is love, joy, peace, longsuffering, gentleness, goodness, faith, meekness, temperance: against such there is no law," (Gal. 5:22-23).

In standing fast in liberty, Paul explains in verse 1 of this chapter that the Christian is made free by Christ. The freedom of God applied in the Covenant, frees men. And if the Son sets you free, you are free indeed. If one is freed by Christ then retreating back to doing work in the Law for righteousness, for justification, is a distortion of the Gospel; it is no Gospel at all. There is a great difference between legalism, to earn salvation by works, and obedience, to live before Christ in holiness and the sanctifying influences of the Spirit. These concepts are very much muddled in the church today. People think obedience is legalism. But legalism is *working for salvation. Obedience* is doing what the King says to do. Generally, when people do not like the things the king says, they pass it off as legalistic, or simply something they do not care to abide by and in. But it is not legalism at all – that excuse is merely a cloak for their sinfulness.

When people attempt to work their salvation out by

their own means, even if it means like the Judaizers going back to shadows of the old law in ceremony, they reject Christ, and they attempt to shackle themselves again in bondage which they cannot fulfill. Christ becomes of no effect to those working for their salvation. And it is not so much that extravagant means are used, extensive means, to work before God in a certain manner. Paul says in verse 9 that only a little leaven leavens the whole lump. It does not take much to bring forth a different Gospel. A little leaven changes the Gospel to something other than the Gospel. This is why precision in such things is important. This is why the Galatian church ought to be an example to today's Evangelical church. A little error removes the Gospel and curses people. And it is not only doctrinally important, but as with these Galatians, it is practically important. People change in their behavior, in the practical outworking of their faith, if the Gospel they believe, or not, is twisted, warped or changed, or not.

In contrast, to changing the Gospel to go back to the Law, to do things to earn salvation instead of being justified by Christ's work and merit, Paul explains the difference between trying to keep the Law perfectly, or adding even a little to it, to walking in the Spirit. This walking in the Spirit is a direct result of the benefits of being converted through this Gospel. It is a benefit of the intercession of Christ who freely justifies people by his grace. People in Christ are called to liberty in Christ, abundant life, victory in the Spirit, bound by the walk they have in the Spirit, not bound by the yoke of bondage that is impossible to bear in retreating back to the Law for salvation.

Obedience to Christ in the Spirit is in direct opposition to working salvation in one's own strength according to the Law. Trying to walk according to the Law fuels knowledge of the flesh, and the lust of the flesh not being subdued, but stirred, has certain qualities about it; qualities like, "Adultery, fornication, uncleanness, lasciviousness, Idolatry, witchcraft, hatred, variance, emulations, wrath, strife, seditions, heresies, envyings, murders, drunkenness, revellings, and such like: of the which I tell you before, as I have also told you in time past, that they which do such things shall not inherit the kingdom of God," (Gal. 5:19-21). The flesh is stirred up by its original sin, and it births all kinds of wicked actions that disqualify one from entering heaven which aggravate their state. Reveling? Envy? Contention? Excess? People forfeit heaven on such things as these; they do not have to be really big sins, so to speak, in the mind of man. But the walk of the Christian, the one justified by Christ and his free grace, now has a vital life principle in them by the baptism, anointing, unction and indwelling of the Spirit.

As a result of this, the Spirit, through the direction of Jesus Christ, sanctifies the believer by producing in them fruit. All the originating qualities of the believer that tend towards holiness and righteousness come from the Spirit. It is, in fact, his fruit: *the fruit* (*singular use* of the work of the Spirit. All kinds of works of the flesh (plural) are fruits of the wicked. The fruit (singular) of the Spirit are these nine points that all come together in the Spirit's motion in the born-again soul.

These nine fruits are grouped together into three sections. The first, "love, joy, peace, the second, "long-suffering, gentleness, goodness," the third group, "faith, meekness, temperance." The "fruit" of the Spirit is singular. It contrasts the *works*, plural, of wickedness. All the fruit, the nine marks which make up this fruit, come from the fruit, singular, of the Spirit, and are entirely bestowed on all those this Spirit indwells. They are arrested by this Spirit, and they then produce this fruit of the Spirit to some degree. Nathaniel Vincent said, very astutely, in summing up this fruit, "And well may the apostle say, that the "fruit of the spirit is peace

Chapter 11: The Fruit of the Spirit

and joy," (Galatians 5:22) since Christ brings the affections of Christians into captivity."[1] This is in contrast to being captive to the Law; or the works of the flesh. One kind of person is captive to the Law and the flesh. The other is captive to the Gospel and the fruit of the Spirit which comes from the merits and work of Jesus applied to them in redemption. Let's keep this idea simple and just surround our thoughts on the fruit of the Spirit in general.

All spiritual fruit in a justified Christian is produced by the indwelling Spirit as a result of the virtue of Christ's merit. All spiritual fruit in a believer is fashioned and produced by the Spirit. It is all *his* fruit *in* them. Interestingly, the use of the idea of fruit is appealing to the senses. Good fruit tastes good. Good trees bear good fruit. Good fruit has life in it. It gives life. It gives abundant life. Rotten fruit, not so much. It smells. Its rancid. It makes one sick. It cannot be eaten. It is no good for life. The fruit of the Spirit not only presses the Christian to look at the outward performance of some holy duty, but also the inward nature of how that duty will be performed. Fruit is the evidence of the kind of tree that fruit hangs on. It shows whether the tree is a living and good tree, or one that produces bad fruit, which is a bad tree, which will make one sick or even kill them. "...a tree is known by its fruits," (Matthew 12:33). The fruit never makes the tree good or bad, but simply points out the kind of tree it is. This fruit of the Spirit in a Christian is an evidence showing what kind of tree this Christian is to other people. God already knows, but do other people know? Does the Christian himself know? Is there a good judgment given about trees by other trees? That in and of itself is an interesting note. Fruit is sanctifying, but it is also a marker, a non-negotiable marker for other Christians to see. Not only the inward principle comes from

---

[1] Vincent, Nathaniel, *The Day of Grace*, (Coconut Creek, FL. Puritan Publications, 2012) 111.

the Spirit, which exercises these things, but every good work stems from the Spirit.

The Christian exercises himself in the Spirit, in the fruit of the Spirit, by the Spirit. And not only is their vital principle of Spirit-fruit infused into the Christian, but all their acts, in all their exercise, they are all from the Spirit. Every act of faith is from the Spirit. Every act of love is from the Spirit. Every act of every fruit is the fruit of the Spirit. What will the Christian take credit for? What can the Christian take credit for? What kind of a doctrine is it that gives all the glory and all the honor to God, to Christ, to the Spirit? Will the Christian take credit for being humble knowing that everything that they accomplish is the fruit of the Spirit indwelling them? They do the Spirit an injustice if they think they produce that sense of humility in themselves, knowing that Christ produces that fruit of humility in them by his Spirit as well. It is all *his* fruit. People often do not like to think about things like that because it takes all the glory out of it for them. It gives all the glory to God. Eph. 5:9 echoes this in Galatians, "The fruit of the Spirit is in all goodness, and righteousness, and truth." In goodness, in righteousness, in truth, according to the Gospel of Jesus Christ, these three things are all acts of unmerited favor, produced through the supplies of the Spirit in the Christian. Because they are joined to Jesus Christ and his work and his merit, Christians have the covenant blessing of being engrafted into the same root as father Abraham (Romans 11), to produce the same fruit that the Spirit worked in him.

This fruit of the Spirit is a mark of covenant blessings. Ezek. 36:27 says, "I will put my Spirit within you, and cause you to walk in my statutes, and ye shall keep my judgments and do them." God requires as he did with Abraham, to "walk before him and be blameless," and so such walking is by the Spirit, and fashioned in all believers by him for it is his fruit. It is all of free grace in Christ, as a benefit of his merit in the believer due to his justifying them, and further sanctifying them. "If we live in the Spirit, let us also walk in the Spirit," (Gal. 5:25). As a consequence of this engrafting due to Christ's justification of them, to make them righteous in God's eyes and accepted by crediting their account with God with Christ's work, the Spirit makes them fruitful by way of sanctification, in setting them apart for holy service to God. This is the Spirit's job. It is *his* work. "They are Christ's." He purchased them by his blood, delivered them from hell, indwells them by his Spirit and has total dominion and authority over them as his treasured possession. They are in this, communing with him through his Spirit because of what he does to them and in them and for them.

    The Christian has communion with Christ in his merit and by his Spirit. His merit is applied to the Christian by way of being justified, and his Spirit by way of being sanctified. From that communion (that drawing near to him) with Christ, and from that fruit of the Spirit, they serve God acceptably with reverence and godly fear. Listen to this right from the beginning: "God had a respect unto Able, and to his offering," (Genesis 4:8). God respected Abel in his justification, and then his sacrifice in acceptable service. Abel had to be justified for his sacrifice to be acceptable to God. And it was acceptable because he had the Spirit of God dwelling in him to produce such fruits. Abel could not produce that righteous fruit on his own. Now Cain had none of this, and was not accepted by God. Keep in mind, this first commentary by Moses is on the *worship* they offered in service to God. Why? Because any good works are only such as God has commanded in his holy word, and not such as, anything without its warrant, are devised by men out of blind zeal, or upon any pretense of good intention. Earnestness in sincerity to God though idolatry is always idolatry; and it is always hated by God.[2] But the fruit that comes by the Spirit, is always accepted by God because it is God's fruitfulness in the prescribed action. And so Christians have this sanctifying affect, this setting apart in everything they do as a Christian, from the Spirit's application of Christ's work to them and in them and through them. He works all these good works in and for the believer. He does this so that the Spirit's works are *the Spirit's works and also the believer's works* because of Christ. Jesus gives the believer the ability to claim the works in service to God as those of their very own. But they know, all the power and acceptable rendering of that service is due to Christ through the Spirit. John Brinsley said, the believer is "but a reasonable instrument, acted by the Spirit of God and supernatural performances. So these fruits are most properly the fruits of the Spirit and also of the believer."[3] This fruit of the Spirit is the fruit of Christ's work through the Spirit in believers without which they can do nothing. Their ability to do good works is not at all of themselves, but wholly from the Spirit of Christ; but they do good works...but...the Spirit motions those works. And they are bound to stir up the grace that has been begun in them. And that stirring is also made possible by the Spirit. And so, they can do good works, and they do, but they know their ability is of God alone. "I am the vine, ye are the branches: He that abideth in me, and I in him, the same bringeth forth much fruit: for without me ye can do nothing," (John 15:5). Nothing can be done in their own strength. "Cursed is every one that continueth not in all things which are written in the book of the law to do them." (Gal. 3:10). And none can; none can begin them much less continue in them, or even start them successfully without the Spirit.

---

[2] See Hosea 7:8; Ezek. 8, 23-25; Matthew 15.
[3] Brinsley, John. *The Christian's Union, Communion and Conformity to Jesus Christ in His Death and Resurrection*, (Coconut Creek, FL: Puritan Publications, 2015) 85.

Chapter 11: The Fruit of the Spirit

And God says, "Cursed be the man that trusteth in man, and maketh flesh his arm, and whose heart departeth from the LORD," (Jer. 17:5). It must be done through Christ by faith who became a curse on behalf of all his believers. "Christ hath redeemed us from the curse of the law, being made a curse for us," (Gal. 3:13). It is all of his merit and his free grace. Not even the believer's *reflex* act of faith after being born again is of himself without God's help. He is changed, and by a reflex, believes. Even this is of grace by the Spirit. "For by grace are ye saved through faith; and that not of yourselves: it is the gift of God: Not of works, lest any man should boast," (Eph. 2:8-9).

People love to boast, and they like to take God's credit. God will not let them, it is his Spirit's fruit. All spiritual fruit in a justified Christian is produced by the indwelling Spirit as a result of the virtue of Christ's merit. In other words, believers are accepted through Christ, and all their good works produced by the Spirit are also accepted in Christ. They will have said to them on judgment day "well done thou good and faithful servant" and yet they will know their ability is of Christ; their ability is the fruit of the Spirit. Their good works are hardly perfect, but God looks on those works in his Son and he is pleased to accept and reward that which is sincere as they are prescribed by God, although accompanied with many "weaknesses and imperfections," as the 1647 Westminster Confession of Faith says in chapter 16 on *good works*.

There are three departments of spiritual fruit in believers. The Spirit's work in producing spiritual fruit in a believer is divided into three groups by the Apostle Paul. "Love, joy, peace," which concerns the Christian's relationship to Christ and God. "Long-suffering, gentleness, goodness," concerning their relationship to others. "Faith, meekness, temperance," concerning the regulation and conduct of their walking with the Spirit in the Christian life. It would be impossible to work through all these in one chapter, and so we only touch on them briefly, each in their own place, that we might simply see the Spirit's work in these various areas.

The first department is concerning God. The Spirit produces fruit toward God in love, joy and peace. Love is the foundation, joy is the exercise, and peace is the outcome. All these are adoptive relations to Christ; graces given to sons and daughters. They are all graces worked in the Christian by the Spirit; they are his fruit. The fruit of the Spirit further sanctifies the relationship the Christian has with God.

Love to God. To love God, to love Christ, implies conversion, and enlightenment, both of which we have covered in past chapters on the work of the Spirit. One cannot love God without first being converted by the Spirit, and then being enlightened by the Spirit. They even continually experience spiritual persuasion as they continue to read the Scripture and the Spirit impresses this to their hearts that such things are true concerning them. To love God is that he first loved his people in Christ. Love, or, the manifestation of love to God; its outward and practical working. It must be a supreme love, which understands the object it loves. "Thou shalt love the Lord thy God with all thy heart, and with all thy soul, and with all thy mind," (Matt. 22:37). So, love has as its foundation, knowledge, truth, the communication of that truth to the soul. What will it know to love without knowing and assenting and believing by faith certain truths about God and Christ? In this they believe God's love to them in the Gospel is seen as a fruit of the Spirit. Regardless of the outward condition of the Christian, he professes love to Christ and God over all other things in the world. Love is a choosing of Christ and God for the self. It includes, as Thomas Doolittle said, "a voluntary resignation of man's self to Christ," in all things."[4]

Joy in God. The biblical words imply its foundation, love, and its outward expression, "to be excited." Joy is the mark both individually of the believer and corporately of the church. "...ye rejoice with joy unspeakable and full of glory," (1 Peter 1:8). It is a quality as much as it is an emotion, because it is grounded on God, and rejoices because of what God has done in saving them.[5] "Rejoice in the Lord alway: and again I say, Rejoice," (Phil. 4:4). It characterizes the entire Christian life on earth. It anticipates the joy of being with Christ forever in the kingdom of heaven (*cf.* Rev. 19:7). It is not a passing notion. It is cultivated by the Spirit in a believer towards God "that your joy may be full," (1 John 1:4). It is predicated on knowing God. Love or Joy cannot be had with knowing what Christ has done or who God is; and what do these produce?

Peace with God. If one loves God, and has joy in Christ, they cannot but have peace. "The LORD lift up his countenance upon thee, and give thee peace," (Num. 6:26). This looks to harmony, completeness in Christ. It is the Messiah's peace given by his Spirit, his way that leads to salvation, where the soul is set in the tranquil state of assuredness because of Christ's work; they have peace in abundant life. It is based on that justified state. And it is promised in full, and experienced day by day, degree by degree as love to God and joy in Christ is cultivated. Love and joy work peace into the soul. "For the kingdom of God is not meat and drink; but righteousness, and peace, and joy in the Holy Ghost," (Rom. 14:17).

The second department concerns others in long-suffering, gentleness, goodness. The Spirit produces fruit toward others. The fruit of the Spirit further sanctifies the

---

[4] Doolittle, Thomas, *Love to Christ Necessary to Escape the Curse at His Coming*, (Morgan, PA: Soli Deo Gloria, 1997) 26.
[5] Psa. 16:11; Phil. 4:4; Rom. 15:13.

relationship the Christian has with others, long suffering or patience towards others. "But thou, O Lord, art a God full of compassion, and gracious, longsuffering, and plenteous in mercy and truth," (Psa. 86:15). God is longsuffering towards his people and the Christian is to be as well. It's a slowness when people wrong one another. They aren't immediately harsh. They esteem others better than they think of themselves. It houses in it the ability to be steadfast in being patient, which in in turn, in my assessment, is that they must have a godly contentedness generally about them; we have yet to enter into the application but consider, are you generally content? "...longsuffering, forbearing one another in love," (Eph. 4:2). It's a fruit of the Spirit, because its widely known in Christendom, people don't like to do this. Patience is a hard rock to roll uphill for the Christian; that is because they are often not content with life.

Gentleness. This is integrity with one another, kindness toward one another. "Now I Paul myself beseech you by the meekness and gentleness of Christ," (2 Cor. 10:1). "Take My yoke upon you, and learn from Me, for I am gentle and humble in heart; and you shall find rest for your souls," (Matt. 11:29). "Let your moderation be known unto all men," (Phil. 4:5). This gentleness is linked to having compassion, because no one would ever be gentle to others unless they had some kind of compassion towards them. Have you ever heard anyone, ever, preach on gentleness? God's gentleness? "...thy gentleness hath made me great," (Psa. 18:35). The gentleness of Christ?

Goodness. This is uprightness towards another. It is kindness exercised. "And I myself also am persuaded of you, my brethren, that ye also are full of goodness, filled with all knowledge, able also to admonish one another," (Rom. 15:14). "For the fruit of the Spirit is in all goodness and righteousness and truth," (Eph. 5:9). It is goodness to people, righteousness to God. Believing the truth by faith.

The third area concerning themselves is faith, meekness, temperance. The Spirit produces fruit toward themselves. The fruit of the Spirit further sanctifies the relationship the Christian has in both belief and conduct.

Faith or faithfulness. This is not the body of faith, but in the exercise of faith, as Paul outlined in Galatians to the justification of the individual, and the continued belief in the work. Continued service to God through Christ in the power of the Spirit. It surrounds the conviction of truth. Faith in those things to be faithful in. It respects man's relationship to God and divine things, generally with the idea of trust and holy zeal born of faith and joined with it. It leads one to press into the kingdom or to take the kingdom by violence. It is belief with trust (or even the idea of confidence in God and Christ, springing from faith. "For ye are all the children of God by faith in Christ Jesus." (Gal. 3:26). It is to believe in the one who justifies the ungodly, and brings them into a union with himself. "But to him that worketh not, but believeth on him that justifieth the ungodly, his faith is counted for righteousness," (Rom. 4:5).

Meekness. This differs from moral integrity in gentleness, by a mild disposition in one's walk. It moderates anger. It houses a teachable spirit. It removes rashness. Gentleness is towards others, and here, meekness is towards one's walk in general. They are not contentious, they have an air of contentment about them. "Now the man Moses was very meek, above all the men which were upon the face of the earth," (Num. 12:3); afflicted in soul to remain humble. It is to know one's place, to recognize in one's self that they know their place, and consider what the outcome of being another's property is. Being bought with a price, being owned by the King, not being one's own king; cultivates the idea of meekness.

Temperance. This is self-control or the mastery of one's desires. Especially of sensual appetites, but, there is no link to a specific duty here. It's just the idea of being temperate. It is a mastery of life over sin. How about a sermon on that work? "If thou doest well, shalt thou not be accepted? and if thou doest not well, sin lieth at the door. And unto thee shall be his desire, and thou shalt rule over him," (Gen. 4:7). "But I keep under my body, and bring it into subjection," (1 Cor. 9:27). It delivers from all excess, in recreations, in eating and drinking, in fashion and apparel, in passions of the mind, and in those things that respect chastity. It has mixed in it wisdom and sobriety, or simply *temperate.*

All Good works, in this way, towards God, others and concerning the self, are fruits of the Spirit and they all shine a light on Jesus Christ. Good works merit nothing when it is applied or compared to the requirements of justice of God and the work of Christ. Though believers do good works, they do those works by the Spirit's vital principle, and leading. The Christian owes their entire life to God without any possibility of meriting anything before him. Their strength to perform good works is accomplished only in the strength which God imparts to them from day to day. There is no credit that they can claim for them. "For it is God which worketh in you both to will and to do of his good pleasure," (Phil. 2:13). In Christ and him alone is the believer accepted and loved. And it is only through the glasses of his beloved Son that the good works of believers are received though tainted with sin.

Acceptance with God may be illustrated this way: God is like the grandfather who receives the drawing from his grandchild and is exceedingly excited about it. Yes, the coloring of the crayons on the page is severely poor. The grandchild has not kept within the lines, and the page looks like a giant scribbled mess. And yes, God is still pleased with it. But *why* is he pleased? Why does he take such joy at the scribbled mess? Why does he parade the poor attempt and display it for all to see upon the refrigerator? Not because it is a complete and whole masterwork of art. Far from it! But he does this because he loves what he sees. And what is this? The grandchild has brought his grandfather a drawing drawn with the "crayons of the Holy Spirit and blood of Jesus." He has the prescription, the artwork outlined on the page for him to color. He is not doing something he shouldn't. He is not doing something not asked of him. The child is doing their best with the crayons. It is not a master work, but God sees the colors of his Son, and so, it looks to be a master work through those glasses. It is accepted as if it was done by God's Son. Christians give to God work done by the power and motioning of the Spirit of God. They are their crayons. Christ died to give them those crayons, but they are the work of Christ and the power of his resurrection in them. Christians utilize these crayons in their vast array of spiritual colors—love, joy, peace, patience, kindness, *etc*....all these which make up the fruit of the Spirit, and create our best drawing of God in us, and then we hand it to the Father and he is well-pleased. The Father is well pleased in the faint reflections of his son in them, but not with them apart from Christ. Christians are decrepit and wicked, saved only by the merits of Christ. They are *piles of dung covered in gold* as Martin Luther said. Could they add anything to God's pleasure in their weak works? No. Only Christ is pleasing to God; only the reflections of himself. Such good works are the fruits and evidences of a true and lively faith. They are those zealous for good works in the sight of God and of men (Titus 2:14).

  Bringing forth the fruit of the Spirit in your life is an important outward mark of your conversion. Ask yourself, "Do I bring forth fruit?" Is it the fruit which flows from Christ's Spirit? "Even so faith, if it hath not works, is dead, being alone," (James 2:17). Again, "as the body without the spirit is dead, so faith without works is dead also," (verse 26). What is dead faith but dead as to justification and salvation which Paul was arguing for. Some might object, "well, am I a robot? The Spirit just works all these things in me and anything I do doesn't even count?" I ask you, "do you feel like one? Do you *feel* like a robot?" You will answer, no. Then what is the issue? Give glory to God. He works his will through you. They are your works, but they are the Spirit's fruit.

Your good works are not a cause for justification, for justification comes by faith alone in Christ alone. But that faith is not alone. It has annexed to it works; and those works are bubbling up by the stirring of the Spirit. John Brinsley said, "If faith justifies the person, it is works that must justify that faith. James says, "Show me thy faith without works, and I will show thee my faith by my works," (verse 18). The former is impossible, if the latter is infallible."[6] Your obedience in all this to Christ's will and word shows forth a testimony to saving grace. Evidence of a true saving justifying faith are good works which are the fruits of the Spirit. "That ye might walk worthy of the Lord unto all pleasing, being fruitful in every good work, and increasing in the knowledge of God," (Colossians 1:10). ἀξίως τοῦ Κυρίου, *worthy of the Lord*; that is, those who have drawn close to Christ in the assurance of faith. How will you do this? Paul says, then, being fruitful in every good work; being *fruitful* in good works. Plants planted by God, vines attached to the true vine of Christ, bring forth fruit; that they may bring forth fruit, and much fruit, and good fruit. "Ye are his workmanship, created in Christ Jesus unto good works," (Ephesians 2:10). People think that mere church attendance is their good works for the week. No, what Paul speaks about in these 9 qualities of the Spirit's fruit is every minute of every day. Growth should be seen. Does Christ not

---

[6] Ibid, *Union and Communion*, 86.

require this of you by his Spirit? He, "looked that it should bring forth grapes," (Isaiah 5:2). Christ looked at the fig tree that from afar off it looked good as if it should have fruit based on its outward appearance, but upon further investigation, and closer examination it was found to have no fruit on it (Mark 11:13). He *cursed* that tree as you might recall. God's judgments are always hanging over the heads of hypocrites.

The parable of the vineyard, sending forth his servants to gather the fruit of the vineyard, even demands fruitfulness. "And at the season he sent a servant to the husbandmen, that they should give him of the fruit of the vineyard," (Luke 20:10). Even John the Baptist preached to the Pharisees and Sadducees, "bring forth fruits meet (necessary) for repentance," (Matthew 3:8). What happens if there is no fruit? Christ says, "Cut it down, why cumbreth it the ground?" (verse 7). Trees and plants and such that do not bear fruit, they are good for nothing but to be cut down, thrown onto the fire and burned. Not only are they a burden to the earth in their lack of fruit, and stealing away of soil nutrients, but they are cumbersome to God; God sees unfruitful trees as cumbering the ground. "Every branch in me which beareth not fruit, my Father taketh away," (John 15:2).

How shall *your* fruit grow? The easy answer is by the Spirit. "I just need to be connected to the Spirit...I just have to feel the power flowing through me...I just need to be plugged into God...." But the harder answer is, by the Spirit through the word. There is much in the word to consider and learn. Christ never gives us the right to be wrong about his word. A right ordered faith and understanding produces much fruit. When you plant a tree or plant in the garden, it produces only one kind of fruit. Figs, oranges, tomatoes or the like. But Paul lists for you many kinds of fruit, and you are to bear them all, and more. *Fruit*, singular, of the Spirit is to be shown. Even John wrote, "In the midst of the street of it, and on either side of the river, was there the tree of life, which bare twelve manner of fruits, and yielded her fruit every month: and the leaves of the tree were for the healing of the nations," (Rev. 22:2). This is being in Christ, abiding in him; "abide in me, and I in ye. As the branch cannot bear fruit of itself, except it abide in the vine; no more can ye, except ye abide in me," (John 15:4). John says, "he that saith, he abideth in him, ought himself also so to walk, even as he walked," (1 John 2:6). Peter says of the passive obedience of Christ, "he suffered for us, leaving us an example, that we should follow his steps," (1 Peter 2:21). Jesus Christ is our pattern to be imitated. Did he not have the Spirit without measure, and did he not perfectly exemplify the fruit of the Spirit? Consider your fruit, the fruit of the Spirit working through you.

The lost have no fruit of the Spirit. Lost people cannot do *any* good works. If they profess Christ, and do that without the Spirit, they still have nothing. There is no power and life of Christ in them. There is no Spirit working his fruit in them. All they can say for themselves is what the Pharisee said, "God, I thank thee, that I am not as other men are," (Luke 18:11). They might even be free from certain sins, but yet, they have no Spirit of Grace working in them. All the works of holiness and righteousness, works of personal devotion, love, gentleness, temperance and the like, they have no relation to them. They are, instead, fruitful in the works (plural) of the flesh, such as those listed by Paul previous to our verses. "Now the works of the flesh are manifest, which are these, adultery, fornication, uncleanness, lasciviousness, adultery, witchcraft, hatred, variance, emulations, wrath, strife, seditions, heresies, envyings, murder, drunkenness, revelings, and such like," (Galatians 5:19). This is the quality they belong to who do not have the Spirit, for it is the quality of their father, the devil, stemming from original sin. The old Adam, the fruit of a corrupt nature and the foundation of all actual sins. Where a man is justified, filled by the Spirit, engrafted into Jesus Christ, the grace of God which is ministered to him will teach him to "deny ungodliness, and worldly lusts, and to live soberly, and righteously, and godly, in this present world," (Titus 2:12). Again, Brinsley said, "All of us must put ourselves on trial, and pass sentence according to evidence."[7] Why would anyone want to deceive themselves in considering this. It would only be to their eternal detriment. All spiritual fruit in a justified Christian is produced by the indwelling Spirit as a result of the virtue of Christ's merit. Then, the Spirit works through us by his fruit, and some fruit excels, and that fruit is called *gifts*, which we will study in the next chapter.

---

[7] Ibid, *Union and Communion*, 87.

Chapter 12:
Exercising the Gifts of the Spirit

"Now concerning spiritual gifts, brethren, I would not have you ignorant," (1 Cor. 12:1).

In the letter to the Corinthians church, the writer, the Apostle Paul, wrote to this church, of which required a tender and pastoral care having so many difficulties. The church was experiencing all kinds of trauma after his departure. There are a number of special topics that Paul deals with, particular to the body of Christ which strings together the whole letter. Consider first, that Corinth was a wealthy city in Achaia. It had the Aegean Sea on one side, and the Ionian on the other, being an important port city. One can imagine what a sailor's paradise this place would have been, or maybe even at the time, a pirate's paradise. Paul, after teaching there for a year and a half, as Luke mentions in Acts 18:11, 18, left to go to Syria to escape the treacherous Jews. When Paul left, all manner of evil infiltrated the church: wicked doctrines, extravagance, pride, vanity, effeminacy, covetousness, and ambition and the like. Calvin makes note in his commentary on Corinthians that the doctrine in the church so declined after Paul left that discipline in the church became laxed, and that the purity of doctrine had already begun to decline, so that a main article of religion — the resurrection of the dead — was called in question. He says, "The first step towards serving Christ is to lose sight of ourselves, and think only of the Lord's glory and the salvation of men." And this is what Paul desired to instill in this church.

In this letter Paul reproves schisms and factions and listening to ambitious, treacherous false teachers, chapters 1-4. He reproves incest and fornication, chapter 5. He deals with

Chapter 12: Exercising the Gifts of the Spirit

what it means to go to the Law in chapter 6. He disputes about marriage, chapter 7. He speaks about various miscellaneous notes, chapters 8-10. About the sacrament of the Lord's Supper in chapter 11. Then, he discusses the orderliness of the church, and about the right use of spiritual gifts, chapters 12-14. After this he discusses the resurrection, chapter 15, and concludes about financial collections for the saints and miscellaneous matters of salvation, chapter 16.

There is a connection of Corporate Worship that also strings together these ideas. In chapter 12 it is not simply answering a few questions about spiritual gifts. He is dealing with the manner in which the body functions together in worship. Where is Christ's body together? When is Christ's body together? Why is Christ's body together? This answers the need for those gifts, knowing that the entire corporate gathering cannot function without the work of the Spirit in them during worship. There are no Christians allowed to sit back and enjoy the ride. They are all part of the body, and the body must function in a certain manner. Each part is to do its duty before God. In time, certainly, but in duty, assuredly. Once these believers at Corinth come forward with a proclamation of their allegiance to King Jesus, once they as a covenanted body come together to discern the nature of their gifts, then, as Paul instructs, one must covet the greater gifts to do the most good in the body as God so grants.

Many at this point want what they deem the greater gifts like miracles, knowledge, wisdom, even preaching and exhortation as *most* important. Such people want a fantastical gift, some *super hero-like* gift. Paul will explain, the greatest of all the gifts, the greatest exercise of any gift, is always accomplished in the gift of love, or charity; love is a gift, but it is also a fruit of the Spirit (1 Cor. 13; 2 Peter 1:7; Rev. 2:9). There is a greatness to gifts, but there are three which abide in the church militant. Faith in God and Christ, and what a *grand gift* that is. Hope, to be so assured in the hope of Christ, another grand gift. Yet, the exercise of the Spirit's motions in the body of Christ, and the badge of the disciple, love, excels them all.

All those who are indwelt by the Holy Spirit have spiritual gifts, for they are baptized in him, are now considered a spiritual person controlled and influenced by the motions of the Holy Spirit. They are in fact, then, to be useful to the body of Christ with those gifts. They are gifted in a certain way for the good of the body. Every Christian receives the entire spiritual blessing in Christ, and is gifted. Does a Christian need a special outpouring of the Spirit after conversion to have the gift of faith, hope or love? No. There is no such thing. Love is *the greatest spiritual gift, and evidence of being a Christian, and having the Spirit of God.* There is no other eternal evidence of giftedness, or the Spirit's indwelling as it relates to gifts, other than love (love exercised in good works). Love to God and love to one's neighbor. Love to one another. That does not mean they all have the same degree of giftedness, and who knows how the Spirit will then work out faith, hope and love in other lesser gifts.

"Now there are diversities of gifts, but the same Spirit," (1 Cor. 12:4). Διαιρέσεις δὲ χαρισμάτων εἰσίν. The word *diaerasis* means a variety or difference of appointment. The word *charismaton* is a gift or favor freely given by the Spirit. This is particularly, though, as a spiritual gift, in a special sense, distributed to the body of Christ by Christ through the Spirit. Unity in church activity occurs when the Spirit enables a variety of gifts, so that the people can work harmoniously together for the good of the kingdom. Like an orchestra that plays together with various notes, so the church comprised as a whole makes a symphony. The one in charge of dispensing these gifts is Christ, through the power of the Holy Spirit. Regardless of where one finds the church, whether it is in the Old Testament or the New Testament, the same unifying Spirit works in the church to bring about its diversity in spiritual gifts. But *at no time* as the church militant is on earth do they ever do without faith, hope and love.

The office of the Spirit is to apply the blood of Christ to all his people, to convert his people, baptize his people, give them an anointing, unction, power, and enable them with giftedness for their usefulness in Christ's kingdom. He does this upon their regeneration, upon being born again. "But all these worketh that one and the selfsame Spirit, dividing to every man severally as he will," (1 Cor. 12:11). Having dealt with so many divisions in this Corinthian church up to this point, Paul is arguing that the Spirit gives to everyone in the church their giftedness as he wills.

As mentioned a moment ago, this is part of the office of the Spirit, in the economy of salvation, and it is described here in verse 11 by the word ἐνεργεῖ, *worketh*. The Spirit works. He works in such a way as to will a diversity of gifts to different people for different reasons for the good of the body of Christ and the expansion of the Kingdom of God. *Dividing* means distributing to each one as he wills. To will here is to deliberately purpose to do it according to the Spirit's wise use of the gifts in his people; he is the Spirit of wisdom and knows the proper distribution to the proper people. He knows what the body needs, and brings people together to work those gifts in unity and harmony among one another. God does not "spiritually gift" a woman to preach or teach in the church, for that is not her role as Paul explains the pre-creation ordinance of Adam and Eve's union before the fall, that man is the head and the woman is under the man. Nor does he gift a deacon to preach and teach. He does not gift a man to take on a role he does not give the skill to accomplish; or at least the ambition for it. If one desires the office of an elder, for example, that is noble, but desire does not mean that the elder is gifted for that task. They must be tested and evaluated. There is a harmony where the Spirit gives gifts to people in the church to complement the church in all its parts. These professing Christians were brought together to accomplish good works, ordained for them in Christ. They are unable to do anything without Christ, for without him they can "do nothing," as Christ says, (and you have been so reminded throughout these chapters about this point). So they must have the Spirit in them, gifting them, working in them these diverse powers for the good of the body. No one person has all the gifts of the body, as much as people would like the pastors to have that; thinking that religious exercises are for the pastors alone. Pastors have a particular function, and each person in the body has a particular function. This is willed to them, applied by the work of Christ, through the Spirit, for the good of the kingdom of God. The covenant community benefits by the Spirit's work in them as they work with and towards one another in the church for the glory of God.

Allow me a moment to consider a side note on the kinds of gifts the church has for today based on 1 Corinthians 13:13. "Charity never faileth: but whether there be prophecies, they shall fail; whether there be tongues, they shall cease; whether there be knowledge, it shall vanish away. For we know in part, and we prophesy in part. But when that which is perfect is come, then that which is in part shall be done away. When I was a child, I spake as a child, I understood as a child, I thought as a child: but when I became a man, I put away childish things. For now we see through a glass, darkly; but then face to face: now I know in part; but then shall I know even as also I am known. But *[And]* now abideth faith, hope, charity, these three; but the greatest of these is charity," (1 Cor. 13:8-13). Listen to what Paul is saying here. "But now" — "In this present state" in contrast to the extraordinary gifts.

Chapter 12: Exercising the Gifts of the Spirit

Paul uses three examples of the whole of what I'll call temporary extraordinary spiritual gifts. The gifts of "prophecy," "tongues," and "knowledge." These are examples of the whole class of extraordinary but temporary spiritual gifts during the time of establishment of the Christian faith right after the departure of Christ into heaven. All the extraordinary and temporary gifts are listed in both Mark 16:17-18 and 1 Cor. 12:7-11. They are:

casting out demons
speaking new tongues
interpretation of tongues
the power to pick up serpents
immunity to poison
healing the sick
word of wisdom
word of knowledge
special faith
working of miracles
a word of prophecy
the ability to distinguish between spirits

Special extraordinary gifts were given to the Apostles and those ordained by the Apostles at that time.[1] These extraordinary gifts are always connected with the Apostles in the New Testament and the book of Acts. They are even called "signs of the apostles," "and many wonders and signs were done by the apostles." (Acts 2:43). "And by the hands of the apostles were many signs and wonders wrought among the people," (Acts 5:12).[2] And what purpose did they serve in the

---

[1] Acts 2:1-13; 3:1-8; 8:14-17: 9:32-34, 40-41; 10:44-46; 19.6; *etc.*
[2] Compare Matt. 10:1-2; Mark 16:20; Acts 2:43; 14:3; 2 Cor. 12:12; Heb. 2:3-4.

early church? They served to attest the divine authority of the messengers sent from Christ to preach the Gospel in establishing the finality of the Christian faith and truth of the Good News once delivered.[3] The apostles are the foundation of the household of God. "And are built upon the foundation of the apostles and prophets," (Eph. 2:20). This foundation is only set down by them, (Rom. 15:20; 1 Cor. 3:10-12; 2 Tim. 2:19). But those extraordinary gifts, Paul says, *will fail.* They will fail when there are no more apostles, and when the "but when" gifts (verse 13) take over. Fail means to dissolve into inactivity or to be abolished. Those gifts are now abolished. There abide permanently in the place of those extraordinary gifts, three important gifts—faith, hope, and charity. When the end comes, and the church is raptured into heaven for all time, faith will turn to sight, and hope will turn into forever, (Romans 8:24; 2 Cor. 5:7). Those will cease. But love never fails, even in heaven love will continue. But now, Faith, hope and love abide. When do they abide? It cannot be heaven? Only love will abide forever in heaven. Faith and hope will be finished in heaven. The "but now" is now. But now, is the time when the extraordinary gifts of the church have ceased. Only those ordinary gifts surrounding salvation and maturity in Christ are necessary. Faith, hope and love are now necessary, and faith, hope and love are the *badges* of the Christian. The extraordinary gifts are no longer necessary because the church is established and the Apostles are dead. Instead, the church now has the full, inscripturated word placed together at the finality of the canon of the bible to guide them by the Spirit in faith, hope and love. Yet, there are some ordinary gifts which need to be understood.

The Holy Spirit equips every true believer with ordinary spiritual gifts for the good of Christ's church. First, I

---

[3] See John 3:2; 10:25; Matt. 9:6; 14:33; Acts 2:22; 3:11; 5:13; 9:35, 42.

give you an initial notation, there are ordinary saving gifts and extraordinary special gifts. Some people had the extraordinary gifts of the Spirit in the early days of the Apostles and the church, without being saved. Heb. 6:4-6, "For it is impossible for those who were once enlightened, and have tasted of the heavenly gift, and were made partakers of the Holy Ghost, and have tasted the good word of God, and the powers of the world to come, if they shall fall away, to renew them again unto repentance: seeing they crucify to themselves the Son of God afresh, and put him to an open shame." These people had professed Christ, but had no saving influence, (*no* faith, hope and love,) yet they partook of something of the Holy Spirit, and heavenly gifts. Jesus testifies that, "Many will say to me in that day, Lord, Lord, have we not prophesied in thy name? and in thy name have cast out devils? and in thy name done many wonderful works? And then will I profess unto them, I never knew you: depart from me, ye that work iniquity," (Matt. 7:22-23). These lost people had certain extraordinary gifts among the covenanted members of the church, and so exercised them as the Spirit gave them power to do so; charismatic gifts. But they were not baptized by the Spirit in faith, hope and love. Judas, *the son of perdition*,[4] had extraordinary gifts, but did not have faith, hope and love, the ordinary saving gifts. In sending out the 12 Apostles, Mark records, "And they went out [*that included Judas*], and preached that men should repent. And they cast out many devils, and anointed with oil many that were sick, and healed them," (Mark 6:12-13). Judas was a great preacher; he cast out demons, healed people, but did not have a *different* heart. This argues greatly for the work of the visible church comprising both saved and lost in a professed covenant with God. Those who came to Christ, and said, "Lord, Lord, we have

---

[4] John 17:12.

prophesied in thy name, and in thy name have cast out devils," *etc.* Extraordinary gifts don't make a Christian a Christian, or even one that is Spirit filled; grace from Christ and the power of the Spirit makes a Christian militant as they reside in faith, hope and love in the "church militant."[5] Did not Judas himself have a very convincing profession of godliness about him? He followed Christ, left everything like the other disciples for Christ, he preached the same Gospel of Christ, he cast out demons in the name of Christ, he ate and drank with Christ for three years, *and yet Judas was a hypocrite.* But these extraordinary gifts now not only cannot be coveted because they have ceased, but ought not to be coveted since the greatest gifts are those of *faith, hope and love,* those are *saving* gifts, which Judas knew nothing about.   What ought to be coveted is faith, hope and love. These are the gifts continuing "but now" and are enhanced by the Spirit's work among people to gift them according to the ordinary saving gifts that benefit the body.   Second, spiritual giftedness is Trinitarian in nature. "Now there are diversities of gifts, but the same Spirit. And there are differences of administrations, but the same Lord. And there are diversities of operations, but it is the same God which worketh all in all," (1 Cor. 12:4-6). Spiritual gifts must also be understood as coming from the triune God (1 Cor 12:4-6). All three Persons of the Trinity are actively involved in spiritually gifting each believer for ministry in the church.   *The Spirit.* God the Spirit empowers all believers with a variety of different abilities but all by the same method of powerfully working within and through them. These are not natural abilities which can be separated from the Spirit who gives these gifts in his willful choice and diversity. These gifts are enabling abilities (*cf.* 2

---

[5] The *church militant* is the theological term used of the church as it is in the world fighting the world, flesh and devil militantly as Christian soldiers.

Cor 3:4-6) body-enhancing abilities that are a direct result of the Spirit's indwelling and abiding presence (Rom. 8:9-10). They are part of his baptizing and what might be called, his occasional filling for a particular ministry or gift (Acts 4:31). He gives people power in the skills needed to accomplish in the church whatever Christ directs.

The Lord. The name above all names is not Jesus, but "the Lord," the essence and nature of the Christ. Christ is the sovereign Son of Man who dispenses gifts in his church since he has merited these gifts for his church in dying for lost sinners. He does this through sending his Spirit and empowering these newly converted individuals as a result of all his work and merit. In Ephesians 4:7-11 Paul explains how the gifts of grace, received by each believer individually, are given by the exalted and victorious Christ, as a result of his merit and finished work. He is exalted to the right hand of the power of God. All his works, all his spiritual giftedness, flow from this completed perfection. He gives his people these gifts, these benefits, as the King who sovereignly dispenses his rule and reign over his subjects, which are in fact his body, which he is the head, in his church by his Spirit (1 Peter 1:10-12). And think, that such a diversity of gifts, to members of the body, using their skills and abilities for the good of the church, how is such distinguished by the people in the church? How do the people know Christ is gifting them in the church by the Spirit in a certain area? Part of this rests through the ministers and elders he has appointed in his church, who in turn are equipping believers for growth. They build up the body. They must be discerning to see where members in a church fit in and how they might be used. Through these leaders who should be in tune with the work of Christ in his people through the Spirit, demonstrates Christ's governance by the power of the Holy Spirit in recognizing their giftedness. Christ in using his mouthpieces, governs all spiritual gifts within his church; they are not gifted to go off on their own; they reside in the body to benefit the body. This work of Christ the Redeemer, through the Spirit, is a work of his sovereign authority in growing up the church under his headship.

God. God the Father is the sovereign giver who makes each gift effective. Man's capacity to function in the church and God's prerogative to bless them in their gifts, is a direct result of the Father's decreed blessing in Christ, not simply a result of some skill or ability they have apart from God. The Spirit is sent of the Father and the Son. The Father, Son and Spirit are all directly working in the spiritual giftedness of the people to mature the bride of Christ for her wedding day.

Third, spiritual gifts must be distinguished from the gift of the Holy Spirit. Gifts (plural) of the Spirit are not the Galatians fruit (singular) of the Spirit. Every repentant believer who believes on the Lord Jesus Christ alone for salvation, immediately receives the gift of the Holy Spirit when they are regenerated by his power, or born again by him (Romans 8:9-10). "Then Peter said unto them, Repent, and be baptized every one of you in the name of Jesus Christ for the remission of sins, and ye shall receive the gift of the Holy Ghost," (Acts 2:38). "And they of the circumcision which believed were astonished, as many as came with Peter, because that on the Gentiles also was poured out the gift of the Holy Ghost," (Acts 10:45). Spiritual gifts are certainly a Spirit-related function in the church, but they are not the fruit of the Spirit (Gal. 5:22-23) which all believers receive upon their Spirit baptism in regeneration; gifts are a fruit of salvation, but are not classified as the fruit of the Spirit. People may have many *gifts* of the Spirit, but all Christians have *the gift* of the Spirit, the gift of salvation through Christ. Sanctification, being set apart to be more holy, usefulness in Christ's kingdom and church, is different for every believer at various phases of their life. Gifts will be cultivated throughout their life, but their usefulness will depend on the extent the work of the holy Spirit in that gift being used; or if it is used. This will be very different from those who profess they are Christians, say they have gifts, but produce no fruit. When a limb of the vine produces no fruit, it is cut off and thrown into the fire. Producing spiritual fruit is a way that the church considers the truth of a professing Christian. For, "faith without works is dead," (James 2:20).

Equally, usefulness in the church is also a way that the church considers the truthfulness of a profession. Each part bears the mark and work of the Christ, and the Spirit works fruit and gifts in all true believers. Hypocrites, or false professors, will never show forth the fruit worthy of repentance in trusting in the Lord Jesus; and they will have counterfeit gifts, or things they do in their own strength, or by the power of the devil.

Fourth, the Holy Spirit empowers believers with spiritual giftedness in order to build up and mature the body of Christ. Different spiritual gifts are given by the Spirit for different ministry purposes. These in turn are managed for different pursuits in the church. Ephesians 4:11-16 speaks to this very clearly.

> "And he gave some, apostles; and some, prophets; and some, evangelists; and some, pastors and teachers; For the perfecting of the saints, for the work of the ministry, for the edifying of the body of Christ: Till we all come in the unity of the faith, and of the knowledge of the Son of God, unto a perfect man, unto the measure of the stature of the fulness of Christ: That we henceforth be no more children, tossed to and fro, and carried about with every wind of doctrine, by the sleight of men, and cunning craftiness, whereby they

> lie in wait to deceive; But speaking the truth in love, may grow up into him in all things, which is the head, even Christ: From whom the whole body fitly joined together and compacted by that which every joint supplieth, according to the effectual working in the measure of every part, maketh increase of the body unto the edifying of itself in love."

Pastors and elders are given to direct and instruct the church, and this is for perfecting the saints, the ministry which they have in the church. It is to edify the body, or cause the body to be further matured in Christ. The goal is not to be thrown about by bad doctrine, "But speaking the truth in love, may grow up into him in all things, which is the head, even Christ." These Christians have been accepted in the Beloved, in Christ, and receive from him all the spiritual blessings he gives. They are indwelt by the Spirit sent from Christ (Eph. 1:13-14; 2:20-22). They gain a new perspective on life in obedience to King Jesus (Eph. 4:1ff). They are not to grieve the Spirit (Eph. 4:30) and his work in the church. That they might come to be imitators of God as dear children, (5:1-2). But, they are described as those filled with the Spirit (Eph. 5:18) having faith, hope and love as the greatest of gifts. Spiritual gifts, then, are distinguished and pointed out in specific individuals for various tasks in the church. They are then empowered for that service, which in turn leads to practical godliness in edifying the body, and ultimately to reverse the fall in the bride of Christ. They are given for the common good of the body of believers. Even esteeming others better than themselves. They are given gifts to promote unity, and so that all members will mutually care for each other in love, in the truth of love. They build up the church, the body of Christ.

Fifth, the Bible does distinguish between believers who have the Spirit of God, and unbelievers who do not have the Spirit. All true believers, regardless of their time of conversion or present state of spiritual obedience, or weakness, are members of Christ's body and have faith, hope and love. They are all endowed with the Spirit of God and with spiritual gifts. They not only show forth the fruit of the Spirit, but they will exercise the gifts of the Spirit as the Spirit so administers them. Maybe they are an encourager. Maybe they are an exemplary prayer warrior. Maybe they are helpful, or hospitable, or naturally giving. Some elders are gifted to teach Scripture, others are more endowed to biblically counsel, and maybe others are more inclined to work with children. For elders, there are a host of spiritual qualifications that they must all have in a non-negotiable manner, but that does not mean that in a group of elders one might be more gifted in some things, than others. The *Spirit* determines such things.

Real spiritual gifts are given to the church solely on the basis of Christ's righteous merits, and they are housed within the authority of the church. They are not merely for personal use, but exercised under the authority of the church leaders he has appointed to help the body mature. Consider a young fellow who desires the ministry; maybe the Spirit has set this fellow apart with the necessary gifts, but they have not been exercised. Various kinds of work go into not only distinguishing that, but after training and such, placing them in a position where they minister in that capacity must be done with wisdom. It isn't something to be taken lightly. There is direction needed.

Sixth, spiritual gifts are always set in the context of the glory of Christ. "...even so minister the same one to another, as good stewards of the manifold grace of God," (1 Peter 4:10). It does not matter what the Spirit gives a person to do in the church, they are to do everything they do for Christ's glory. He is the focus. They are his benefits, from his work, from his death, from his resurrection, from his ascension, from his exaltation, from his intercession, from his Spirit, from his throne, from his power, from his love, to his people. All eyes are on him in faith, hope and love.

Seventh, all of this spiritual giftedness occurs inside the church. People often say, "I don't like organized religion. I don't go to church but I'm a Christian. I won't join a church but I'm a Christian. I don't want to be a member of the church, but I'm a Christian." *No, no,* Christ doesn't allow for that. John says, "They went out from us, but they were not of us; for if they had been of us, they would no doubt have continued with us: but they went out, that they might be made manifest that they were not all of us," (1 John 2:19). Paul says, "This know also, that in the last days perilous times shall come. For men shall be lovers of their own selves, covetous, boasters, proud, blasphemers, disobedient to parents, unthankful, unholy, without natural affection, *trucebreakers,*" (2 Tim. 3:1-2). A *truce breaker* is what Paul uses as akin to "covenantbreakers," (Rom. 1:31). Such thinking is what the bible calls *apostasy.* How can one love Jesus and not love his church? Jesus came to *die* for his church. "...which he hath purchased with his own blood," (Acts 20:28). He died to save it. He rose from the dead to gift it and equip it and bless it. It is *within* the church that the Spirit is dispensed by Christ, not outside of it. There is *no* salvation outside the church. There are no sacraments outside the church. There are no ordained men to the ministry outside the church. Only robbers and thieves are found there.

Eighth, to neglect using one's gifts, is to sin against both Christ and the body. How can people really be concerned about salvation, about Christ, about godliness, who neglect the use of that which God commands and bestows? If they are not so concerned, then it is evidence that they are not concerned seriously about salvation. They are not really concerned about Christ, about sin, about godliness and such things. If they are not solidly convinced of sin, and neglect the use of these gifts, or prove to be unconcerned about their success in their use of them, it is sure that they have not laid salvation to heart yet. Certainly, the children of the king will be remiss in using spiritual gifts from time to time, but to entirely neglect the means of grace given to them in their exercising gifts in the body is to sin against the body by stealing from them. They do not do what the body needs, and so steals from them. They come to church, think they have done their duty and leave. By neglecting the use of their gifts, they rob Christ of the glory he should receive. Even Judas did more than such people, that hard hearted serpent, went out to preach and heal and cast out demons. What do most people in church do? *They sit in the pew week after week.*[6] Such a neglect of using one's gifts is to be unconcerned about that which the Spirit is very concerned about. It is to grieve and quench the work of the Spirit in the body. It is being unconcerned about Christ's means and manner of salvation.

Christ endows with the Spirit for service to the body. The most Spirit-endowed person that ever walked the face the earth in exercising spiritual gifts was Jesus Christ. He exercised his spiritual gifts in full capacity. To be gifted is to be filled with the Spirit, and Christ, in his incarnation, was filled to capacity, filled even, without measure, where he taught the people not as the scribes and Pharisees, but with power. He demonstrated wisdom, healed, performed miracles like raising the dead, created earthly sustenance in the multiplication of loaves and fish, directed fish in the sea to swim into the nets of his apostles. He walked on the water, cast out demons, and in so many other spiritual ways manifested the realities of the one who is immeasurably anointed by God to fulfill the work of saving his people in the

---

[6] Have they, "turned the world upside down?" (Acts 17:6).

covenant of grace because he alone is the God-man and covenant Mediator. Even from his youngest days, "did you not know I must be about my Father's business?" Though Christ was endowed with the Spirit without measure, every believer is endowed with the Spirit in good measure. In a lesser degree, in just the right measure, Christians are also filled with the Holy Spirit and they too demonstrate the presence and power of the Spirit in their lives "by word and deed," through the power of the Spirit. Christ supplies them of his inexhaustible fountain. "Thou hast ascended on high, thou hast led captivity captive: thou hast received gifts for men," (Psa. 68:18). Christ is the only fountain of saving mercy and spiritual giftedness. Zechariah 13:1, "In that day there shall be a fountain opened." Joel 3:18, "A fountain shall flow from the house of the LORD." Christ is the only Savior...Redeemer...Satisfaction before the face of God, the only one who can bear the wrath of God for sinners and give an inexhaustible fountain of faith, hope and love in gifting his people for service. The only one who can take the debt and do away with it. He is the Lamb, the sacrifice once for all. There is no other name under heaven by which men must be saved. Any other mercies which God bestows upon the sons of men are nothing in comparison to the saving mercy of Jesus. How can they compare? Yet, Christ gives even more than merely salvation. He sends his Holy Spirit to make people more holy by giving them gifts to operate in the midst of the church.

    Christ is such an inexhaustible fountain that sinners cannot ever out desire the mercies and gifts of Jesus Christ. He is an overflowing fountain of infinite mercy and a storehouse of power. Such a storehouse enters into eternity and can never be exhausted. The believer is filled with the Spirit, filled with mercy and grace, filled with power to exercise gifts, filled with fruit and filled with thanksgiving and joy. They are filled, and are directed to be filled daily. "Being filled with the fruits of righteousness," (Phil. 1:11). "...filled with the Spirit," (Eph. 5:18). "...filled with joy, and with the Holy Ghost," (Acts 13:52). It is from the Lord Jesus Christ that this Spirit is to be communicated to believers in order to empower the church. The Spirit is even called "the supply of the Spirit of Jesus Christ," (Phil. 1:19). And what a great supply he gives!

Christ purchased, not only the church, not only the benefits given to the church, but the Spirit was purchased by his blood as well. He is a great benefit bestowed on the believer and dispensed by Christ's crimson hand. All of the beneficial functions produced by his Spirit are attributed to Christ. The Spirit certainly does many things as a result, but the Spirit shines the light of the Gospel of Christ on everything; every work, every good deed.

What is your spiritual gift? If you think to yourself, "I don't have a gift..." that's certainly *not true* if you are a believer. Every believer is endowed by the Spirit with the gift of salvation and gifts of service. Everyone has a gift that flows out of faith, hope and love, which are in fact gifts to you as well. If you think to yourself, "I don't know what my gift is..." that's far better than saying you don't have one. What will you do to find out what that gift is? Will you sit with an elder to consider it? Do you even want to consider it? Those who do not want to consider it, there a difficult problem arises. If they are a Christian, why would they not want to do good in the body. And will you not reap a harvest if you do not give up, as Paul exhorts in Galatians? You must find out what your gift is so that the body of believers can benefit from your selfless actions in working on behalf of their good.

It is called a *Spiritual gift* because the Spirit is needed by you to function in it. It is his gift working through you. It is a privilege for the Spirit to work in and through you for the work he sets you to do. Did you think that the Christian walk was just about hearing sermons and coming to prayer meetings? There is kingdom work to be done. Christ's kingdom is to be expanded and enlarged, and it is so interesting that he does this for his glory, through his Spirit, in you. The church, the people of the church, readers like you, are living stones, built up together in Christ, and set on his foundation. One of the means by which he makes you useful in the church, and communicates grace to you in the assembly of saints, is by the communication of such spiritual gifts. He builds you as stones into a temple for the living God to dwell in. He spiritually unites you into one mystical body, under the Lord Jesus who is the head, by the greatest gifts of faith, hope and love. He gives you gifts and spiritual abilities. Every one of you is a part of the body of Christ, of its essence, by the same quickening of the Spirit of Grace. But each of you are parts to the whole. Who is the eye, the hand, the foot? "...unto every one of us is given grace according to the measure of the gift of Christ," (Eph. 4:7).

What is your motivation in gifts? Maybe you know what your gift is, but you use your gift, not for the glory of God, but for the satisfaction of the work itself in your own heart. Maybe it is some selfish desire. When you use your spiritual gifts, you ought to be thinking, first, that they are to be used for the good and profit of others. The Spirit was given to the church so everyone could profit. Are you to light your candle and put it under a basket? What good would that do? But what if you lit your candle and stood together as a corporate body, what would that unified light do to passersby? Would it not shine so that the collective light might be seen? In speaking of spiritual gifts, Robert Sanderson said, "These graces are of the number of those things that communicate themselves by multiplication, not division, and by diffusion without waste."[7] They should be multiplying,

---

[7] Sanderson, Robert, *The Works of Robert Sanderson*, Volume 2, (London: Oxford University Press, 1854) 102.

being used, being furthered, not being wasted. You ought never to exercise any spiritual gift, or any encouragement, any help, any aid, for the sake of pride or applause to yourself. There is a great amount of selfishness in exercising spiritual gifts. You do it to glorify God, but also to better the body. If the body is bettered, then you, as part of the body are bettered and all of you grow up into maturity. Do you want that, or not? But gifts need certain things. They need discernment, what a gift might be. They need opportunity. I only make note of that. They need prayer to discern God's will, and an emptying of pride.

There are steps to further spiritual gifts in the church. Negatively – they are not accomplished in your own strength. Because you wish something, does not mean God bestows it upon your wish. Simon the sorcerer thought that gifts of God might be purchased with money; we call that Simony as a result (Acts 8). To acquire something in your own work or strength has a flavor of his sin in it. Spiritual gifts can never be purchased with human labor. God is the one that both administers the seed to the sower, and multiplies the seed when it is sown. The seed are his, and the growth is his. Pray about it. "Open thou mine eyes, that I may behold wondrous things out of thy law," (Psa. 119:18). Consider what the word of God says about these gifts, and be open to the Spirit's leading to direct you. That may take much prayer and much time. It may, consequently, take little time because it is at the sovereign disposition of the Spirit. It is his diversity of gifts, and his work nonetheless.

It takes discernment. Like the man on the roof that has the three means of escape from the flood. He was not discerning. Maybe you hope to have certain gifts, but the Lord has other plans. What gifts will God give you? Whatever they are, you will love them ultimately, and be the best at them because the Spirit works them in you. "A man's gift maketh room for him, and bringeth him before great men," (Prov. 18:16). And God never says don't exhaust yourself in the service of the King. He expects your full use, knowing that the work that is done further expands and increases the work of the Kingdom of God. Cultivating enjoyment in using them is part of spiritual giftedness because the Holy Spirit equips every true believer with ordinary spiritual gifts for the good of Christ's church.

One note of warning: beware of spiritual pride in using gifts. Francis Roberts said, "The more gifts, graces and mercies we have from God...the more humble we should be, as being greater debtors to God, and under deeper obligations. But alas, how hard is it to have spiritual gifts: and not to be puffed up?"[8] Spiritual pride and vain-glory, in regard of men's own, or others spiritual gifts whom they admire, is a pitfall. "Knowledge puffeth up."[9] The Corinthians themselves excelled in gifts, and their many ministers excelled in gifts. These people were vainly puffed up against one another, and carnally gloried in various teachers. Paul clears it all up by saying, "who maketh thee to differ from another?" Spiritual pride, and vain-glory of the Corinthians in their own gifts caused divisions in the body. Roberts said further, "Pride makes a man think himself singular; and puts a man upon such singularities of way, that others may think him singular."[10]

I know you would much rather have me expound gift by gift so you can, like a soldier walking into an armory, choose whatever gift might well suit you, or that you might like. Romans 12 teaches about encouragement, giving, leadership, mercy, service, teaching. 1 Corinthians 12 about administration, discernment, helps. Ephesians 4 about

---

[8] Roberts, Francis, *Mystery and Marrow of the Bible*, (London: R.W., 1657) 1180.
[9] 1 Cor. 8:1.
[10] Ibid, 1181.

Chapter 12: Exercising the Gifts of the Spirit

pastoring and teaching. Some other New Testament letters speak about celibacy, hospitality, and even martyrdom. But this was not the purpose of this chapter to go over a list of various possibilities. It was merely to tell you that you do have gifts, that the Spirit gives them to you and that you are to exercise them. The greatest gifts are faith, hope and love. Love will never fail. Exercise your gift in love to others. It may take some time to find out what those are, but they are certainly there stemming out and growing up from faith, hope and love to Christ.

The next chapter will be the final summary of all that we have learned so far, which is, *walking in the Spirit*. All these things, everything we have learned about the abundant life and victorious living in the Spirit is summed up in the phrase, "walking in the Spirit."

Chapter 13: Walking in the Spirit

"If we live in the Spirit, let us also walk in the Spirit," (Gal. 5:25).

By way of reminder to the letter of Paul to Galatia, the apostle writes to call the church at Galatia back to the Gospel which they had at the first received from his preaching. Remember that in Acts 15:1 Judaizing trouble was stirring at Antioch, "certain men coming down from Judea." They were troubling people about the meaning of what justification is, looking to go back to the law instead of the fulfillment of the law in Christ. Looking to do good things to gain justification by works, instead of looking for the declaration of God through Christ about the sinner. Certainly, good works are to be present in the sinner, but not until justification saves them. This doesn't mean that God does not require good works from sinners, he certainly does, but they have no ability to perform them until they are converted because they are fallen. Why then would one walk according to the rule of the law for justification, by works, since they have no ability to actually fulfill them? What is on the line is the eternal Gospel; this was heralded by Paul as a result of God's eternal covenant through Christ, the only means of salvation or justification for that matter. It is the unchangeable Gospel of justification by the free grace of God, through faith in Jesus Christ that brings forth the fruit of the Spirit in contrast to all the fleshly works of darkness. Such a Gospel cannot be had by sinners through returning to the works of the Law. It is not by works, *lest any man should boast*. It cannot be twisted into a work of the Law. Men are unable to do those good works apart from Christ's work in them by his Spirit. Again, such a Gospel is set

Chapter 13: Walking in the Spirit

in his overarching principle in 1:8-9, "But though we, or an angel from heaven, preach any other Gospel unto you than that which we have preached unto you, let him be accursed. As we said before, so say I now again, If any man preach any other Gospel unto you than that ye have received, let him be accursed," (Gal. 1:8-9).

 This Gospel not only saves through Christ alone by faith to justification, but it also produces, from that justified position before God, a righteous fruit in the lives of those that have been saved. It is not merely about what professing Christians say, but much about what professing Christians then do after being saved. What they do stems from what Christ has first done in them. It stems from what Christ gives them and empowers them in the Spirit. They are enlisted in the army of Christ, and are to set forth a standard, a way of living, that follows the fruit of the Spirit, in contrast to their former works of darkness that they worked in their lost condition. This is a great sticking point for a good number of people, because before their conversion, they don't see they were so bad, which argues, they may have not been converted in the first place. The fruit of the Spirit in a Christian is set in direct contrast, opposition, where the Apostle speaks about it as the flesh warring against the Spirit.

 Justification, rightly understood, leads to a proper sanctifying effect that produces fruit in contrast to the works of the flesh. Works of the flesh hold all kinds of wickedness in them. Instead, these Galatians are to walk in the Spirit. "If we live in the Spirit, let us also walk in the Spirit," (Gal. 5:25). Living in the Spirit is demonstrated by not only what one believes, or what one says, but by what one does. It is an exhortation to follow in the steps Christ has laid out in his word through the empowerment of the Spirit of grace. It is not about joining a church to join a club. It is about walking. Walking is part of salvation. Without walking, one cannot be saved. And there is much controversy about that, because people immediately misrepresent salvation, with proven consequences of salvation. If one is saved by grace alone, they will have a faith that is not alone. It will indeed have works. It will indeed walk in a certain way before God. When a person is converted by Christ, and endowed with the blessings and benefits of Christ's work and merit, this is applied to them by the Spirit. This Spirit changes them, baptizes them, enables them to repent, enlightens them, gives them unction and power, illuminates them to the truth of the word of God, equips them in spiritual usefulness, enables them to pray in the Spirit, and to exercise all manner of godliness, which is here translated, live in the Spirit. If they are born again by the Spirit, and all those blessings accompany them, they will in turn live in the Spirit. They no longer live according to the deeds of the flesh. This does not mean they are perfect, but it does mean that the overall desire of that changed Christian is to strive toward perfection. Jesus said, "And that which fell among thorns are they, which, when they have heard, go forth, and are choked with cares and riches and pleasures of this life, and bring no fruit to perfection," (Luke 8:14). He assumes the plants that grow in his garden come forth striving towards the fruit of perfection.

If one surveys historical theology, what people believed through the history of the church and why they believed it, they would find that this little phrase, "live" is very useful in understanding what God requires of the Christian. William Ames said, "Theology is doctrine or teaching of living to God." Peter van Mastricht further edits this and said, "Theology is doctrine or teaching of living to God through Christ." In expounding this I will take this one step further. "Theology is doctrine or teaching of living to God through Christ in the power of walking in the Spirit." Paul says, if one lives in this way, then, there should be a certain outcome; with

Chapter 13: Walking in the Spirit

a certain godly perspective. If we live in the Spirit, *i.e.* changed by him, baptized, enlightened, given unction and power and illumination, to the truth, equipped with spiritual gifts, then, we also should walk in the Spirit. Now this term walk, στοιχῶμεν (Gal. 5:25), is not merely walk, (there is another Greek word for that elsewhere), but this word means *walk orderly, or march*; it is used as a military term. As a good soldier in Jesus Christ, Paul says that Christ has given his people marching orders. If they profess to live in the Spirit, if they have been born again, and all the benefits of King Jesus have been given to them, then they will walk in the Spirit. They will march with those orders from the King into spiritual battle daily. Such talk, daily spiritual battles, walking in the Spirit, these are foreign to those who do not live in the Spirit. These Galatians are not only to march, but they will walk orderly, following the steps laid out by the Spirit for their good. This kind of walking contrasts those works of the flesh, by living in the Spirit, and being fruitful, following the marching order of Christ by the Spirit, found in Scripture. It is, in fact, a term that denotes *discipleship*. Being a good disciple under the authority of Christ, is to be led by Christ, through the Spirit, to conform to him in character and conduct.

Also make note, that this, marching in order for king Jesus, is in contrast to verse 26, "Let us not be desirous of vain glory, provoking one another, envying one another," (Gal. 5:26). In contrast to pride of all kinds, Christians walk in the Spirit. They are gifted by the Spirit not to render pride or selfishness in their work in the church, but in living to God through Christ in the Spirit, they put to death the deeds of the flesh, and instead of vain glory, or provoking, or envying or any other relational sin in the body, they all walk in the Spirit together.

Walking in the power of the Spirit is the duty of every

Christian who is living to God through Christ. The Bible is filled to the brim with a theology of walking. What exactly does walking with God or walking in the Spirit mean?

The idea of "walking with God" is mentioned in various ways and in various scriptures over 200 times. This is no small amount. God places his covenant promises to his people in the midst of walking with him through Christ in the power of the Spirit. That is where one finds all the promises of the Christ as yes and amen for them. From the very beginning of time, people walked with God. Walking with God in a positive way was synonymous with being in a saving relationship with him. To walk against God was to be at enmity with him. In the garden of Eden, Adam communed with God as God walked in the garden with him, and when the fall occurred, that relationship was torn asunder. "And they heard the sound of the LORD God walking in the garden in the cool of the day," (Gen. 3:8). But they went hiding due to their fall. Their communion of walking with God was disrupted by sin.

Various members of the church throughout the ages were said to walk with God. "Enoch walked with God three hundred years," (Gen. 5:22). "Noah walked with God," (Gen. 6:9). Abraham was commanded by God in this theology of walking, by engaging Abraham in covenant with him. "I am Almighty God; walk before Me and be blameless," (Gen. 17:1). God continually tried his people as to, "whether they will walk in My law or not," (Exod. 16:4). Material blessings were even attached to this walking. "If you walk in My statutes and keep My commandments, and perform them, then I will give you rain in its season, the land shall yield its produce, and the trees of the field shall yield their fruit," (Lev. 26:3-4). Disobedience to God's commands brought cursing. "Then, if you walk contrary to Me, and are not willing to obey Me, I will bring on you seven times more plagues, according to your sins," (Lev. 26:21).

In contrast to false worship, God required the people to follow his word and walk in accordance with his commandments at all times as they were to fear him with a godly fear. "You shall walk after the LORD your God and fear Him, and keep His commandments and obey His voice, and you shall serve Him and hold fast to Him," (Deut. 13:4).

In difficult circumstances, or frowning providences, or even danger, the Christian is required to walk with God. "Yea, though I walk through the valley of the shadow of death, I will fear no evil; For You are with me; Your rod and Your staff, they comfort me," (Psa. 23:4). Those who walk with God walk in the truth of his word. "Teach me Your way, O LORD; I will walk in Your truth," (Psa. 86:11).

The prophets are filled with godly examples of walking in the right way, whether with God, or with others according to truth. "Can two walk together, unless they are agreed?" (Amos 3:3).

Now, as the Old Testament is filled with myriads of verses on this topic of walking, the New Testament is equally clear that walking with God in the Spirit is a duty. Those who walk contrary to God walk in darkness, and those who walk in the truth of Christ, walk in the light. "Then Jesus spoke to them again, saying, "I am the light of the world. He who follows Me shall not walk in darkness, but have the light of life," (John 8:12).

Proper walking is walking in the opposite direction of sin and wickedness. "Let us walk properly, as in the day, not in revelry and drunkenness, not in lewdness and lust, not in strife and envy," (Rom. 13:13).

Walking with God is done by faith. "For we walk by faith, not by sight," (2 Cor. 5:7). Walking by faith is walking by a higher level and in a higher plane of heavenly conversation. "Walk in the Spirit, and you shall not fulfill the lust of the flesh," (Gal. 5:16). Walking with God is walking according to the Spirit, and so we have our verse. "If we live in the Spirit, let us also walk in the Spirit," (Gal. 5:25).

There is a great worthiness in walking with God in the Spirit according to the example of Christ, to increase in holiness. "...that you may walk worthy of the Lord, fully pleasing Him, being fruitful in every good work and increasing in the knowledge of God," (Col. 1:10). Walking in the Spirit is walking in the light, and it is a means of fellowship with God, and with the saints. "But if we walk in the light as He is in the light, we have fellowship with one another, and the blood of Jesus Christ His Son cleanses us from all sin," (1 John 1:7). Walking in the light means Christians have fellowship with God by the blood of Christ. If Christians say they love God, if they live to God, then they walk in the Spirit and walk with God, according to his commandments, and his word.

What is love to God in this way? People *say* they love God? "This is love, that we walk according to His commandments," (2 John 1:6). Even ministers have no greater joy than to know that their people are walking with God, in Christ, according to the truth, in the power of the Spirit. "I have no greater joy than to hear that my children walk in truth," (3 John 1:4). Such people are imitating God, and acting as children of God who walk with God and imitate Christ in their walk. "Therefore be imitators of God as dear children. And walk in love, as Christ also has loved us and given Himself for us, an offering and a sacrifice to God for a sweet-smelling aroma," (Eph. 5:1-2).

The Bible is filled with a theology of walking in the Spirit and with God. It is a supernatural and eminently important topic. It is the great excellency and commendation of a godly person to walk with God. It is the highest testimony that God gives a person in Scripture that they walk with him in the Spirit. The duty is a reward in and of itself because walking in the Spirit, is *walking in the Spirit;* is that not an amazing thing? One does not wish to walk outside of the Spirit. To walk in that way is to walk according to the flesh. Such wages of the flesh are death and hell. But to walk in the Spirit, that is not only to be holy and happy, but to receive the leading and guidance of the Spirit in all things as one lives to God through Christ. Let's consider, then...

What does it mean to walk in the Spirit? Walking itself is motion; generally speaking, a *forward* motion. John Howe, a very famous puritan preacher, said that walking, mere walking, "is a self-motion, a voluntary motion, an orderly motion, a pleasurable motion, a continued motion, and a progressive motion."[1] When people walk, they tend to house all these things in their walking. He even distinguished walking from traveling, one being pleasurable, and one being a task. But to walk in the Spirit, is to apply that spiritual principle, that principle of glorifying Christ and God in everything in that forward motion of walking. If general walking is orderly, continued and progressive, so spiritual walking in the Spirit may be said to do the same but with a spiritual principle that far exceeds regularly walking because it causes the one walking in the Spirit to walk closer to Jesus Christ in grace.

By way of a side note, there is often a great controversy about good works, and walking in the Spirit, as it relates to Christ and salvation. People often say, that good works are necessary for salvation. That is true, but not the *cause* of salvation. Christ's good works for his elect are the meritorious cause of all the Spirit's work in a believer. It is all of Christ, and only Christ believed on by faith. But, is this all that there is? What happens is that people often misunderstand how to rightly apply certain hermeneutical principles to the

---

[1] Howe, John, *The Works of the Rev. John Howe*, (New York: E. Sanderson, Printer, 1836) 538.

discussion of good works. In one sense, called the compound sense, when dealing with things like election and such in God's eternal counsel, good works play no part in electing a believer to saving grace in Christ, because salvation rests on Christ alone. Yet, in another sense, called the divided sense, as Christians perceive the working world around them, and the general nature of life in the church, good works are most necessary to being saved, for they show forth who is saved and who is not. At no time is justification by the works of a believer, but rather, works demonstrate *that one is justified.* This is the grand difference between Paul, "justified by faith alone" and James, "not by a faith that is alone." At no time can works be added to Christ's holy merit for salvation, but good works by Christians demonstrate that Christ has saved them. "These good works, done in obedience to God's commandments, are the fruits and evidences of a true and lively faith."[2]

So, I want to give you 6 points of walking that follow in the real-life sense of understanding how to live before God. I say *real life* as that which points to the practical, every day, walking of the Christian as a proof of their salvation.

[1] Walking in the Spirit is to walk in submission to Jesus Christ. This houses the principle of grace. "Submit yourselves therefore to God," (James 4:7). Jesus is the King, because he is the only Savior, God's perfect servant, the God-man who fulfilled the entire covenant of the Lord, the counsel of peace, that men might have eternal life who believe in him and repent of their sin to live a godly life. Men cannot be saved through pride. They are only saved when they have submitted themselves before king Jesus and bowed the knee to his majestic person and will. If a person vows allegiance to the Christ, they submit to him, even to gain him as a friend instead

---

[2] *The 1647 Westminster Confession of Faith* 16:2.

Chapter 13: Walking in the Spirit

of an enemy. If a person is not submissive to God, God never calls such people friends, but rebels and enemies to his will and his word. A man who repents and turns to Christ is never prideful. *Pride cometh before the fall,* not before salvation. They must be placed by the Spirit, first, in an inferior position before God, governed by God's will and pleasure. They find this will and pleasure in the word. He has laid out for them there, everything they needed for life and godliness. They do not look for their own will, but "thy will to be done."

[2] Walking in the Spirit is to walk in the light of Jesus Christ, on the principles of truth (precept upon precept). The biblical idea of "light" is synonymous with knowledge and wisdom. Being enlightened is associated with "seeing," because people are unable to discern anything in the dark. Light is necessary for seeing, and the more light a person has, the better they can see. Scripture refers to both God's nature and God's will as light. "that God is light, and in him is no darkness at all," (1 John 1:5). "...the Father of lights," (James 1:17). This God dwells in "unapproachable light," (1 Tim. 6:16). Christ refers to himself as the "light of the world," (John 8:12). And the Apostle John encourages believers to walk in the light as God is in the light (1 John 1:7). Which is walking in the Spirit according to the will of God, according to his truth, according to the word. To walk in the light, to walk in the Spirit in the light, is to walk according to the truth of the word. This means Christians must have a good knowledge of the word to know how to walk in it. Many think that walking in the Spirit is being zapped in some way and simply instantaneously knowing everything, or simply having some connection to God *regardless* of how one lives; or even just knowing enough of Christ to have some religious knowledge. It is not that. Christians are to have a knowledge of God, a knowledge of the truth of God, to understand the word of God. They walk in the light of the word, in the light of the

truth, in the light given by the power of the Spirit. It is true, they sin. They fall, sin and displease God many times, even though they are commanded to walk in the light, yet, they often fall into the darkness of sin and grieve the Spirit and his work. But, to live in the Spirit, to walk in the Spirit, notwithstanding walking in the light, upon their repentance from those sins, the blood of Christ cleanses from all sin, and so their fellowship (their friendship with God continues).

[3] Walking in the Spirit is to walk in the conformity of Jesus Christ. The principles of the pattern, the pattern of the Christ, "that in me first Jesus Christ might shew forth all longsuffering, for a pattern to them which should hereafter believe on him to life everlasting," (1 Tim. 1:16). The Lord Jesus, as the God-man of utter perfection in all things, was the perfect pattern of all things according to godliness and holiness. He is to be followed. He is to be imitated. "And we know that all things work together for good to them that love God, to them who are the called according to his purpose. For whom he did foreknow, he also did predestinate to be conformed to the image of his Son," (Rom. 8:28-29). Conformed, changed into, made like the pattern. They walk in the Spirit to conform to Christ. They want to be like Christ. A continued walking is a continued conformity. A continued conformity is a continued sanctifying influence. In the truth, in the precept of what God says, and in the pattern, the Christian has both – pattern and precept for everything they might ever do laid out in Scripture, and demonstrated by Christ's pattern in Scripture. Walking in the Spirit, where the Spirit highlights and shines on Christ, this is to, day by day, conform to his pattern and his precepts. What he did and what he says. It's the grand curse on people to not do this. It is the hypocrite's plea. "And why call ye me, Lord, Lord, and do not the things which I say? Whosoever cometh to me, and heareth my sayings, and doeth them, I will shew you to whom

he is like: He is like a man which built an house, and digged deep, and laid the foundation on a rock: and when the flood arose, the stream beat vehemently upon that house, and could not shake it: for it was founded upon a rock. But he that heareth, and doeth not, is like a man that without a foundation built an house upon the earth; against which the stream did beat vehemently, and immediately it fell; and the ruin of that house was great," (Luke 6:46-49). There is a great chasm between wise and foolish builders. The fall of the foolish is very great. It is their walking that shows forth their wisdom or foolishness.

[4] Walking in the Spirit is to walk in union with Jesus Christ. This is the principle of unity. Union with Jesus Christ is the height of all joy and pleasure for the Christian. From Christ, from his intercession in heaven for believers, he sends his Spirit and all his spiritual benefits to those who believe. To be joined to the vine, and to receive life-giving sap, is life. And when the believer is joined to Jesus Christ, he is joined to that life-giving power, that spiritual power, that continually transforms him into a better Christian day by day, a more obedient, submissive Christian that God can use for the good of the kingdom endowed with the spiritual giftedness to make them useful. And what does God chiefly look for? Worshippers who worship the Father in spirit and truth (John 4). Walkers who walk according to the precepts and patterns of the Christ for God's glory. "But he that is joined unto the Lord is one spirit," (1 Cor. 6:17). This is a like-mindedness, and powerful spiritual union that is eternal, even the end of which is eternal life.

[5] Walking in the Spirit is to walk in the power of Jesus Christ. This is the principle of *enablement*. What are they enabled to do? Everything opposed to sin, and everything acceptable before God. The Father seeks those worshippers who worship him and the Son and the Spirit in truth. He

enables them to do this in every area of the Christian walk, as well as in the worship of God. The Spirit of Christ enables them to walk worthy of the calling by which they were called to holiness. They know they are imperfect. The Christian who walks in holiness by the power of the Spirit is much like Samson. The enemies of the truth feared him. But when he gave himself up to things that were unclean and unholy, he found that grieving the work of the Spirit was a hard road to walk. Christians ought to be carrying the gates of Gaza on their back, so to speak, not wandering into sin. But even in their imperfections, the power of Christ's eternal Spirit moves and motions them to work good works. "Make you perfect in every good work to do his will, working in you that which is well pleasing in his sight, through Jesus Christ," (Heb. 13:21).

[6] Walking in the Spirit is to walk in the love of Jesus Christ. This the principle of love and joy. Love and joy coexist at the same time to give the Christian a life that is abundant. "Herein is love, not that we loved God, but that he loved us, and sent his Son to be the propitiation for our sins," (1 John 4:10). And, "We love him, because he first loved us," (1 John 4:19). Love *and then* joy. Christians ought to be the happiest people on earth. "And the disciples were filled with joy, and with the Holy Ghost," (Acts 13:52). "For the kingdom of God is not meat and drink; but righteousness, and peace, and joy in the Holy Ghost," (Rom. 14:17). *Joyous.* "Even them will I bring to my holy mountain, and make them joyful in my house of prayer," (Isa. 56:7).

Walking in the power of the Spirit is the duty of every Christian who is living to God through Christ. It is part of the character of the Christian before Christ, and it is the most joyous life that can ever be lived. It is accomplished in the Spirit for the glory of God. And so, it comprises everything the Christian would do to give God glory as a redeemed sinner. Being regenerate, baptized, indwelt, anointed, with a divine and supernatural light, filled, given power, led and guided, praying and being fruitful in the Spirit, with a diversity of gifts in the body, all of this, (if the Christian is mindful to these ideas), are all wrapped up in one package as *walking in the Spirit.*

    In the midst of a fallen world, you must be walking in the Spirit. What an odd thing it is for a wicked person to hear that your life-long goal is to please Christ and walk in the Spirit. They want to please themselves. Yet, there is great hope and satisfaction if you walk in the Spirit. You must necessarily differ from wicked men, by forsaking the course of this world, and walking according to the world to come, which is walking in the Spirit. That is pressing into the kingdom. That is taking it by violence. You are men and women of the Bible; and this book commands you to walk with God, through Christ, in the power of the Spirit. *It is your life.*

    Enoch was so blessed of God to walk with him, that in a special manner, God took him that he would not taste death because he walked faithfully with him. Genesis 5:24, "And Enoch walked with God; and he was not, for God took him." Noah walked with God and was rescued by God in the ark. Abram, Moses, Joshua, Caleb, David, Solomon, Asa, Hezekiah, Paul, Peter and the like, all the saints, walked with God in the Spirit. *You* must walk in the Spirit. You see, you must have a hearty theology of walking. In 2 Chronicles 7:17 God says, "As for you, if you walk before Me as your father David walked." In Psalm 1:1 it states, "Blessed is the man who walks not in the counsel of the ungodly." Paul tells us in Romans 13:13, "Let us walk properly." And in 1 Corinthians 7:17 he says, "But as God has distributed to each one, as the Lord has called each one, so let him walk." Those all have a great weight on the reality of salvation they profess. Yes, we ought to have a theology of walking with God through Christ in the Spirit all the days of our life; in submission to Christ, in the light of Christ, in conformity to his image, in union with him, in the power of Christ, and in love to Christ. The puritan Robert Bolton said, "That walking with God is the crown of the Christian's Character."[3] It is the crown of your character. People often spy out a crown on a king's head. What do people spy out about you? What do they see about you that they would want to be encouraged to walk in the same Spirit that you demonstrate? Walking in the Spirit is not necessarily easy; who said it was? Roads that reach destinations may be long and arduous, but in many cases the arrival is worth the journey. For you to walk properly before Christ in the Spirit is to hold a continually reforming outlook on holiness with God. That requires your dealing well with fighting the likes of sin, and the further enhancement of walking in holy duties of all kinds. God does not want you to simply walk with God, you are to comfortably walk with him in the Spirit in and to abundant life. So, you walk, and then you walk comfortably. It means you walking in the Spirit for however long God gives you as a life here on earth in a most contented manner. Leviticus 26:3 says, "Walk in my statutes and commandments and perform them...I will walk among you and be your God." Paul exhorts us in Col. 2:6, "As you therefore have received Christ Jesus the Lord, so walk in Him."

When you walk in the Spirit, you are regarded as Christ's friend, walking in the same direction as God, a comfortable walking with him no matter the providence, no matter the task at hand, no matter what he requires of you. That means you have to know what direction God goes in. God's direction can be summed up in one word – holiness. You can measure your walk in the Spirit to a certain extent by seeing if what you do, and who you are, reflect an attitude and an example of holiness as God desires it. When you walk as

---

[3] Bolton, Robert, *General Directions for a Comfortable Walking with God*, (Morgan, PA: Soli Deo Gloria, 1997) 30.

separate from the world, and separated to Christ, that is where you are the mirrored reflection of God's character. This is very pleasing in God's sight; he loves to see more of Christ in you. Walking in the Spirit means you forsake everything to walk alongside of Christ, whatever he would have for you. Thomas Mockett taught in his work, *The Christian's Duty to Forsake All for Jesus Christ*, "That every Christian should, and the wise Christian will, willingly part with all for Christ and the grace of the Gospel."[4]

Are you willing to walk in the Spirit in this way? Check your devotions. Check teaching your children. Check your heart and its disposition at worship. Check your manner of taking the supper. Check the way you deal with others in the church. Check your exercise of spiritual gifts. All of this tends toward walking in the Spirit. It's doing what the Spirit wants you to do for the glory of the Redeemer. And you must remember that everything you have learned so far in the Spirit, is part of that walking.

If you walk away from Christ then you walk with the devil. There is no middle ground. Walking in the Spirit means that you are not spiritually dead, but spiritually alive. But if you are not walking in the Spirit, that could show that you do not have the Spirit. Christ must be in all our thoughts, captivated by him always, focused on him, seeking him, resting on him, trusting him, and following him in everything by walking in the Spirit. *Live* in the Spirit. That's the idea behind that word. He does not occupy a portion of our life, but all our life. We are to live in him, live in the Spirit, live in the ways, will and pleasure of God, we then live in the Spirit and walk before God in Christ. "If ye then be risen with Christ, seek those things which are above, where Christ sitteth on the right hand of God. Set your affection on things

---

[4] Mockett, Thomas, *The Christian's Duty to Forsake All for Jesus Christ*, (Crossville, TN: Puritan Publications, 2015) 24.

above, not on things on the earth. For ye are dead, and your life is hid with Christ in God," (Col. 3:1–3). That means we are to be engaged for Christ in all we do. We have no time to be idle. Did you know that Jesus said He will judge us for every idle thought we have? (Matthew 12:36). We are to be engaging in the violent takeover of the kingdom, in the power of the Spirit. This is taking the kingdom by force, and pressing into it.[5] These things are only done in the power of walking in the Spirit.

No one can do these things if they are not in the Spirit. Our minds ought to be overrun with thoughts of the Savior and what he has done for us in saving us from the curse, and bringing relief, giving us the great blessing of living to God and walking in the Spirit. Everything you do ought to have that connection with Christ. Nothing you do should be done apart from Christ. You should not be able to go anywhere or do anything that is not in connection with Christ. Psalm 1:2 says our meditations about God and His ways are to be done, "day and night." You cannot even eat a snack without walking in the Spirit, for "Whether therefore ye eat, or drink, or whatsoever ye do, do all to the glory of God," (1 Cor. 10:1). That is, walking and living in the Spirit. It is a constant endeavor.

When we walk in the Spirit it hurts us to fall into sin and we cannot rest until the relationship with Christ is reconciled again. Paul said, "O wretched man that I am. Who will deliver me from this body of death?! Thanks be to Christ Jesus our Lord!" (Romans 7:24–25). We willingly give ourselves to the Spirit as an open book for him to examine us. "Search me O God, and know my heart..." (Psalm 139:23). "Examine me O Lord and prove me; try my mind and my heart," (Psalm 26:2). We are always striving to conform to Christ's will and his way searching for every morsel of hope

---

[5] Matthew 11:12; Luke 16:16.

Chapter 13: Walking in the Spirit

and relief we can glean from Jesus Christ while we live in the midst of a fallen world, and so King Jesus bids us to take up the duty of walking in and according to the Spirit. For, walking in the Spirit is the duty of every Christian who is Living to God through Christ.

Our final chapter will consider rejoicing in the abundance of Christ and the Spirit. Abundant life, Spirit-life, Christ conforming life, is one of *rejoicing* and the abundance of grace.

Chapter 14:
Rejoicing in Abundance in Christ

"And the grace of our Lord was exceeding abundant with faith and love which is in Christ Jesus," (1 Tim. 1:14).

In 1 Timothy Paul gives two reasons for writing to the young pastor. He directed Timothy to give forceful opposition to the false doctrine which was growing in Ephesus (1:3). He instructed Timothy about the behavior that should characterize believers as members of "God's household" (3:15).

Interestingly, the *Pastoral Letters* house a number of important doctrinal points, including the Trinity, the Gospel, the work of Christ, and the work of the Holy Spirit. It is not merely about elders and deacons. Our verse falls in the beginning of the letter, which Paul addresses Timothy, wishing him grace, mercy, and peace (1:1–2). In 1:3–20 Paul demonstrates three important tasks for Timothy. Against false teaching (1:3–11). Thankfulness to God for grace in salvation through the Gospel (1:12–17). Charging Timothy to stand in truth, pursue godliness and avoid the destructive examples of Hymeneus and Alexander (1:18–20). "And the grace of our Lord was exceeding abundant with faith and love which is in Christ Jesus," (1 Tim. 1:14).

Set in the context of his writing to Timothy, his ministerial son, he gives a witness to his conversion. "Who was before a blasphemer, and a persecutor, and injurious: but I obtained mercy..." Paul says, (1 Tim. 1:13). ὑπερεπλεόνασε δὲ ἡ χάρις τοῦ Κυρίου (1 Tim. 1:14a). *The abundance of grace* of Christ. This word "abundance" is only used here in the entire New Testament but is linked with worship and the ability to come into the presence of God through grace. It is echoing, and possibly quoting, "But as for me, I will come into thy house in the multitude of thy mercy: and in thy fear will I worship toward thy holy temple," (Psa. 5:7). The word itself is taken from that idea of an overflowing fountain coming from God. God is an inexhaustible fountain of grace to believers. Paul certainly had found an abundant mercy, and he uses this special phrase to express an abundant grace. Paul ponders here how grace could come to such a vile and despicable man as he was, and still transform him into a Gospel minister. This grace was given by God, and given to Paul. It was in Paul. It was more than necessary. It was not only grace, but abundant grace. The grace conferred on Paul was so abundant, that it could convert everyone in a million billion worlds if that were God's plan. However, God never speaks in the realm of possibilities concerning the Gospel. He speaks in directives and promises. *Repent* and *you shall* be saved. *Come* and *you will* find rest. *Seek* and *you will* find. *Pray* and *God will* hear.

    This abundant grace was of our Lord. The Gospel comes in no other way, no other manner, but by God. Knowing the depravity of men's souls, the only way a person may be saved if "of the Lord" something gracious occurs. God must rescue men from sin and death, and the manner in which he does this is through faith and love in Christ Jesus. Both of which are part of the fruit of the Spirit. Both are gifts given by the Spirit at the command of Christ. It is nothing men can work for. It is nothing Paul did in converting himself. His entire testimony, was a *wonder* at what God had done in him, as something Christ must do, not what *Paul might have done.*

    Paul was on the Damascus road going to kill Christians. God was on that road with the Gospel and the transforming power of the Spirit of truth, for another reason. God arrests Paul, as Paul was out to arrest Christians. Would Paul have ever come to this on his own? *Not a chance.* From this transforming Gospel power in the Spirit, flow, faith and love. Not only are faith and love deposited in the apostle as a result of his conversion, but in like manner, the reflex act of faith and love back to God is reciprocal. As a result of being transformed, faith and love are exercised in service to God. And this faith and love from Christ, is again in Christ. ἡμῶν μετὰ πίστεως καὶ ἀγάπης τῆς ἐν Χριστῷ Ἰησοῦ (1 Tim. 1:14b). This is with faith and love, in Christ Jesus, which are the greatest of gifts by the Spirit. Love and faith, along with hope, now abide. They are inseparable in the true Christian. Once the Spirit changes and transforms that soul, faith to God, and love to God are inevitable and instantaneous. They immediately start growing in that new soul. They are graces and they are gifts.

Focus on the words, "In Christ Jesus." In Christ believers receive a great number of Spirit worked graces. They receive "faith" in Christ (Acts 24:24; Galatians 3:26), redemption in Christ (Romans 3:24), life in Christ (Romans 6:11; 8:2), love in Christ (Romans 8:39; 1 Timothy 1:14), sanctification in Christ (1 Corinthians 1:2), hope in Christ (1 Corinthians 15:19), justification in Christ (Galatians 2:16), kindness in Christ (Ephesians 2:7), consolation in Christ (Philippians 2:1), perfection in Christ (Colossians 1:28), boldness in Christ (1 Timothy 3:13), grace itself in Christ (2 Timothy 2:1), salvation in Christ (2 Timothy 3:15), and peace in Christ (1 Peter 5:14), to name a few. Ephesians 1:6, "...to the praise of the glory of His grace, by which He has made us accepted in the Beloved." Adam is accepted in the Beloved after the fall in Jesus Christ. People today are also made accepted in the Beloved, through the blood of Jesus Christ. The promises of God's covenant with men are all included in the comprehensive formula, so often occurring in the Scriptures, "I will be your God, and ye shall be my people," in the Beloved, that is, in Christ, in the true Messiah and only in the true Messiah.

Chapter 14: Rejoicing in Abundance

And then, because of this Messiah, there is spiritual power given in the Spirit, *through the Spirit*. From his exalted position, faith and love as worked in believers through the sending of the Spirit is given in abundance of grace and great rejoicing. They live in the Spirit. They walk in the Spirit. They produce fruit by the Spirit. They engage in a life in Christ that is of great abundance, by the power of the Spirit.

The Christian's abundant life is solely by grace in Christ alone, through the power of the Spirit, and the cause of great rejoicing. This is seen in six ways.

Abundant Living. This is more than just living or existing. Christ comes to give, by grace, the life of the Spirit, and that abundantly. This is not merely something that is found in the New Testament, as a matter of fact, the New Testament is a commentary and exposition of the Old Testament applied in Jesus Christ. Abundant living occurred all through the Old Testament. Consider when Moses wanted to see the glory of God, "And the LORD passed by before him, and proclaimed, The LORD, The LORD God, merciful and gracious, longsuffering, and abundant in goodness and truth, Keeping mercy for thousands, forgiving iniquity and transgression and sin..." (Exod. 34:6-7). Did not Moses experience the abundance of goodness and mercy? Does not David's cup overflow? Did not lives covered in the grace of Christ demonstrate abundance? Noah, Abraham, Isaac, Jacob, Joseph, Joshua, Hannah, Ruth, Asaph, the prophets, Mary, Elizabeth, Paul. Paul equally writes in the New Testament to Titus, "Not by works of righteousness which we have done, but according to his mercy he saved us, by the washing of regeneration, and renewing of the Holy Ghost; Which he shed on us abundantly through Jesus Christ our Saviour; That being justified by his grace, we should be made heirs according to the hope of eternal life," (Titus. 3:5-7). "For all things are for your sakes, that the abundant grace might through the thanksgiving of many redound to the glory of God," (2 Cor. 4:15). Abundant living in Christ through the Spirit is not to be thought of as a special occurrence in the life of the Christian. Salvation is special. *Do not mistake that.*

Abundant living, though, is not special in its experience. As if some Christians are given the ability to live, and others the ability to live abundantly. All of them are. It is the daily reception of such things as converted individuals, from Christ, through the Spirit. It is not something they get once and then never again, or only in spurts. The waters of the Spirit are abundant all the time, and Christ sends his Spirit abundantly, so that day by day, he intercedes on behalf of his people so that they may know God more intimately, more abundantly.

How will they know him more abundantly without being given an abundance of the Spirit? This abundance of the Spirit is given to them in the greatness of the blessing itself. This is the greatness of the blessing. This shows the greatness of God in *blessing abundantly.* God does all things in perfection, and with great abundance. He does not do things so small and insignificant to cause the Christian to wonder what they might have or might not have. They have Christ and the Spirit and all blessings abundantly. God covenantally blesses his people by bestowing on them the fullness of the spiritual blessing that they obtain in Jesus Christ by the work of the Spirit on their soul. It is no small blessing. It is an *abundant* blessing. It had to be an abundant blessing to rescue men from the fall; such a blessing must have *fall-reversing power.* Christ is an abundant Savior in this way. He had to deal with sin in a way that vanquished the curse for his people. This was not something he would do in any small measure. He would go to the greatest lengths and greatest straights to even die for them, and be buried in a tomb for them, to die in their place for them. He does this to take the curse and wrath of

Chapter 14: Rejoicing in Abundance

God for them. He does not give sparingly, for God did not spare his only Son in coming to save them. He gives liberally. Like David says in his cup being not only full in Psalm 23, but it overflows like a fountain that never exhausts itself in Christ. He receives more than he can possibly hold of the greatness of such a blessing.

Christians, as Paul said, receive more than they can possibly hold. It is infinite blessing given to finite creatures. How can the finite possibly contain the infinite blessing of God in Christ? It cannot, but it may be thought about as drinking the waters of life, as much as might fit in a person's mouth, while standing under Niagara Falls; water still winds up in the mouth, but there is an abundance of it that never stops. God is a continual fountain. This does not mean that what the Christian has overflowing about, around and in him is lost, for it is an abundant spring and foundation of blessing that God gives, with rivers of living water that no man can contain in himself and that can never be spiritually exhausted.

The fountain of blessing is full in God; and God is infinite; and the cup is full and overflowing to those who partake of that great blessing. It is an infinite blessing of the greatest and highest magnitude that men can only apprehend as a glimpse. It overflows, it is abundant, but it is never ceasing because it is an infinitely great blessing that cannot ever be exhausted. And the Christian lives directly under that fountain, in its midst, and they walk in it, led by the Spirit of God. "And God is able to make all grace abound toward you; that ye, always having all sufficiency in all things, may abound to every good work," (2 Cor. 9:8). Grace abounds even to the chief of sinners, so that the Christian always has a sufficiency in God, never lacking any storehouse of anything he needs or might lack for that acceptable service to Christ as he lives in him walking in the Spirit and living in the great blessings of God abundantly. He looks to serve God acceptably with reverence and godly fear, and he is so covered in the fountain of Christ's blood that such a service is always empowered to its fullest, if they will merely tap into that power by following God as he so directs – both by precept and pattern in his word. Who God is, what God says, and what Christ has done. These are the chief studies of the Christian. That all the works and duties he engages in are filled with an abundance of grace, in their abundant lives. God, out of his great storehouse of abundance bestows on his children, in converting them and sanctifying them, faith and love to such a great extent, that the only recourse the Christian has is to magnify the work of Christ in praise and thanksgiving daily.

In faith Christians reciprocate love. This is why Paul said, "The grace of God was exceeding abundant toward me," it was over-full. It was over-full and abundant in Christ through faith and love. And, as every Christian is given this faith and love in their conversion, so they are given it greatly in the blessing of salvation. This is not only converting grace, but it is sanctifying as well. This is where the Christian lives and moves and has their being. Faith to trust in him, love to please him and be pleased in him. All this is solely by Jesus Christ.

Solely by Jesus Christ? Yes, utterly. There is no other way to abundant life in the Spirit than through Jesus Christ. Christ is called the Christian's Surety because he made satisfaction to God for them. It is true, Christ is the Christian's Surety in which they stand sure of their salvation, from beginning to end. They are, for all intents and purposes, helpless in every way, and utterly destitute of anything pleasing to God aside from Christ in them through the power of the Holy Spirit. Take Christ out of the Christian, take the

Chapter 14: Rejoicing in Abundance

Holy Spirit out of the Christian, and what is left?[1] The totality of the principle of eternal life and salvation is gone with the theoretical removal of Christ and his Spirit from the Christian. All that is left would be the depraved sinner on his or her way to hell. So when Christ is present in his people as the Surety, as the Messiah, as the intercessor, and His Holy Spirit is in them, and working through them, God is pleased with his people and all those works and spiritual activities accomplished in his power and according to his prescription. The work of Christ brings his people into a relationship with God so as to perform that which God desires of them through the power of his Spirit.

It's the Spirit's power. They have no power. They live and walk in the Spirit to have power. If they are saved, if they are born again, they are obliged to keep covenant with God, though the power of "keeping" rests in the motions of the Spirit in them mortifying sin and pressing them to sanctifying duties. Christ is the "surety" or the promise of God to salvation for God's people. Christ's satisfaction for sin surrounds "complete satisfaction." To play on the word, he makes *eternal life very sure*. Christ came in the place of his people to save them completely and wholly. Christ, the Messiah, comes and offers up a complete satisfaction for sin – that which is acceptable to God. He did this abundantly, for without fulfilling every jot and tittle of the Law, there could be no salvation. If there was something lacking, there would be no salvation. Without complete satisfaction, there would be no salvation, for men cannot fill up the infinite sacrifice that God required for sin on their own.

Christ performed his task perfectly. He is the Lord of

---

[1] "I am the vine, ye are the branches: He that abideth in me, and I in him, the same bringeth forth much fruit: for without me ye can do nothing," (John 15:5). "How much less man, that is a worm? and the son of man, which is a worm?" (Job 25:6).

life, able to lay his life down, that others might be filled up with abundant life. John 10:18 says, "No one takes it from Me, but I lay it down of Myself. I have power to lay it down, and I have power to take it again. This command I have received from My Father." In the totality of his personhood, and all the work he accomplished, he did it all in perfect love to God his Father, and for his bride, in whom he loved. Romans 5:8, "But God demonstrates His own love toward us, in that while we were still sinners, Christ died for us." God abundantly accepted this sole satisfaction of Christ because it satisfied the character and nature of the infinite God. It satisfied the Law of God and requirements of God's Covenant. It manifested the truth of God in that it promised justice in the law; it manifested the goodness of God since it reconciled men to God; it manifested the justice of God since it could not clear the guilty without proper means to do so; it manifested the holiness of God since it did not allow man into God's presence without cleansing him first of sin; and it demonstrated the glory of God in his all-sufficiency and perfections ... HOW? ... *in abundance.* In every way and every action, Christ's work was abundantly beneficial for his people.

The obedience of Christ was performed by him in the stead of his people in order that they might receive eternal life. Romans 5:19, "For as by one man's disobedience many were made sinners, so also by one Man's obedience many will be made righteous." The sinner's work, as sinful as it is in the eyes of God, is not bigger than Christ is a Savior. Their sins are, as it were, "overwritten" by Christ's work. The merit of Christ's work is "imputed" to them, his work is credited to their account.

The 1647 Westminster Confession of Faith says in 8:5, "The Lord Jesus, by his perfect obedience and sacrifice of himself, which he through the eternal Spirit once offered up unto God, hath fully satisfied the justice of his Father, and purchased not only reconciliation, but an everlasting inheritance in the kingdom of heaven, for all those whom the Father hath given unto him." God accepts the sinner as a result of Christ alone. The obedience of Christ was sufficient for all his people, and that abundantly. He offered such a sacrifice of inestimable worth for them, that they cannot contain it, but necessary as an infinite sacrifice because God is infinitely angered by sin. Isaiah 53:10, "Yet it pleased the LORD to bruise Him; He has put Him to grief." It pleased the Lord to bruise his Son so that sinners might live abundantly in the Spirit, and Christ did this willingly. John 10:15, "As the Father knows Me, even so I know the Father; and I lay down My life for the sheep."[2] Those with a real interest in Jesus Christ, depend on Christ alone for salvation which is by grace alone, through faith alone, to the glory of God alone. Everything that could be good in or for them is through Jesus Christ. All the benefits of salvation that God has for them are found in Christ alone. They must have an absolute dependence on Jesus Christ alone in their redemption. This is the enlightened mind resting on the work of the Holy Spirit in their heart through the message of the Gospel of Christ's grace. It is exclusively accomplished from God's Holy Spirit that they receive the ability to exercise faith in order to have a true interest in him, "For by grace ye are saved, through faith; and that not of yourselves, it is the gift of God," (Eph. 2:8).

Christians are totally reliant on God's power through every step of their redemption in Christ alone. It is never works, lest any man should boast. They rely on the power of God to convert them, and give them true faith in Jesus Christ, and the new nature by the power of the Holy Spirit. They rely on him daily for power, for living to God. It is *all* of him. This Christ gave himself up solely as God's perfect sacrifice for sin,

---

[2] *cf.* 1 Peter 3:18; Colossians 1:21–22; Romans 5:10; Hebrews 9:15; Romans 8:34.

and all this by abundant grace.

By Grace. It is a supply of the greatest grace from the throne of Christ to the pardoned soul. People sometimes think they are the greatest sinners in the world, as if they could out-sin Adam or Manasseh or the Apostle Paul (chief among sinners). And yet, these were all saved by abundant grace. Grace - the unmerited favor of God in Christ to those who do not deserve it. Stephen Charnock said, "Suppose you are the greatest sinner that ever was yet in the world, do not think that God, who has snatched so many firebrands of hell out of the devil's hands, will neglect such an opportunity to make his grace illustrious on your humble soul. If God has given you repentance, it is a certain evidence he will follow it with a pardon, though your sins are of a deeper scarlet than ever yet was seen on the earth."[3] There is never an excuse that Christ cannot forgive. He is willing that sinners come to him to find rest, to find life, and that more abundantly. It is true that sinners do not deserve anything. It is true that God would have been just to send the whole lot of mankind fallen in Adam into hell for all eternity. It is true that there would not be a single mouth able to say anything against God for doing it if he so desired to act justly in this. But, he decided, out of his mere good pleasure, to save some out of that mass of perdition, through Christ, and the abundance of grace. And he did this...

Through the Spirit. Salvation is through the Spirit, and in the power of the Spirit, the one sent of the Father and the Son. On account of the Father and Christ, by their direction, but through the Spirit in faith and love. Sanctification through the Spirit is the abundant life of holiness. It is the increase of faith. It is the increase of love. It

---

[3] Charnock, Stephen, *The Complete Works of Stephen Charnock*, Volume 5, (London: Printed for Ben. Griffen and Thomas Cockeril, 1684). Reprinted., ed. T. Smith, intro, by James M'Cosh. 5 vols. Edinburgh: James Nichol, 1864-66), 457.

is the engagement of holy duties that one might be conformed into the image of Christ. Christians often think that grace means they are not responsible for working righteously before God now. But this is to confuse the Apostle Paul's argument in Ephesians 2:8-9, and it also shows that the Christian is forgetting the argument of the Apostle James in James 2:16-24. In Ephesians 2:8-9 Paul says, "For by grace are ye saved through faith; and that not of yourselves: it is the gift of God: Not of works, lest any man should boast." This is extremely clear. Regeneration, salvation, redemption, (all that God requires to be accomplished to be saved) has been given to Christ's chosen people by the Covenant of Grace, through Christ's grace, work and merit and in the power of the sanctifying Spirit.

Such unmerited favor towards the individual is by grace, by Christ, applied by the Spirit. It is not by any works. It is not by being baptized, or reciting catechism questions, or church attendance. Salvation is wrought by Christ alone and is held steadfast in their heart and mind through faith. God promises and accomplishes specific undeserving acts for us, and we, with a regenerated heart and renewed mind simply believe him at his promise and word. In this way, men cannot boast that they walked down the aisle before their friend Bob, that "they" believed and their friend didn't. They can make no claim to any work. It is not by any works. It is by faith and love. And faith and love are given to the Christian by the Spirit sent from Christ. Oftentimes, this is where the Reformed Christian plants his flag and completely forgets Paul's next statement. They think it is all of grace, and they have nothing to contribute, as if faith and love are some robotic reflex that they have no control over. "For we are his workmanship, created in Christ Jesus unto good works, which God hath before ordained that we should walk in them," (Eph. 2:10). Without going into a long exposition on this verse, it should suffice to point out that Christians were saved by grace in order to do good works. Why? That's where James 2:16-24 comes into play. James says, "And one of you say unto them, Depart in peace, be ye warmed and filled; notwithstanding ye give them not those things which are needful to the body; what doth it profit? Even so faith, if it hath not works, is dead, being alone. Yea, a man may say, Thou hast faith, and I have works: shew me thy faith without thy works, and I will shew thee my faith by my works. Thou believest that there is one God; thou doest well: the devils also believe, and tremble. But wilt thou know, O vain man, that faith without works is dead? Was not Abraham our father justified by works, when he had offered Isaac his son upon the altar? Seest thou how faith wrought with his works, and by works was faith made perfect? And the scripture was fulfilled which saith, Abraham believed God, and it was imputed unto him for righteousness: and he was called the Friend of God. Ye see then how that by works a man is justified, and not by faith only." Did you know Martin Luther had a problem with this section of Scripture for quite a long time during his younger years? He was so overwhelmed with justification by faith alone that it was cloudy to him why James would say that we are justified by faith and works. But this presses the abundant life of the Christian in the Spirit led by the Shepherd and rejoicing in the truth walking by faith and love, to duty in God's covenant. Their duty? Why do they have to "do" something if Christ finished everything on the cross? Didn't Christ say, "It is finished?" James says that faith *without works is dead.* He tells Christians that true faith must have works to show itself to be real, and that in the eyes of men; faith must be accompanied by works. Men must not only hear their lip service to God, such as when people say, "I'm a Christian," but their works must be seen as well. Those works show forth true faith and love. They don't create true faith and love. One can't outwardly tell people that they are a Christian simply by what they say, yet, they must show forth accompanying signs that such faith is actually real faith, and that the Spirit of the living God resides in them through their good works.

Now, works do not save, rather, those works justify the faith people have been exercising due to Christ's power in saving them and regenerating them in the Spirit. Like Abraham, *one sees faith working*. There is no contradiction between James and Paul, nor between the Christian belief in justification by faith alone, and what James teaches, that works come along side of faith to demonstrate that a person actually is justified, and that men can see that. Sanctification, then, takes a whole new turn here since it is not simply something a Christian does in private. True faith will show itself in the works of the Christian being accomplished in the sight of God and in the sight of the Church. James uses the illustration of Abraham, the father of our faith, demonstrating that Christians see his faith as active and not passive in offering up Isaac before God, on God's command. Such a faith in working itself out by the Spirit of God is a justifying faith which is accompanied by works.

Faith which is not accompanied by works is false faith. There is no Spirit there. It is what hypocrites and heathen do to be seen by others in their statements, in their profession, but not seen in as works in their lives which remain unchanged. Christians are certainly justified by faith alone, but not by a faith that is alone. It is a faith that is linked intrinsically to works: faith and love in the Spirit, which breed hope in Christ. And if there are no works, then James tells us, it is a dead faith. It is simply not saving faith.

There will be a day where the Christian enters into a complete glorification through the Spirit. The removal of faith to sight. The increase of love apart from faith and by sight. Hope is no longer present, for faith is made sight, and now the greatest spiritual gift, the gift of love, will continue into eternity. Yet, now, there is hope, faith and love. Yet, now, the Christian must cultivate the truth of this abundant life in the Spirit, in Christ, with great rejoicing.

Great Rejoicing. The Christian rejoices in God. In living an abundant life, the true saint rejoices in God. "...the joy of the LORD is your strength," (Neh. 8:10). What do people think *strength* is? Muddling their way through difficult times? What doesn't kill you makes you stronger? No. Strength is found *in joy*. They have their minds and hearts set on the enjoyments and wonders of the Almighty God. This argues that they must know this God. They are not merely rejoicing because of things God does in lavishing upon them various spiritual blessings. Certainly, the spiritual blessings God lavishes in them and on them are far different from what the world thinks is lavishing. They rejoice in God for things like a contrite spirit, a humble disposition, an unworthiness, a delight in holiness, and in God's other attributes. The world will be excited with temporal blessings, but the Christian is delighted in the Blessed God, the one who bestows all blessings. In him they rejoice. "I will greatly rejoice in the LORD, my soul shall be joyful in my God; for he hath clothed me with the garments of salvation, he hath covered me with the robe of righteousness, as a bridegroom decketh himself with ornaments, and as a bride adorneth herself with her jewels," (Isa. 61:10). It is true they rejoice in things God gives them. "And thou shalt rejoice in every good thing which the LORD thy God hath given unto thee, and unto thine house," (Deut. 26:11). But their rejoicing is first and foremost in the sweet delights of God himself.

The Christian rejoices in Christ. The soul which comes to Christ abandons everything for Christ. It comes away from all things in the world, as from, "a barren wilderness," leaning on Christ alone. It rejoices in, "Christ and has no confidence in the flesh," (Song of Songs 8:5; Phil. 3:3). He has no confidence in anything that is not Christ, nor in Christ. He does not dare place his confidence in anything else. They do not place confidence in anything they do externally or internally. It is not by way of duty. It is not by way of affections. They rejoice in duty and cultivate godly affections only through the Spirit of Christ. They rejoice solely in him. It is the peculiar excellency of faith and love to disregard itself, and all its works, and instead rejoice in Christ. "But God forbid that I should glory, save in the cross of our Lord Jesus Christ," (Gal. 6:14).

In Christ is found the abundance of life and grace in the Spirit. It is the Spirit's job to apply the work of Christ to the soul, and that daily. It is the Christian's motto, "I must decrease, and he must increase." But it is not a mere humility, but a mourning which is set in the context of eternal rejoicing. They rejoice in Christ who is suited to the work of redemption and of which they are made partakers in abundant living. They look to rejoice in Christ, worship Christ, love Christ, set their affections and faith on Christ alone for all their salvation, from its beginning to its ending. He is God, *full* of all things for them, God filling all in all; and he is the perfect man, heaping up on them spiritual realties that the Spirit ministers to their soul because of his work.

The Christian rejoices only through the Spirit. They not only rejoice in the Father, in the Son, but in the Spirit and through the Spirit. How happy is the one who sees the Spirit of God working in and through them. They are confident that Christ has sent this Spirit to them to work his work in them. They rejoice in this. He is a Spirit of grace. He is a Spirit of holiness. He is a Spirit of joy. In his fruit, they have joy. If they have gained the love of God, and the peace of salvation through Christ, this peace turns quickly into joy in the Holy Spirit. Can he not be but filled with joy in the Spirit, in abundant life in the Spirit? When the soul is born again, when it is passed the line of the new birth, it is bathed in the blood of Christ, set secure in the heart of God's mercies, and secured by the application of all this in the Spirit. It necessarily follows that such a new disposition has these new saving tendencies worked in their heart by the Spirit, and they rejoice in it. What do everlasting pleasures taste like? How does the Christian rejoice over such things they now come into contact with? The Christian rejoices in abundant life *now*. Christ, through his Spirit, by decree of the Father, has restored his people to an abundant life. Now, they live in abundance. They live in the entirety of the spiritual blessing now. Their lives, then, ought to exemplify this great rejoicing in abundant life in Christ now. They are not waiting for another day. Today is the day of grace. Today is the time they rejoice. This does not mean that later on their rejoicing will not grow. It does not mean that eternity will not be more glorious. It will be very much glorious. But the substance of that glory will not change. The same salvation they have in Christ now, will continue. It will merely go through a transformation in the way that such a life is communicated.

So there is never a time in their life that the Christian can use any kind of excuse not to live an abundant life now. They do not bite their upper lip and merely press on through life to a better life, muddling through it. They have a life now that is not only life, but abundant life in Christ through the Spirit. Christ's special errand in his covenant before the Father was to give his people a more abundant life. And all the benefits of that life are those special blessings of a loving savior to his bride. These are benefits and blessings to be rejoiced in. What cause do they ever have not to be under the rule of their king, to reside in contentment and joy in the Spirit? What rejoicing could ever cease now? This rejoicing even cultivates a longing for the new world to come, to rejoice there for all of eternity.

The Christian rejoices in the abundant life to come in heaven. Paul tells Timothy just a few chapters later that "godliness is profitable unto all things, having promise of the life that now is, and of that which is to come," (1 Tim. 4:8). A life now. A life to come. Such is the cause of rejoicing. In the life to come the persecutions and sufferings of this world will be done away with, and it will be only worship and rejoicing. The abundant life given to believers in the Spirit press the soul to desire that day, for it cannot come quick enough. "And the Spirit and the bride say, Come. And let him that heareth say, Come. And let him that is athirst come. And whosoever will, let him take the water of life freely," (Rev. 22:17). Both the Spirit and the bride say this. They long and thirst for that day when it will all be completed and perfected. Such causes the Christian to rejoice even now.

Christ will receive the most wicked sinner who comes to him by faith and love in the grace of God and give them abundant life. Your greatest sins are met with Christ's abundant grace; it was his work to bring such life and grace, which was the overarching point of victory in the Spirit. It is abundant, more than is necessary, overflowing. Those of you who have the least measure of grace, still, you have it in abundance. No matter what you think you have, as a Christian, if you are a believer, you have grace in abundance. It is not a little thing in you; it is eternal life- and is that a little thing? It is the spark of the divine influence implanted and engrafted and sealed in your soul. It is only a matter of understanding it and trusting Christ for its growth. It is only a matter of tapping into the abundant power of the Spirit in you through the word in all the means of grace. The goofiness of the charismatic movement in trying to place some special, superhero like ability in those who walk in the Spirit, or live in the Spirit in comparison to others, is to distort and disfigure what Christ has most assuredly done in every believer who believes in him. It causes many people to think that they don't have something special. They seem unable to discern what they think they "should discern" that those "high-test Christians" have that they do not. But it is not like that at all. There is real power in the Spirit to reverse the fall. There is real spiritual abundance. But it is based, not on a super power, but in rightly understanding exactly what Christ has done for you, and supplying you with the Spirit to walk before him in godliness and holiness in the implanted word able to save your soul.

When Christ forgives you as a sinner, you are forgiven of everything that has ever been or will ever be; that is the beginning of the abundant life; it is the crux of justification in Christ. Your sin is but a drop in the ocean in comparison to the abundance of grace found in Christ and ministered to you. And when you are forgiven, you are forgiven of everything, sins past, sins present, sins future, in regards to being justified before the face of God. He forgives you and justifies you which is something God declares about you, done upon faith and repentance, in trusting Christ for salvation through the Spirit. This declaration by God happens once. You can be no more justified today than you are tomorrow as a believer; for that matter, into eternity. In heaven you will be no more justified than you are today. Christ does not forgive only some sins and not others in his children; he forgives them all. He forgives them not only of their sins, but he forgives abundantly, more than is even needed, so to speak.

And then, because you are not instantaneously brought to heaven, and made perfect in glory, you still have to deal with the remaining sin in you in order to be more sanctified. It is never to be more justified in God's sight. It is to be more separated to him from the world, to be more holy. This is a life-long process, no matter how long that life is;

everyone gets one life; don't waste yours. Yet, that life, is an abundant life in the Spirit. Hosea 14:4, "I will heal their backsliding, I will love them freely." God's love is a free love, having no motive or foundation but God himself and his good pleasure. All the links of the golden chain of salvation (Romans 8) are made up of free grace in Christ, and they give you abundant life in the Spirit. The people of God are freely loved (Deut. 7:6-8), freely chosen, (John 15:16-19, Eph. 1:4); freely accepted, (Eph. 1:6); freely adopted, (Eph. 1:5, Gal. 4:5-6); freely reconciled, (2 Cor. 5:18-20); freely justified, (Rom. 3:24); and freely saved, (Eph. 2:5); "By grace ye are saved," Titus 3:5, Again, "Not by works of righteousness which we have done, but according to his mercy he saved us." Thomas Brooks said, "So you see that all the golden rungs in Jacob's ladder, that reaches from heaven to earth, are all made up of free grace. Free grace is the foundation of all spiritual and eternal mercies; free grace is the solid bottom and foundation of all a Christian's comfort in this world. Were we to measure the love of God to us by our fruitfulness, holiness, humbleness, spiritualness, heavenly-mindedness, or gracious carriages towards him, how would our hope, our confidence every hour, yea, every moment in every hour, be staggered, if not vanquished! Rom. 4:16. But all is of grace, of free grace, that the promise might be sure, and that our salvation might be safe."[4] Has not Christ most readily, tenderly and compassionately received even the greatest and most heinous sinners who have come to him by faith and given them abundant life? Who has Christ so tenderly received and given abundant life? We certainly do not have time to consider them all, but only hear the names of some.

Consider Adam, the most heinous of sinners, saved by God. Samson, that champion of champions who failed in every

---

[4] Brooks, Thomas, *The Complete Works of Thomas Brooks*, Volume 3, (Edinburgh: Banner of Truth Trust, 1980) 484.

way before God. Solomon, he whom God loved, though Solomon did not restrict his flesh from anything. Manasseh, that wicked and heinous king, converted by grace in a jail cell. The Prodigal, (Luke 15:20ff). Matthew the tax collector, (Matt. 9:9). Zachaeus the oppressing Publican, (Luke 19:5-11). The notorious sinful woman that washed Christ's feet with her tears, *etc.*, (Luke 7:37ff). The woman caught in adultery to be stoned. The thief on the cross, (Matt. 27:44 compared with Luke 23:40-44). Saul, that persecutor and a blasphemer, (Acts 26:9-11; 1 Tim. 1:13-14, 16), who by our very text says that he has received abundant grace, abundant life in Christ.

When Christ receives and accepts such who come to him by faith, who would not come to him? Who has any cause to say that Christ will not save, or cannot? He not only saves, but gives life by the Spirit. He not only gives life by the Spirit, but eternal life. He not only gives eternal life, but abundant life, both here, now, on this earth, and even into the age to come.

Be exhorted then, this is a cause of rejoicing. Rejoicing in God's salvation. Rejoicing in Christ. Rejoicing in the Spirit. Rejoicing in having an abundant life rather than an ordinary life, or a common depraved life. Can the greater sea of people in the church today testify to the abundant life of Christ in the Spirit? I don't think they can, nor know how. I don't think most preachers know how. Can they explain what Christ has done in this way through the victory of the Spirit, and can they show forth this abundant victorious life in Christ through the power of the Spirit of living to God. More than a mere feeling. More than mere outward duties. More than mere personal devotion. More than church membership.

> God's decree and oath are set in stone,
>   to send his Christ to save alone.
> Christ from heaven came to earth,

Chapter 14: Rejoicing in Abundance

        to give us life by Spirit-Birth.
Abundant life, to Christ we go,
        its width, its depth, the word does show.
Uncommon joy abundantly,
        that's measured in infinity.
Rejoicing now the Christian can,
        for them to hope in heaven's land.
To love Christ now most lavishly,
        that Flowing Fountain eternally.
And all by Spirit, not by men,
        and so it presses me to say again,

...the Christian's abundant life is solely by grace in Christ alone, through God's power, and the cause of great rejoicing; there we find the believer *walking victoriously in the power of the Spirit*. Do *you* walk this way?

FINIS

Other Helpful Books by C. Matthew McMahon

5 Marks of a Biblical Church

5 Marks of a Biblical Disciple

5 Marks of a Biblical Commitment to the Visible Body of Christ

5 Marks of Biblical Reformation

The Wickedness, Humiliation, Restoration and Reformation of Manasseh

Seeing Christ Clearly

The Lord's Voice Cries to the City: A Biblical Guide for Hearing the word of God Preached

The Reformed Apprentice Series Volumes 1-4, Workbooks

The Two Wills of God Made Easy

A Treatise on John 3:16

A Practical Guide to Primeval History

John Calvin's View of God's Love and the Doctrine of Reprobation

Augustine's Calvinism: The Doctrines of Grace in Augustine's Writings

A Simple Overview of Covenant Theology

Covenant Theology Made Easy

The Reformation Made Easy

Historical Theology Made Easy

Systematic Theology Made Easy

The Two Wills of God Made Easy

Gradual Reformation Intolerable

Psalm 96: A Theology of Praise

Bah Humbug: How Christians Should Think About the Christmas Holiday

How to Live Every Day in the End Times

Eternity Weighed in the Balance

The Two Wills of God: Does God Really Have Two Wills?

A Heart for Reformation

www.ingramcontent.com/pod-product-compliance
Lightning Source LLC
Chambersburg PA
CBHW020325170426
43200CB00006B/271